D1482828

# THE IMPRINT OF TIME

# THE IMPRINT OF TIME

*Childhood, History, and*
*Adult Life*

M. E. J. WADSWORTH

CLARENDON PRESS · OXFORD
1991

Oxford University Press, Walton Street, Oxford OX2 6DP
Oxford New York Toronto
Delhi Bombay Calcutta Madras Karachi
Petaling Jaya Singapore Hong Kong Tokyo
Nairobi Dar es Salaam Cape Town
Melbourne Auckland
and associated companies in
Berlin Ibadan

Oxford is a trade mark of Oxford University Press

Published in the United States
by Oxford University Press, New York

British Library Cataloguing in Publication Data
Data available

Library of Congress Cataloging in Publication Data
Wadsworth, Michael E. J. (Michael Edwin John)
The imprint of time: childhood, history, and adult life / M. E. J. Wadsworth.
p. cm.
Includes bibliographical references and indexes.
1. Children—Great Britain—Longitudinal studies. 2. Education—
Great Britain—Longitudinal studies. 3. Children—Health and
hygiene—Great Britain—Longitudinal studies. I. Title.
HQ792.G7W28 1991 305.23'0941—dc20 91–10159
ISBN 0–19–827360–6

Typeset by Pentacor PLC, High Wycombe, Bucks.
Printed and bound in
Great Britain by Courier International Ltd.,
East Kilbride, Scotland

# Foreword

Parents and grandparents, politicians and policy makers are all concerned in different ways about the future of children as they grow up. Parents and grandparents wonder what will become of them, how they will earn their living, what sort of people they will be, what sort of interests they will have and how they can best be prepared for the future. Politicians and policy makers wonder how children should best be educated and prepared to become valuable members of the work-force, how their health and welfare should be cared for, how they might best learn to contribute what they can to the community, and how they should be prepared for life in a rapidly changing world.

This book describes a study which has followed the development of nearly five and a half thousand English, Welsh, and Scottish children from the time of their birth to age 43 years. The children were born in 1946 and information was collected on their health and development and their education and family life eleven times during infancy and the school years. In adult life information was collected on nine occasions on health, family life, work, and interests. Information on study members' concerns as parents was collected when their first born children were aged 4 years and again at 8 years. More details of the methods used to collect information and to maintain contact with the study population are given in Appendix 1. All this information has been used to ask, for instance, about the associations of childhood development and health with adult health and life, about what happened to bright children who did not get on in school, about the adult life of children who were seriously ill, about the extent to which those from poor home circumstances were able to improve their chances, about relationships between the generations, and about a wide range of related topics.

The study members were children during a period of great innovation in education and in health care. During this time new techniques and ideas for keeping the population healthy were developed, and the National Health Service was started two years after the study began. Two years before the study began the 1944 Education Act sought to eliminate barriers to educational opportunity and to introduce new methods of educating children to become highly contributing and constructive members of a changing society by matching 'aptitude' with type of school. This was also a time of rapid technological and medical advances, and of extensive change not only in material terms and in the kinds of work available, but also in such less tangible but equally influential respects as relationships between the sexes, between professionals, and between those in 'authority' and lay people, in leisure time activity and in entertainment, and in ideas about the value of education and the ways to remain in good health.

The study is by no means complete. More information was collected when the study members were 43 years old, and current work is still fundamentally concerned with how the imprint of each stage of the individual's development affects later life and is, in turn, affected both by previous stages and by previous generations in the same family, and by the world in which development is taking place. The present concern is with the processes of getting older, and how they are affected by earlier and present life and circumstances. Current work, for example, involves measuring the rate of change with increasing age of blood pressure, of short- and long-term memory, and of respiratory function, as well as study of the experience of illness and the maintenance of health and the care of now elderly parents and of children.

Findings from the study have been published in five books and 188 papers and chapters. The purpose of this book is to bring together all these findings, to present them in a concise and accessible way in order to show the importance of childhood in the development of the individual, the influence of the previous generation on children's health and education, and thus the importance of the impact of circumstances at the time of childhood. All these influences leave their imprint on childhood, and so the findings on the development of men and women in this study are described in the context of their time.

# Acknowledgements

The study described in this book has continued for over forty years primarily because Dr J. W. B. Douglas, its originator and director for thirty-three years, had the imagination, foresight, and persistence to guide it fruitfully, and to maintain its funding. It was begun under the auspices of the Population Investigation Committee and the Royal College of Obstetricians and Gynaecologists, and funding during the subsequent infant, childhood, and early adolescent years was generously given by the Nuffield Foundation, the Population Council (Inc.), the Board of the Hospital for Sick Children (Great Ormond Street), the National Birthday Trust Fund, the National Spastics Society, by fourteen Regional Hospital Boards, the Ford Foundation, the Eugenics Society, and the Medical Research Council. In 1962 the Medical Research Council established the Unit for the Study of Environmental Factors in Mental and Physical Illness, and the study was part of that unit. Medical Research Council support, with regular peer group review, has continued to the present day. The Medical Research Council's imaginative long-term funding has enabled analyses and future plans for the study to be undertaken on an appropriately long time scale.

The study has also flourished because of the stimulating surroundings in which it has taken place. It began in what has since become the department of demography at the London School of Economics, but what was then the Population Investigation Committee, which was directed by Professor D. V. Glass. Between 1954 and 1962 the study was housed in the department of public health and social medicine in the University of Edinburgh, and returned to being an autonomous unit in Professor Glass's department from 1962 to 1979, when Dr J. W. B. Douglas retired. The study moved then to the department of community medicine in the University of Bristol, under the honorary directorship of Professor J. R. T. Colley, and in 1986 moved to become a Medical Research Council external scientific staff research team in the department of community medicine at the University College, London, and the Middlesex Hospital Medical School, where it is now directed by Dr M. E. J. Wadsworth.

After more than forty years the list of acknowledgements to all the individuals who have worked on the study, advised on its concerns and analyses, and supported its efforts to continue is too long to give in detail, but their invaluable help is recognized with much gratitude, and their published work is summarized and referred to constantly in the text. I would like to acknowledge my gratitude to past and present colleagues on the study and to friends in Bristol, Giessen, and London, and in particular to Dr J. W. B. Douglas for his guidance and help during the eleven years I had the privilege of working on the study under his directorship, and during the subsequent eleven years.

All through the childhood, adolescent, and earliest adult years the study relied for data collection on the help of professionals in the National Health Service, in schools and in the Youth Employment Service. Health visitors, school nurses, school doctors, teachers, and youth employment officers asked questions, undertook measures, and administered tests with much patience; without their help the study would not have continued, and collection of information during the fast changing years of childhood could not have been as frequent as appropriate. During the adult years information was collected once by professional interviewers, and recent contacts have been carried out by sixty research nurses who were briefed for the work over a period of three to five days. Their skills in interviewing and measuring, and their persistence in finding addresses and 'lost' study members have been invaluable, and are most gratefully acknowledged. Information on the study members' upbringing of their first born offspring was collected by a team of fourteen interviewers who were recruited and trained specially for this aspect of the study, and their sensitive work is also most gratefully acknowledged.

The greatest debt of gratitude owed by all those concerned with the running and continuation of the study is to the parents of the study members and to the study members themselves. Mothers and fathers agreed to one of their children being in the study, and answered many questions at home and at medical examinations during the school years. The study members themselves have been remarkably patient, perhaps particularly during the school years, when for many the embarrassment of being singled out for medical examinations and tests of attainment, usually as the school's only study member, is still remembered. Their patience has been evident again in adult life, when they have agreed to be interviewed at home, to be weighed and measured, and to take tests of memory and cognition. None of the study's work would have been possible without their continuing help and interest, and all those who have worked on the analysis of findings are deeply indebted to the members of the study and to their parents.

# Contents

List of Figures                                                    xii

List of Tables                                                     xiii

1  INTRODUCTION                                                      1

2  BIRTH                                                            17

3  THE PRE-SCHOOL YEARS                                             33

4  FROM 5 TO 11 YEARS                                               57

5  FROM 11 TO 18 YEARS                                              84

6  ADULTHOOD                                                       124

7  GENERATION DIFFERENCES                                          164

8  CONCLUSIONS                                                     195

APPENDIX 1    Study design and management, and
              some comments on the use of this
              research method.                                     207

APPENDIX 2    Descriptions of social class
              measures and tests of attainment.                    223

References and Author Index                                        227

Subject Index                                                      247

# Figures

2.1  Live birth rate per thousand population in England and Wales, 1841–1980

3.1  Decrees nisi granted in England and Wales, 1936–1983

6.1  Cumulative death rates from birth to 35 years in men and women according to the social class of their family of origin

6.2*a*  Cumulative death rates in men, comparing the social class of the family of origin, and those with and without chronic illness in childhood

6.2*b*  Cumulative death rates in women, comparing the social class of the family of origin, and those with and without chronic illness in childhood

7.1  Average scores (and confidence intervals) on tests taken at 8 years

# Tables

2.1  Comparison of study infant death rates with those in England, Wales, and Scotland 1987

4.1*a*  The influence of parental interest on 8-year-old boys' and girls' reading average scores

4.1*b*  The influence of parental interest on 8-year-old boys' and girls' picture intelligence average scores

4.2  Social group by level of attainment at age 11 years; percentage of 15-year-old children attending grammar schools

5.1  Percentages of children who achieved O level examination passes, in relation to the social group of their family and their attainment tests score at age 15 years

5.2  Types of schools attended by girls and boys at age 15 years

5.3  The association of educational attainment at 8 years with educational outcome

5.4  The relationship between parents' and children's qualifications

5.5  Educational attainment of boys and girls from different social backgrounds, according to their experience of parental divorce or death whilst 0–15 years

6.1*a*  Employment of men (and women, in brackets) who scored in the top third on attainment tests at 8 years, and the home and school routes to employment

6.1*b*  Employment of men (and women, in brackets) who scored in the middle and lowest thirds on attainment tests at 8 years, and the home and school routes to employment

6.2  Family origins and educational attainment of high earning (top third) men at age 36 years

6.3  Leisure time activities of men and women at 36 years, according to their class of origin and their education

7.1  Expectations of life at birth and at 40 years, and gains in expectations, for males and females in three generations of the United Kingdom population

7.2  Employment and unemployment amongst study members and their parents

7.3*a*  Women's employment and unemployment at 36 years, and the social class origins of those in each group

7.3*b*  Men's employment and unemployment at 36 years, and the social class origins of those in each group

9.1  Contacts made with the whole population selected for follow-up after the birth survey of 1946

9.2  Contact with the cohort at age 43–4 years

# 1
## Introduction

Thinking back, most people seem to remember the last war as
times when community spirit and friendliness flourished, both
in civilian and in forces life. They remember those times too,
and the pre-war years, for closer family ties and greater family
proximity than are usual nowadays (Young and Wilmott 1962),
helped no doubt by the relatively small amount of movement
away from home which made two- and three-generation
families living together or close by a quite common family
arrangement. Yet the wartime community spirit is often
remembered because it brought together from different social
class backgrounds people who would not normally before then
have communicated or known much about one another's way
of life. For women wartime and forces work gave a new
freedom to make choices in life which had usually been
regarded as unattainable in pre-war years. After the Second
World War people from all parts of society were determined
that life should not return to 'the poverty and unemployment of
the 1930s, and the pre-war division of Britain into two nations'
(Addison 1985: 6); and as Addison (1985) summarized, the
wartime and immediate post-war 'change in relationship in the
classes was forcibly underwritten by the economics of scarcity'
(p. 6), for instance in the form of post-war rationing of food,
clothing, and petrol. The extent to which these perceived
changes in relationships between classes were maintained in
later years is, of course, a topic of considerable dispute
(Summerfield 1986). Such thoughts and hopes of change in the
minds of many people seem also to have been prevalent at the
end of the First World War (Stewart 1988).

Looking back with the help of documentary evidence it is
clear that, apart from the conflict, this was also in many respects
a time of progress. In medicine, for instance, considerable
advances were made in surgery, skin grafting, and treatment of
burns, in the control of infection and the development of
sulphonamide and antibiotic medicines, and in appreciating

the importance and feasibility of maintaining a healthy population through adequate nutrition and through the Emergency
Medical Service's planned distribution of medical care. Industry discovered the skills and versatility of female labour and
the mass production that permitted the rapid output of complex
equipment, such as aircraft, by semi-skilled workers and those
with a minimum of training. In an editorial on the 'Condition
of the People' published in *The Economist*, and written to
coincide with the centenary of Engels's *The Condition of the
Working Class in England in 1844*, a short stock-taking exercise
compared the circumstances of 1942 with those prevailing one
hundred years before. The achievement of greatly improved
survival rates, the system of factory inspection, the forty-seven
hour week, and the national system of pensions and social
insurance were all praised but, the author noted, 'whatever the
improvements in health and nutrition, the problem of the rich
and the poor, the inequalities of wealth have not been
eliminated' (*The Economist* 1944). Despite improvements,
continuing large-scale housing problems were noted, and so
were sharp social class divisions in opportunities for achievement in education. The shock was recalled of the conditions
revealed in the Evacuation Survey of 1943, when people were

appalled at the descriptions, unemotionally related by trained social
workers, of the dirty and verminous children, ridden with scabies and
other skin diseases, with disgusting sleeping and feeding habits, of
the negligence and fecklessness of their parents. It showed how
ignorance and poverty were exploited by all kinds of money-lenders,
clothing clubs, insurance touts, quack doctors and vendors of patent
medicines. (*The Economist* 1944)

Bartlett (1977) noted that 'as late as 1946 the Curtis
Committee had to report that some children under the care of
local authorities were still living in nineteenth century all-
purpose workhouses' (p. 6).

   *The Economist* editorial concluded that

The Government is now pledged to introduce far-reaching reforms in
education, health, housing and social insurance, and is planning to
bring in family allowances and to regulate the wages and conditions
of the lowest-paid workers. Whatever Government is to return to
power it will be committed to this programme of social reform. But to

say that there has been progress since 1844 is not enough; the question is whether the advances in social conditions have been commensurate with technical and scientific progress or the nation's productive capacity, and the answer, on all the evidence, can only be in the negative. (*The Economist* 1944)

This evidence, and the way that people remember the war, reflect the changes in the organization of society which were then beginning, and which were foreshadowed by the wartime community spirit and the nationwide organization of services for welfare, scientific, and industrial purposes.

In some respects these changes originated before the Second World War, and were hastened by the social upheaval of the conflict. For example, Lowndes (1969) noted that the appointment of welfare officers to help with the evacuation of children from cities

marked the beginning of a much more general appreciation of the value of the trained social worker over wide fields of government and local authority activity. Hitherto this field had been covered—in so far as it had been covered at all—by those who had grown up under the arid conception that the only proper sphere of government intervention was to ward off distress (thought of as a kind of symbol of social incapacity), in the case of the poorest citizens. (Lowndes 1969: 207)

Similarly, the rapid expansion of nurseries for the care of children whose mothers had been pressed into working for the war effort and an increased uptake of immunization for children were greatly speeded by the war, and had extensive post-war consequences.

In education there was a similar process. Before the war it had been calculated that one in four pupils left school before the official leaving age, in higher education there were seven fee-paying students for every one who was grant aided, and there was little state or local authority financial help for undergraduates (Lowndes 1969). The discussion document that was the forerunner of the Education Act of 1944 was concerned with 'the social ideal the Prime Minister has set before us of establishing a state of society where the advantages and privileges, which hitherto have been enjoyed only by the few, shall be more widely shared' (Barnett 1986: 277).

Much of the debate about the Education Act was concerned

whether its first and guiding priority should be the development of the individual in mind, body, and spirit, or the
education of the nation's individuals to 'promote national
capability and success' (Barnett 1986: 277). A vociferous lobby
for the priority of individual development was led by the
Church of England and by those in the education and political
establishment who were in favour of building what they called
a post-war 'New Jerusalem' which would perpetuate 'the
national unity achieved in this country during the war through
a social and economic structure designed to secure equality of
opportunity and service among all classes of the community'
(Barnett 1986: 20).

There were others, all too aware of the serious lack of skilled
manpower during the war, who urged the government to
recognize that

A highly trained scientific technical personnel is of course a
prerequisite; and although the universities provide the initial
training of a small minority, our existing technical colleges, on which
the bulk of training for industry falls, are neither equipped nor staffed
to deal adequately with modern demands (Barnett 1986: 288).

In health and welfare there was much greater agreement
about plans for the future, in the shape of Beveridge's
proposals to free Britain as much as possible from the 'five
giant evils' of Want, Disease, Ignorance, Squalor, and Idleness,
by providing children's allowances, a comprehensive health
service, and a higher rate of employment. There was, of course,
rather less agreement about the details of how this could be
achieved.

Such plans and pressures resulted in the Education Act of
1944 and the National Health Service Act of 1946. In the 'flurry
of legislation carried through by the Labour Government'
(Marwick 1982: 61–2) newly elected in 1945, many other Acts
of Parliament were also passed which were designed to
increase accessibility to benefits of all kinds, and to improve
the standard of living of people in all social classes. The
National Insurance Act (1946), the National Insurance (Industrial Injuries) Act (1946), the Family Allowance Act (1945), the
National Assistance Act (1948), the National Parks and Access
to the Country Act (1949), the Town and Country Planning Act

(1947), the New Towns Act (1946), the Housing Act (1949), the Legal Aid and Advice Act (1949), and in 1946 the establishment of the Arts Council were all passed during the term of office of the Labour government, although all were the culmination of ideas from many sources and from earlier times. Howard (1986) observed that in electing a Labour government with a mandate for such change

the 1945 voter was not so much casting his ballot in judgement of the past five years as in denunciation of the ten years before that. The dole queue was more evocative than El Alamein, the lack of roofs at home more important than any 'national' non-party edifice, the peace that might be lost far more influential than the war that had nearly been won. (p. 4)

In America Vatter (1986) describes a comparable post-war process of development of measures to redistribute income, to improve the nation's health and education, and to repair the social divisions inflicted by the pre-war Depression.

Thus there was a strong desire for post-war reconstruction and change, and above all for improvement. In Britain the changes in community spirit and in medical and industrial techniques revealed what could and what needed to be done, and with quickening technological innovation, barriers against the idea of change were gradually reduced, so that nowadays, more than ever before, many aspects of life seem to be very different when generations are compared; but not without an awareness of the dilemma of wanting improvement yet at the same time feeling reluctant to abandon many aspects of the remembered past.

The purpose of this book is to describe the life and development of a large group of children who were born in 1946, in that immediate post-war time, and who therefore lived their childhood through a period of immense social change. They were selected randomly from all the births in Britain that took place in one week in March of that year, and they have been studied ever since, so far for more than 40 years. A certain amount of information was collected from their parents, who were born over a wide range of years from 1882 to 1931, and this provides some comparative material on an earlier generation. A study of ways in which the study population, born in

1946, went about bringing up their children has also been undertaken to look at relationships with the following generation. The design of the study is described in Appendix 1.

Such a research design provided the chance to study the development of the children and to make evaluations of post-war innovations in education and health, by comparing these children with those born at earlier and later times. This kind of study offers the opportunity to consider three aspects of time and change.

## DEVELOPMENT OF THE INDIVIDUAL

Time passing may be investigated in terms of the development of the individual. In biological terms, for example, the passage of time in childhood is of great importance, since by the late teenage years physical development will be practically complete; failure to develop during these years is, in most respects, a permanently lost opportunity (Bock and Whelan 1991). The potential for such development is genetically determined as well as influenced by the environment that parents, especially the mother, provide both before and after birth (Emanuel 1986, Butler and Golding 1986). There is growing evidence that the risk of ill health in adult life is associated not only with the current environment and the individual's choice of health habits, but also with health in childhood. Levels of adult blood pressure and adult respiratory functional ability, for example, both seem to be associated with childhood levels. Although the reasons for these observed associations in blood pressure (de Swiet 1986, Berenson 1986, Medical Research Council 1987, Barker *et al.* 1989, Bock and Whelan 1991), and in respiratory function (Britten *et al.* 1987, Barker and Osmond 1986*a*, Mann *et al.* forthcoming) are not yet fully understood, there is evident importance of such findings for the development of health services, particularly for children. There is also some evidence to show associations between adult smoking and exercise habits and those of parents (Golding 1987, Fenner 1987, Mann *et al.* forthcoming). It may therefore be that in some important respects during the time *in utero* and childhood the stock of health resource and potential is laid down, which may be augmented or depleted later in adult life (Bock and Whelan 1991).

Childhood, adolescence, and early adult life are also vital times for educational attainment in our society, since although it is possible to obtain educational qualifications later in life, it requires an unusual effort of will, and relatively few people do so at later ages. Whether or not these are years of unique opportunity to develop intellectually is hard to know, since attitudes form an important aspect of such development. Many books of advice for parents claim 'that the preschool years are vitally important in influencing the intellectual growth and curiosity of a child, and that by the age of five the measure of his intelligence gives a rough estimate of his future performance' (Jolly 1977).

Good evidence for such a statement is, however, hard to find. Douglas and Cherry (1977) and Rodgers (1986) found that, contrary to the assumptions of many in education, one aspect of intellectual functioning, namely reading skills, continued to improve after school leaving in practically all the children who are the subject of this book. It is therefore not possible simply to regard intellectual development in the same terms as biological growth, although many of its components, such as intellectual interests, motivation to learn, and attainment in educational terms, are powerfully influenced during childhood.

Childhood and adolescence are also times of development of tastes, self-perception, styles of coping in emotional and other terms, and many aspects of identity formation, as well as times of gradually increasing independence from the family of origin.

Development is thus a process of accumulation of experience modified by inherited characteristics, two components of which tend to change in relation to one another as time passes. Studies that compare twin and singleton development show that

younger children, regardless of their genetic relatedness, resemble each other intellectually because they share similar rearing environments. Older adolescents, on the other hand, resemble one another only if they share genes. Our interpretation is that older children escape the influences of family and are freer to select their own environment. Parental influences are diluted by the more varied mix of adolescent experiences. (Scarr and Weinberg 1983)

Thus, a study of individual development from birth into adulthood is concerned with how individuals are influenced in their adult life by a whole range of childhood family and environmental circumstances. This is of importance in planning health, education, and welfare services, as well as in the study of the natural history of particular aspects of development and of ageing.

## HISTORICAL OR SOCIAL TIME PASSING

Time and change may also be considered in terms of historical or social time. The children in the study described here lived through times of great change in many things ranging from income to attitudes to sexual behaviour, and from opportunities in education to the changing and increasing types of occupation available. This kind of follow-up study is therefore also a way to investigate how some kinds of changes in society have affected individuals.

For example, attainment of educational qualifications by the children in the study was generally much higher than that of their parents. This improvement was found not only on average in the total population but also within social classes, as a result of changes in the provision of educational opportunities. Findings from the study show how far changes in the educational services brought the benefits intended, the extent to which they were available for all those for whom they were intended, and whether they were of long-term value.

In post-war medical care advances in technical knowledge and in lay people's understanding and improvements in curative and preventive services, especially in nutrition and infant welfare, brought actual increases in children's growth (Kuh *et al.* forthcoming). Beginning well before the Second World War the availability of advice for mothers, the development of child health clinics, the provision of school meals, and for mothers and children of milk, iron, vitamins, and cod liver oil all helped to improve children's growth. Burnett (1989) notes that in 1939 'Twelve-year-old boys attending elementary schools in London were three inches taller and eleven pounds heavier than their fathers had been twenty years earlier' (p. 285). In the follow-up of children born in 1946 rates of growth in height and weight have been studied from birth to mid-life in order to see what happened to children who lived their early years during national food rationing, and their adolescence and adulthood in times of wide choice. The analysis examined whether the potential for height achievement assessed from the combined genetic and environmental effects of parents' heights was reached by individuals from all kinds of social circumstances, and whether the increases in the quantity and quality of food available were equally well managed, in terms of consumption of food and alcohol, by all the individuals in the study; the findings are described in the following chapters.

Changes in society are also important because they bring new ideas and attitudes which affect the individual. In this study, for instance, it is possible to see who changed habits in response to new ideas about smoking or nutrition, and the social circumstances of those who, over time, changed ideas about what was socially acceptable behaviour or about the value of education. It is also possible to compare the effects of changes in public expectations of outcomes of particular childhood problems. For instance, there has been considerable change in notions of what the long-term effects on the child may be of chronic illness in general, and in particular of some serious illnesses, such as epilepsy. It is important to know how far the now much less pessimistic prognoses about the medical and social futures of seriously ill children have changed the observed course of events. Similarly, popular ideas about the effects on the child of parental separation or divorce which prevailed in the immediate post-war years were gloomy about future educational attainment and 'moral fibre'. How far were they right, how did they seem to affect individual children, and how far have improvements in the popular outlook changed the lives of those more recently born?

Comparisons of change over time in health and welfare provisions and in powerful popular ideas need to be carried out, however, not only through the study of individuals born at different historical times, but also by the investigation of generation change and generation difference within the same families. This is especially important, for instance, in the study of educational attainment. In the generations of children born shortly before and soon after the Second World War parental interest in their child's school work and progress was found to be strongly associated with the child's ultimate educational attainment; low parental interest tended to precede relatively poor attainment and high interest was significantly associated with high attainment (Douglas 1964). In the 1930s and 1940s education was seen as practically the only way for the child of a lower social class family to move into a higher earning group, commanding greater respect and greater freedom of opportunity (Jackson and Marsden 1962). Do parents who have good educational qualifications tend now to think of such things as of less importance for their children? Or are parents who themselves made the greatest gain in educational attainment, in comparison with their parents, those who gave the greatest encouragement to their children to do well in school? These are necessary questions about the future pattern of educational attainment and the capabilities of the labour force.

## ATTACHMENT TO A PARTICULAR PERIOD OF TIME

A third way to investigate the experience of time and change combines the two previous methods in the study of the individual's attachment to a particular period of time. Children born in the immediate post-war years grew up in the late 1940s, the 1950s, and the early 1960s, and they are in many respects children of that time. Social factors unique to that period, such as Britain's post-war food rationing, the development of and changes in selective secondary education, widespread cigarette smoking, relatively uncontrolled atmospheric pollution, and rapid changes in attitudes to sexual behaviour, marriage, and religion will have affected individuals' experience and development in a way that is unique to that era.

In biological terms, for instance, adult respiratory abilities and proneness to illness in a generation who lived their developing years at a time of high atmospheric pollution and widespread cigarette smoking may be less good than in those who grew up after the Clean Air Act of 1956 and when changes in smoking habits began to take effect. Children born in 1946 were growing up at a time when ideas about cigarette smoking were very different.

Dr Dalton's autumn budget of 1947 put up the price of cigarettes from 2s 4d for 20 to 3s 4d (they cost one shilling before the war), and in his cheery way he announced: 'Smoke your cigarettes to the butts, it may even be good for your health.' (Howarth 1985: 65–6)

This 'advice' is rather less surprising in its contemporary context; during the war smoking was widely regarded as a rapid and reliable method of reducing tension and of staying awake (Harrisson 1978).

Improved standards of nutrition in childhood, in all social classes, brought increases in average height (Tanner 1962), which may also reflect better development of many other organs. Children in this study, for instance, grew on average to be taller than their parents and were likely to achieve their parentally determined growth potential (Kuh and Wadsworth 1989). Children born more recently have grown to be taller still (Kuh *et al.* forthcoming). Such information is useful not only for the assessment of improvement, or otherwise, in the health of the population, but is a reminder that in many respects health, like education, is an investment in childhood which has long-term consequences both for the individual and for future national well-being. For example, girls who are not well nourished in childhood and who do not develop well are, in due course, at greater risk of problems in pregnancy and of giving birth to a less than optimally healthy baby (Illsley and Mitchell 1984, Emanuel 1986).

There are other very long-term influences of childhood experience which are associated with social and educational circumstances prevailing at the time of the individual's development. It was, for instance, found in this study that a combination of family attitudes to education and the design of the selective system of secondary education available to the study children effectively reduced the chances of further or higher education for children from working class homes (Douglas 1964), and therefore in due course restricted their opportunities in choice of jobs and in income (Cherry 1978, Kuh and Wadsworth forthcoming). Parental attitudes prevalent at the time study children were at school played an important part in the educational opportunities of children in the following generation. In this study, for example, girls' chances of going on to further or higher education were much lower than those of boys. Children of least-educated parents had the smallest chance of achieving any educational qualifications, and children of best-educated parents had the greatest chance not only of qualifications, but of getting the highest qualifications. Improvements in educational opportunities in one generation may therefore improve chances of bringing about an intergenerational rise in skill levels and in occupational adaptability.

We are also attached to a particular time period in that we think of ourselves as 'children' of a particular era. This may be especially true of adolescence and early adult life when individuality and identity are established through first independence from parents and before perceptions of the restrictions of adult life become clear. Childhood, adolescence, and early adult life are naturally not the only times to which we look back and which have a significant impact on the course of our lives, but they usually constitute a particularly salient time. They are remembered by many as the most carefree times, and recollected with varying mixtures of agreeable nostalgia and irritation at opportunities seen as lost. In adulthood memory of earlier life gives access to a period when time and possibilities seemed happily endless. Warnock (1987) quotes de Beauvoir's observation that 'The reason why the emotional memories that restore childhood are so treasured is that for a fleeting instant they give us back a boundless future' (p. 137). As we get older we make increasing use of earlier childhood and adult life to understand and explain what we are. Warnock (1987) writes that 'The sense of personal identity that each of us has is a sense of continuity through time. We could not have this without memory, in the full sense of recollection' (p. 75).

One elderly gentleman said in Blythe's (1979) study, 'I've got no work and no wife, but I've got what I've done, haven't I' (p. 76) Recollection of all kinds of experience in times past is thus an important aspect of life and of identity: a character in one of Katherine Mansfield's (1918) short stories asks, 'Who am I . . . but my own past? If I deny that, I am nothing' (pp. 151–2). Recollection of childhood and adolescence is affected by parents' stories, recollections, values, and interpretations of what was also an important time in their lives, as well as by experiences that took place during the intervening years (Yarrow *et al.* 1970). Consideration of time and change in terms of recollections of childhood, adolescence, and early adult life is therefore necessary in the study of individual development.

Attachment to a particular historical time, during the individual's early life, also emphasizes the difference between generations. In times of great change in environment, in technological achievement, in personal ambitions, or in the common standards of socially acceptable personal behaviour, such generation gaps will seem particularly great. Improvement is nowadays expected within the lifetime of the individual, for instance in material circumstances, as well as between generations in terms of such things as educational and living standards. In a rather homely way Wolfenstein (1955) described generation differences in how parents wanted to bring up their children and how, at that time, parents 'turn to the contemporary expert'.

in a changing culture the elders lose their infallibility. American parents, for instance, do not expect to bring up their children in the way they were brought up, any more than they would want to live in the house in which they were raised or to drive around in the family car of their childhood. They hope to bring up their children better than they were brought up themselves. (p. 145)

Many aspects of the generation gap will look different as increasing age changes the individual's perspective. In middle life, when responsibility increases and there is a growing awareness of mortality, there are changes in styles of beliefs, attitudes, and values. Ingmar Bergman is reported to have said that 'We go away from our parents and back to our parents. Suddenly one understands them, recognizes them as human beings, and in that moment one has grown-up' (Prawer 1988).

Each part of life, from infancy to old age, has to be lived in its historical time. Now there is increasing evidence to show that we carry forward influences of our earlier lives and of the times in which we then lived. Thus, although the elderly now have present day care, some important aspects of their health and chances of survival are rooted in the time of their childhood and adolescence in the early years of this century. It may be that attitudes, expectations, beliefs, and notions of morality are also developed in the context of their time, particularly in adolescence and early adult life, when education and upbringing have their most visible effects on life chances. Later modification of such early life biological, educational, and family effects will undoubtedly occur, but later influences can only operate on existing states of health or attitudes, and chances of encountering later influences may themselves be to some degree dependent on earlier experience. Understanding these interrelationships of influences on individual development and change with age is important for the design of health and education services, for the study of the origins and effects of changes in society, and for the investigation of how developments in medicine, technology, and education affect the lives of individuals and of families.

It is, therefore, of value to explore the processes of physical and mental development and change with age.

Understanding growth and organ development, the origins of vulnerability to illness, and the processes of ageing is important in order to establish how risk of illness increases and how to improve methods for its care and control. The study of a group of people from birth into adult life can provide information on many aspects of these processes for use in health care and planning, and this is particularly necessary now that the prevailing pattern of illness is long term.

Intellectual and cognitive development and their change with increasing age must also be understood for reasons both of health care and of education and training. This is necessary since education and training are vital for the supply of skilled labour, as well as for the development of capacity for fulfilment during increasing leisure time and longer periods of retirement. An understanding of development and change in cognitive processes during the life course is equally necessary in health care plans for the management of problems of degeneration with age in memory and cognition in a national population in which the proportion of elderly people is rising.

Research into these processes must take into account the social and family circumstances of its subjects, since they are very likely to influence both perception of risks, for example to health, and thus attitudes to care, as well as the rates at which biological and cognitive changes take place. For example, the development of high blood pressure will be influenced not only by such intrinsic factors as inherited tendencies, but also by those things from the previous generation which are associated with health and growth in early life, before and after birth, as well as by exercise habits, diet, and the extent of alcohol consumption and cigarette smoking. Changes in cognitive processes are similarly influenced by intrinsic as well as by extrinsic factors.

Whilst biological, cognitive, and intellectual development and change take place the individual is, of course, in many ways far more concerned with such important matters as choice of education and training, of employment opportunities, of partner, of lifestyle, of whether and when to have children, and of how to establish and maintain comfortable relationships with parents. All these things are in various degrees also influenced by family background and own experience and personality, as well as by the opportunities that custom and the structure of society present; they will become influences on health and opportunities in middle and later life. Information about the availability of such opportunities is useful in assessing, for instance, how educational policies work, and whether they favour individuals with particular experience or attributes, or those who are from particular backgrounds.

It is important to undertake research into these processes because times and social circumstances change. Eating and alcohol consumption and smoking habits have altered considerably during the last forty years, and so have leisure activities and the demands made by work in many occupations, the chances of gaining further or higher education after leaving school, and behaviour and expectations in the emotional aspects of life. It is necessary to know how these kinds of changes affect physical and mental health.

The study of change in individuals during their childhood and on into adult life is thus an opportunity to assess the differential strengths of impact of a range of influences encountered at various stages in life. As the study population become parents their influence on the following generation, who begin childhood in a very different world compared with that of their parents, may also be examined. Information of this kind allows us to compare childhood in two generations, and to understand effects of policies and changes which have come about during the intervening time. It is also a source of information on the transmission of personal and family characteristics and values from one generation to another.

We often want to know what happened in the past in order to understand how the present came about, either in ourselves or in society. We can get at the past by asking people to recollect what it was like, but the risk is that they may not remember because they have completely or partially forgotten, perhaps because they do not want to remember, or because they never knew, and they may not properly recall the chronological order of events. In remembering they may inevitably colour how it was with the perception of today, and with knowledge of what happened in the time between then and now. We can also get at the past by consulting records made at the time. Looking back using records we can often recognize a time of progress of one kind or another in health, for example, or education; but progress rarely touches all those for whom it is intended or who need it; records and published statistics usually contain neither enough detail nor sufficient analysis to make this clear. Records can usually only provide snapshots taken of groups at one point in the past, and only from one angle. A more informative record is made by a series of snapshots of individuals taken at frequent intervals, and of many aspects of the same subjects. (See Appendix 1 for comments on research methods used in studies of long periods of time.)

The study described here is in effect a series of snapshots of people born in all kinds of circumstances and in all parts of England, Wales, and Scotland soon after the Second World War. Comparisons of the 'pictures' taken from the time of birth onwards reveal how members of the study population grew up and made their way in the world, and what became of those from every kind of beginning.

# 2
## *Birth*

### INTRODUCTION

It may at first seem odd to have undertaken a study of maternity services, of home help in pregnancy and after childbirth, and of the costs of childbirth, in the turmoil of the immediate post-war years. The study team's report observed that at the time there were

schemes for evacuating expectant mothers, and the control of employment. Moreover there were acute deficiencies in housing, maternity beds and medical personnel also attributable to the war. These deficiencies existed, however, in many areas before the war and are unlikely to be remedied for many years. Consequently it was felt that although this study has been undertaken in an 'abnormal period', it yet gives a substantially accurate picture of the problems of childbearing both today and for some time to come. (Joint Committee (*a*) 1948: 15)

But at that time, plans for the beginning of the National Health Service needed to be as well informed as possible, and relatively little of the necessary information was available. This desire to look forward and to plan for the future characterized the post-war mood, and as Thomson (1981) describes,

the pre-war world of the thirties seemed so insecure and blameworthy that there was little nostalgia for the past. To look back at all was to look back in anger—and in grief. So men looked forward, damning the recent past perhaps too completely, and shunning so vehemently the errors of the past that they were apt to commit an entirely new set of errors of their own. Uppermost in their minds was the desire for fuller social justice, a lessening of class differences, and greater security and peace. (p. 218)

There were also worries about what appeared to have been a continuing decline in fertility in Great Britain since the middle of the previous century, as figure 2.1 shows, and a Royal Commission on Population was considering this and other problems when the study was planned in 1945.

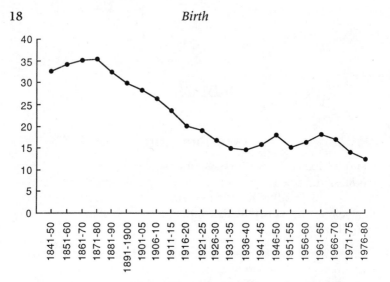

F<small>IG</small>. 2.1 Live birth rate per thousand population in England and Wales, 1841–1980

In 1942 Titmuss and Titmuss had written that

Millions of parents are revolting against parenthood, and these millions of individual decisions are collectively expressed in a falling birth-rate pointing ultimately to extinction. For sixty years, through war and peace, boom and slump, hardship and happiness, the birth-rate has been relentlessly falling. (p. 11)

In fact, as is evident in figure 2.1, the country was on the brink of a baby boom, although this was not yet wholly clear during the latter years of the war even in 1946 when the study described in this book began.

The study was therefore begun not only in consideration of plans for the future Health Service but also because there were anxieties that 'the medical and other costs associated with the birth of a baby may today be a serious deterrent to parenthood, not only for the lower income groups, but for all sections of the community' (Joint Committee (*a*) 1948: 1).

With these aims in mind the study was designed to be representative of births throughout England, Wales, and Scotland. All births in the week 3–9 March 1946 were investigated by means of questionnaires that health visitors asked of mothers at home visits when the selected child was eight weeks old. This age was chosen since by then all costs associated with preparation for the birth and the birth itself were likely to be known, mothers should by then have received postnatal care, and babies should have been taken for their first visit to an infant welfare centre. This time was also soon enough after the birth to avoid problems of recollection. As well as the data collected at these home interviews, health visitors also checked clinic notes, and two members of the study team visited five contrasting local authorities to talk to the medical and nursing staff. A full description of the study design is given in Appendix 1.

The extent of co-operation was remarkable. All 458 local authorities in England, Wales, and Scotland were asked to take part in the study and 424 (93 per cent) agreed to do so. Only 2 per cent of the mothers who had given birth in the chosen week refused to be visited. Some mothers (7 per cent) could not be traced, partly because of house moving, because gypsy mothers were hard to find, and because of emigration and the departure of some GI brides for their new homes in America soon after the birth of their child. But in the end 91 per cent (13,687) of mothers were successfully interviewed.

## CARE BEFORE BIRTH

All but 125 of the 13,687 women who took part in the study received some kind of antenatal care, and for one in four (26 per cent) this was provided privately, perhaps in some cases for reasons expressed elliptically by one lady who said that 'everybody doesn't like to meet what you have to meet at antenatal clinics'.

There was a considerable social class difference in the average number of weeks before delivery during which antenatal care (referred to as antenatal supervision at the time) was from time to time received; they ranged from a period of 25.7 weeks for wives of professional and salaried workers, to 21.8 weeks for wives of manual workers, and to 14.8 weeks for unmarried mothers. Within each social class first time mothers attended for antenatal care earlier than others, and the proportions of fourth or later time mothers who received such care in the first three months of pregnancy fell from 53 per cent of professional and salaried groups to 15 per cent of agricultural workers; it was concluded that 'There is clearly a case here for further efforts at education by health visitors and midwives' (Joint Committee (a) 1948: 33).

The argument for an increased effort to extend the reach of antenatal care to include more women and a greater proportion of each pregnancy received further stimulus from two quarters. Maternal death rates, which had fallen little between 1931 and 1941, had fallen sharply by 1945, and this had generally 'been attributed to improved nutrition brought about by milk schemes, and the addition of vitamin and mineral supplements, together with rationing and the greatly improved qualities of the national loaf' (Joint Committee (a) 1948: 36). But it was argued, 'These measures, however, apart from improving the nutritional condition of expectant mothers, encouraged women to put themselves under supervision early in pregnancy, while a further incentive to early and regular supervision was provided by the growing demand for institutional confinements and the consequent shortage of beds' (Joint Committee (a) 1948: 36). Thus improvements in antenatal care had arguably helped to reduce the maternal death rate, and findings from this maternity study demonstrated a second advantage. In the study week the rates of still-births, prematurity, and deaths in the first month of life (neonatal deaths) for both first and subsequent births were lowest for those who received 'adequate' antenatal care (i.e. at least nine attendances starting in the first three months of pregnancy) and highest amongst those whose care was described as 'inadequate' (attendances only in the last three months of pregnancy). Breast-feeding was also more successfully established in those 'adequately' cared for, particularly for first births, and 63 per cent of mothers who had received 'adequate care' established breast-feeding compared with 47 per cent of mothers who had had 'inadequate care'.

The importance of nutrition was raised again in the interpretation of findings from a national study of perinatal mortality (that is, death of a baby occurring between 28 weeks of gestation and within seven completed days after birth) carried out in one week in March 1958 (Butler and Bonham 1963). That study found after ten years of the National Health

Service, that perinatal mortality was still sharply differentiated by social class, although considerably reduced. It was suggested that this might partly be explained by long-term effects of relatively poor nutrition of women from manual social class families of origin who were children during the Depression. However, although the argument for long-term effects of childhood nutrition on subsequent child bearing has been shown subsequently to be of great importance (Emanuel 1986), it is evidently not the whole explanation for such social class differences in perinatal mortality, which are still striking (see Blaxter 1981 and 'Survival', section below).

More recent studies of attendance at antenatal clinics continue to show social class differences in the use of antenatal care, and particularly in the time of first attendance (Blaxter 1981, Macintyre 1984).

In 1980 the House of Commons Social Services Committee was still concerned about 'long waiting times, difficult access to clinics, lack of continuity of care,' and it is clear from recent studies that mothers' desire to be given more information, and their irritation with the low level of communication at clinics cuts across all social class divisions (Macintyre 1984). It was also found that much of the social class difference in first attendance times may be accounted for by pre-maritally pregnant women delaying their first visit until after marriage (Illsley 1956, McKinlay and McKinlay 1979), although this is now much less likely than at earlier times.


PAID EMPLOYMENT DURING PREGNANCY

In 1946 paid maternity leave was extremely rare, and women with small incomes had to work late in pregnancy and return to work soon afterwards to maintain their income. One mother in the study worked until the day before delivery and returned to work one month afterwards. 'This was the mother's sixth confinement, two of her older children had died in infancy. Poverty is indicated by the fact that the whole family occupied only one room, and it was in this room that the confinement took place' (Joint Committee (*a*) 1948: 170).

Although such extreme cases were few, state financial assistance was very limited. A maternity grant of £2 was available to married employees, in addition to the £2 grant they received under the National Health Insurance (NHI) scheme as workers' wives. This was, even by the standards of the day (see 'Costs', below) a very small sum. Women who were self-employed or in family businesses were not covered by the NHI scheme. The National Insurance Act of 1946 was later to double the maternity grant to £4, and entitle working mothers to a maternity allowance of £1 16s. a week for six weeks before the confinement and seven weeks afterwards. However, the Joint Committee (*a*) (1948) concluded that it was 'highly questionable whether the sum of £1 16s a week is adequate at present price-levels to provide for the full mainten- ance of mother and child' (p. 171).

Full-time paid occupation during pregnancy was most frequently found amongst the unmarried (75 per cent), as compared with 20 per cent of married women. Paid employ- ment was, of course, much more usual amongst first-time mothers (58 per cent) than amongst those who already had one or more children (9 per cent). All but 12 per cent of those who were gainfully employed during pregnancy stopped working during the last ten weeks before the birth of the baby.

Although the relatively small numbers of women in the various occupation groups made the assessment of the effects of paid employment during pregnancy rather difficult, it was concluded that 'there is no reason to believe that work during the first five months of pregnancy increases the risk of prematurity or stillbirth. Work during the last 19 weeks of pregnancy, however, seems to involve an additional risk' (Joint Committee (*a*) 1948: 168). Women in full-time paid employment received antenatal care as frequently as others, but this often necessitated absence from work and therefore loss of income.

Whereas in England and Wales before the Second World War there had been nursery provision for less than 7 per cent of children under five years, the numbers of available places had risen considerably during the war, but were substantially cut back in the immediate post-war years; nevertheless 23 per cent of children of study mothers who were in full-time occupation during their pregnancy went to nurseries. The potential demand, however, was much higher, and 60 per cent of first-time mothers who were wives of manual workers and who intended to return to work after the birth of their baby wanted their child to have a nursery place.

## PLACE OF BIRTH

Nowadays in England approximately 99 per cent of births take place in hospital (Department of Health and Social Security 1985), but in the 1946 study the comparable figure was 54 per cent, and this varied from 58 per cent in county boroughs to 11 per cent in Norfolk. Like antenatal care, this too was class biased, with greatest opportunities of hospital or nursing home delivery for wives of professional and salaried men. Manual workers' wives were not only least likely to have their first baby in hospital, but the chances of this happening for their second and subsequent births fell sharply, compared with the chances for wives from higher up the social class scale.

Giving birth in hospital without the advantages of being in a private ward or nursing home was not likely to have been a wholly relaxing experience, since it was then usual for babies to be left in the wards day and night. Visiting was also inclined to be restricted.

Some hospitals allow visits every day for an hour in the afternoon and an hour in the evening; others rigidly limit visiting to two or three half hours per week. Some matrons feel that even the latter is too much and would prefer to stop visiting altogether. Then, again, visitors are usually admitted singly, but in a few hospitals there is no limit to the number. Often the baby can only be seen once a week by the father, but other hospitals allow all visitors to see the baby whenever they come. (Joint Committee (*a*) 1948: 73)

Visiting restrictions must have been particularly trying when the average length of stay was 15 days; the average length of stay in 1978 was 5.5 days (Macfarlane and Mugford 1984).

Although confinement at home could offer the comfort and reassurance of family closeness, for those not so well off it was likely to be a difficult time, since

many home deliveries still take place in conditions of appalling overcrowding. Midwives interviewed in the local inquiries spoke of women who slept during their confinement in the same bed with mothers, female relatives, or husbands. Similar instances occur in the questionnaire survey. For example, a woman living in her parents' house slept during her confinement in the same bed as her mother and sister. Another, living in a two-roomed house, was delivered in one room, while in the other, her three older children and husband were waiting. Lastly, a Glasgow woman who lived in a single room with her husband and three older children had to be delivered there because she could not leave her family. (Joint Committee (*a*) 1948: 58)

In fact one in five confinements took place in homes where the ratio of people to rooms was greater than two per room, and one in fourteen occurred where the ratio was greater than three persons per room. It was concluded 'that shortages of home helps and residential nurseries result in many women being confined at home who should be confined in hospital' (Joint Committee (*a*) 1948: 63).


## BIRTH

A surprisingly high percentage (64 per cent) of home confine-ments were carried out by midwives alone, and although the chances of the general practitioner being present were highest for first births, nevertheless 'deliveries by doctors are largely confined to the wealthier groups' (Joint Committee (*a*) 1948: 67). In hospital only 19 per cent of deliveries were carried out by a doctor.

This reliance on midwives to carry out deliveries of home confinements was particularly unfortunate, since in 1946 only one in five midwives was qualified to administer gas and air for pain relief, and this could only be done if two midwives or a midwife together with a trained nurse or pupil midwife was present. As a result only 20 per cent of women in the study who were delivered at home received some sort of pain relief, and it was concluded that 'The giving of analgesia in itself involves a certain amount of trouble which some midwives seem un-willing to take unless a mother is very insistent in her demands for relief' (Joint Committee (*a*) 1948: 82).

When a doctor was present 48 per cent of women received pain relief, but only 8 per cent did so when the delivery was carried out by a midwife:

wives of professional and salaried workers are three times as likely to be given analgesia as wives of manual workers. Part of this difference is due to the much higher proportion of doctor deliveries in the wealthier group, but this is not the whole explanation.

If the group of women attended by their own doctors is considered alone, there is still a very great difference between the social classes. It appears that practitioners are more likely to give chloroform to rich than to poor women. This may be because the better educated more insistently demand relief, but this explanation does not excuse a discrimination that has given rise to numerous complaints. Some practitioners seem to under-estimate the need for analgesia. (Joint Committee (*a*) 1948: 82–3)

Even in hospital only 52 per cent of women received pain relief, but for unmarried mothers the proportion was 37 per cent.

Sometimes analgesia is not given because of defective apparatus, but more often staff shortages are the cause. It is not enough to provide sufficient machines; the midwives must themselves be encouraged to give analgesia on every suitable occasion. (Joint Committee (*a*) 1948: 86)

## LOW BIRTH WEIGHT

Of all the single births (as compared to twin or other multiple births) 6 per cent were of low birth weight, that is the baby weighed 5½ pounds (2,500 g.) or less. The proportion of low weight births ranged from 4 per cent of births to wives of professional and salaried workers to 7 per cent of births to manual workers' wives and 10 per cent of illegitimate births, and low birth weight was greatest amongst those who had received 'inadequate' antenatal care (see earlier section on 'Care before birth'). Although the prevailing thought was then that low birth weight was closely associated with poor nutrition during pregnancy, there was some evidence from this study that women who were gainfully employed during the last five months of pregnancy (11 per cent of first time mothers) were at greater risk of a low weight birth. However, it was concluded that 'the data from the present inquiry are insufficient to enable us to say how much of this increased risk is due to employment and how much to the poverty that makes it necessary for expectant mothers to remain at work late in pregnancy' (Joint Committee (*a*) 1948: 144).

The proportion of all babies born who weigh 2,500 grams or less has changed very little, ranging from 8.0 per cent of births in England and Wales in 1955 to 7.2 per cent in 1986 (Macfarlane and Mugford 1984, Department of Health and Welsh Office unpublished). This apparent lack of change, however, conceals the fact that massive strides have been achieved in improving chances of survival in babies of low birth weight. Still birth rates amongst low weight babies dropped from 13.1 per cent of all low weight births in 1963 to 10.1 per cent in 1973 and 5.1 per cent in 1983 (Department of Health and Social Security 1985).

## SURVIVAL

Death rates in the study population for the first year of life are given in table 2.1. Looking back from shortly before the time of the study Titmuss (1943) reviewed the evidence on infant survival and concluded that 'Despite a considerable fall in the absolute rates, the range of inequality for total infant mortality is as great as, if not greater than, in 1911' (p. 57).

Now comparison with recent English and Welsh rates shows

TABLE 2.1   *Comparison of study infant death rates with those in England, Wales, and Scotland 1987*

| Social class | Infant death rates (death in the first year of life) per thousand live births | | |
| --- | --- | --- | --- |
| | 1946 birth Cohort[a] | England and Wales 1987[a] | Scotland 1987 |
| Professional I | 13.3 | 6.9 | 7.1 |
| Salaried II | 27.8 | 6.7 | 7.6 |
| Clerical: non-manual IIINM | 32.3 | 7.1 | 4.7 |
| Skilled manual IIIM | 32.7 | 7.7 | 6.4 |
| Semi-skilled IV | 41.7 | 9.6 | 6.5 |
| Unskilled V | 52.3 | 11.8 | 9.0 |

[a] Legitimate births only. Weighted cohort data used to adjust for sampling effect (Appendix 1).

the very great improvements that have taken place in both the still birth rate and the rates of death in the first year of life. Nevertheless, despite many improvements, social class differences in risk of death in the first year of life are still, nowadays, considerable.

## CARE OF THE MOTHER AND BABY AFTER CONFINEMENT

Although it was well recognized that child bearing was, amongst other things, 'a cause of much avoidable ill health' which postnatal examinations could reduce, nevertheless relatively few women (31 per cent) attended for a check-up, and in some districts this proportion was as low as 11 per cent. Chances of being examined were highest for women having their first child and for those whose confinement had been in hospital, and lowest for those who already had four or more children (22 per cent attended) and amongst those delivered at home (17 per cent). It was concluded that the remedy lay 'in a more positive attitude on the part of doctors and midwives, in reducing clinic waiting and in providing facilities for looking after babies while their mothers are being examined' (Joint Committee (*a*) 1948: 92). It was also recommended that 'postnatal clinics should enlarge the scope of their work to include advice on family planning and periodic reviews of general health during lactation' (Joint Committee (*a*) 1948: 92).

Infant welfare centres were, in comparison, much better used and by the age of eight weeks 57 per cent of children had been for at least one visit. First born children of whatever social class were the most likely to attend (61 per cent), even when compared with those born to wives of professional and salaried workers (44 per cent). However, those least likely to go to infant welfare clinics were those with the greatest disadvantages, that is the unmarried and those with many children, and this pattern has been found continuously in studies of children born at later times (Wedge and Prosser 1973, Ford 1976).

Infant welfare centres were commonly set up for each session in a public hall, and were therefore very often of a makeshift nature.

If there is only a single hall available, it may be divided up by an arrangement of chairs and screens into different 'rooms' for weighing, for health visitors' consultations, for the sale of foods etc . . . . The structure of the halls varies greatly. Some are temporary corrugated-iron huts, while others are mission halls built of brick or stone. Several have been damaged by bombs. Some form of heating is always provided for the main hall, though at one centre the chimney of the coke stove was so blocked during the previous winter that the room is said to have been filled with fumes. The smaller rooms used by the doctor are not always adequately heated; at one Aberdeen centre the doctor could only keep warm by sitting near a lighted gas oven in the consulting room, a small kitchen behind the hall. Several of the mothers in the sample refused to go to the centres because they said it was too cold there. The caretaker is usually responsible for cleaning the hall, and standards vary greatly. Many of the church halls are badly lighted, and the paint-work is often dark, giving the rooms a dingy appearance. There is usually a cold-water tap somewhere on the premises, often in a back kitchen where water can be boiled and instruments sterilised. (Joint Committee (a) 1948: 102–3)

In rural areas transport difficulties were sometimes overcome through the provision of special transport in buses, or even in health visitors' cars, but even so these parts of the country had the lowest attendance.

There was concern about the work of the clinic, and municipal health officers often reported that the emphasis of clinics was insufficiently medical; they described 'stalls and racks full of clothing along one side of the hall and trestle-tables with every variety of baby food along the other; the health visitor sits at a small card table in one corner, advising the mothers' (Joint Committee (a) 1948: 106).

It was feared that because of the emphasis on the weight change of the baby, mothers might come to believe that a gain in weight was the only criterion of progress.

## BREAST-FEEDING

Breast-feeding was urged as the best possible way of feeding both for mother and baby. Liddiard (1944), in a contemporary book of advice for mothers, said that

Almost without exception the mother who happily and successfully nurses her infant benefits her own health as well. She is doing a natural thing, and not drying up a natural outlet. To quote Sir Truby King, in 'Natural Feeding of Infants':

What is best for the child is best for the mother and best for the race, apart altogether from the question of the individual child itself. Every mother ought to be told the full extent of maternal responsibility and privilege. If she really understands in time, she would rarely fail to fulfill the most primitive and sacred of all trusts. (p. 47)

By their eighth week 45 per cent of study babies were being breast-fed. In contrast with the pre-war years when one British study found significantly more breast-feeding by manual social class mothers (Whitehead and Paul 1987), in this study well-to-do mothers were slightly more inclined to breast-feed their children, and were more successful in maintaining lactation.

Second and subsequent babies were more likely than the first born to be breast-fed, and so were those whose mothers had 'adequate' antenatal care. It was thought, however, impossible to say whether 'it is advice on diet and the care of the breasts or whether it is the moulding of the mother's attitude during antenatal consultations that is more important' (Joint Committee (a) 1948: 162); it may simply have been that mothers who were regular attenders at antenatal clinics were the most likely to breast-feed.

This pattern of social class differences in breast-feeding was subsequently found in studies of children born in 1958 (Davie *et al.* 1972), in the early sixties (Newson and Newson 1963), and in the mid–1970s (Coles *et al.* 1978); these last authors felt that breast-feeding could undoubtedly be increased with encouragement, and concluded that 'it is worthwhile mounting campaigns directed at all relevant staff as well as all mothers'.

Information on weaning and on breast-feeding in this study after the age of eight weeks, and on the trends in more recent years is given in the next chapter.


COSTS

From information collected by the study the average annual net salaries for manual workers was estimated as £218, compared with £600 for professional and administrative workers. This last group spent on average £57 (9 per cent of average annual salary) on the first birth compared with £36 (16 per cent of average annual salary) spent by manual workers' families, and although the professional and salaried groups spent as much on second and subsequent births the figure was very considerably lower for manual social class families. In addition to the National Health Insurance benefits described above (in 'Paid employment during pregnancy') some help was also available in the form of extra clothing coupons to help purchase additional clothing, which was then still rationed. Up to 30 per cent of the total financial outlay was for medical and chemists' bills, and although this aspect of the 'economic obstacles to childbearing' was to be removed two years later under the National Health Service, the greatest need was for help with other costs of having a baby.

## CONCLUSIONS

Although it can appear now that the mood of post-war Britain was in many respects forward looking and relatively optimistic, it is clear that at the time everyday life was often uncomfortable and bleak. Before the cohort children were a year old the country was plunged into a

year of crisis, 1947, [which] was preceded by an exceptionally severe winter, bringing a fuel shortage that dislocated production and transport, and greatly hampered the drive for export. Not only was rationing continued, but some foodstuffs (bread and potatoes) were now rationed for the first time. Western Europe as a whole suffered from the same dollar shortage, as well as from the same severe winter. (Thomson 1981: 223)

The power cuts, reductions in gas pressure, and shortages of coal for domestic heating, which made life uncomfortable and difficult during this severe winter, coincided with the Attlee government's decision in the spring of 1947 to authorize the development of nuclear power technology (Robertson 1987).

It is all the more understandable that in such bad times there should have been fears about the falling birth rate. The Medical Officer of Health for Sheffield wondered rather gloomily, at the end of a long and welcoming review of the study's first book (Joint Committee (a) 1948), that it had not approached 'the more fundamental problems of why the human race, despite all its difficulties, continues to reproduce itself' (*Sheffield Telegraph* 1949). Yet the rising birth rate, shown in figure 2.1, and the increasing number of live births in the United Kingdom (702,000 in 1940, 956,000 in 1946 and 1,025,000 in 1947, the peak post-war year—the 1983 total was 788,000) reveal an important aspect of the optimism of the time.

The impact of the first report of the study, published as a book entitled *Maternity in Great Britain* (Joint Committee (*a*) 1948) was considerable both because of the revelations about what the *Observer's* headline called 'Needless Pain' and *The Times* emphasized as the 'Need for Better Care and Lower Costs'. The *Daily Mirror* summed it up in these words: 'Present day maternity services have concentrated on one important object—to make childbirth safe. Now they need to pay more attention to the mother's feelings and her material needs.'

Perhaps the publicity it received was enhanced because, as the *Birmingham Post* observed, 'The birth of a Prince has put maternity in the public eye'. In the House of Commons Mr Gallacher (Communist) said that, while he would make no adverse comments on the birth of the prince, 'there are far too many babies in this country being born in appalling conditions'.

The most practical of the report's recommendations were in some measure acted on, financial resources for mothers were improved, and pain relief in childbirth was rapidly made much more widely available, following a private member's bill in the House of Commons which enabled midwives to administer gas and air without the need for a doctor to be present. Recommendations about changes in staff attitudes have been much more slowly taken up as, for example, Macintyre's (1984) work on antenatal care has shown. Fears about the cost of childbirth, which were amongst the reasons for carrying out the study, seemed appropriate, since they proved to be considerable in relation to income for the majority of families. But the problem was clearly not that costs were a deterrent to parenthood, as had been feared when the study began, but that they were a serious source of hardship for parents and children.

Whatever the publicity at the time about the more immediately remediable aspects of the findings, the report's comments on the inadequacy of official monitoring of rates of progress of change had little impact. Although, as the *Times Literary Supplement* noted, the study 'provides statistics which have not hitherto been available', it is disheartening to find that in their comprehensive review of information nowadays routinely collected on maternity and birth Macfarlane and Mugford (1984) could conclude that still our routine statistics 'neither provide a comprehensive picture of care available, nor is it usually possible to relate the patterns of care provided to the characteristics of the population receiving it' (p. 167).

Nowadays, looking back, the most striking feature of the study's findings about birth is the extent of social class differences in preparation for childbirth, in the circumstances of childbirth itself, and in the chances of the child's survival; and these have turned out to be differences that are persistent and still all too evident.

# 3
## The Pre-school Years

### INTRODUCTION

Mothers of the study children came to child upbringing on the brink of a massive change in ideas.

A surprisingly short time before the war, the Newsons (1973) reminded us, mothers had been advised,

Never play with or excite a baby before bedtime . . . Half the irritability and lack of moral control which spoil adult life originate in the first year of existence. The seeds of feebleness and instability sown in infancy bear bitter fruit afterwards (Truby King, 1937). (p. 61)

Before the war the gurus had been those for whom authority meant not only knowledge but also the tone necessary for its effective delivery. In *Mothercraft* Truby King (1934) wrote that 'a real Truby King baby, then, is one whose mother brings it up strictly according to the Truby King system—*a baby who is completely breast fed till the ninth month*' (his italics, p. 4). Books by Truby King's disciples were still published and widely available in the immediate post-war years; for instance Liddiard's (1944) *The Mothercraft Manual* went into a third reprint of the tenth edition, and was translated also into Siamese, Chinese, and Afrikaans. Newson and Newson (1973) quote the experience of one particular mother;

*I* was caught up in the Truby King Mothercraft doctrine of 1935 . . . The health visitors prated and bullied; one's baby screamed and tears splashed down one's cheeks while milk gushed through one's jersey. But one must *never* pick the baby *up*—it was practically incestuous to *enjoy* one's baby . . . In my day, we were instructed that frost never hurt a baby yet, and if the baby cried it must be *mastered*. Working-class women cuddled their babies up in the warm as women had done for millions of years. We, the young graduate law-abiding wives of the thirties, cried *ourselves* as our babies went blue with cold. (p. 62)

Even in 1947 in the preface to the third edition of *The Care of Children from One to Five* Gibbens (1947) wrote that 'some are bound to dislike the use of the second person and the imperative, but this downright way of giving advice is vivid and it strikes home, and every mother will meet with it when she goes to her doctor for advice'. By the early 1950s there was a considerable change in expert advice, and Dr Spock (1955) in a section of his *Baby and Child Care* called 'Trust Yourself' advised parents not to 'be overawed by what the experts say' (p. 3). Advice in these years became far more concerned with emotional development and less so with discipline, and as Hardyment (1984) describes

the self-controlled, emotionless infant, hygienic in mind and body, was thrown out with its icy bath-water. The new model baby was warmly affectionate, impulsive, dependent, and (preferably) scintillatingly intelligent. Spock talked about the 'daily stimulation from loving parents' which was necessary if 'emotional depth and a keen intelligence' were to be fostered, Jerome Kagan identified the 'two critical concerns of American parents' as 'attachment to mother and rate of cognitive development'. Similarly Martin Richards in England recognized the modern parent's 'preoccupation with children's education and emotional growth'. (p. 223)

With this new concern for emotional well-being, however, came worries about the true meaning of the term. Hardyment quotes Bowlby's (1953) *Child Care and the Growth of Love*; 'Mother-love in infancy is as important for mental health as are proteins and vitamins for physical health, . . . what occurs in the earliest months and years of life can have deep and long-lasting effects' (Hardyment 1984: 236–7).

Some important misinterpretation of Bowlby's original ideas occurred at this time, and seemed to have great appeal. Bowlby's emphasis on the importance for the child of a warm, unbroken, and close relationship with the mother was, as Rutter (1972) notes,

. . . wrongly used to support the notion that only twenty-four hours' care day in and day out, by the same person, is good enough. Thus, it has been claimed that proper mothering is only possible if the mother does not go out to work (Baers, 1954) and that the use of day nurseries and creches has a particularly serious and permanent deleterious effect (WHO Expert Committee on Mental Health, 1951). (p. 15)

Bowlby's work has since been demonstrated in many respects

to be correct, particularly those aspects which were concerned with the likelihood of later distress following either some sorts of separation, or disruptions of affectionate relationships with adults (not only the mother) closely concerned with the child's upbringing. The exaggerated interpretations were seen as authoritative by those who would have liked women not to return to paid work after the birth of their first child, but the benefits of work outside the home had already been discovered by many women during the war. In the late 1940s 'even in what were regarded as progressive occupations, such as the Civil Service women had to leave the Service when they married' (Stevenson 1984: 177).

As compared with indicators of change to be found in comparisons of publications about children's upbringing, it is much harder to know what the daily work of child rearing was really like at this time. Even now mothers who turn to the manuals are relatively few, and ideas about what to do, and why, come from such other sources as health visitors, general practitioners, mothers, grandmothers, and the mass media, and at this time their notions must have represented ideas from both the pre- and post-war schools of thought. Douglas (personal communication) found that the Ministry of Health was promoting good dietary practices by providing information for publication in women's magazines. The relatively recent experience of wartime evacuation must also have been strong in the minds of mothers of study children; as Hardyment observes,

the disastrously clumsy evacuation at the start of the war is remembered with amusement by some of the organisers. It must have shattered the psyche of many of the evacuees, particularly the last to be chosen of the groups of children foisted on half-hearted country matrons. Perhaps the experience of evacuation opened the mind of that generation of mothers to the ideas of the Freudians about 'separation and anxiety'. (Hardyment 1984: 235–6)

It seems clear that the pre-war notions of upbringing were still by no means abandoned. In a study of what he called 'English character' Gorer (1955) asked 2,328 people about their attitudes to 'rearing and training young children', and found that

A metaphor employed with considerable consistency is the training or

pruning of a tree or plant, which will grow misshapen or sport back to
its wild origins if not timely treated and formed ...

There is very little belief in childish innocence or in the innate
goodness of children, views which are strongly held in some other
societies. Somewhat less articulate, but nevertheless apparently
strongly held, is the belief that discipline, habit training, is good in
itself, and valuable for the formation of good character, almost without
regard to the habits trained or imposed. (p. 163)

In the immediate post-war years the daily task of bringing up
children was gradually eased by household improvements. It is
again Hardyment (1984) who has summarized most effectively:

Freud could not have been allowed free rein in the 1950s if domestic-
appliance technology had been less sophisticated. One can plausibly
track permissiveness in feeding, playing and toilet training down the
income levels in company with modern cooking appliances, vacuum
cleaners and washing machines. Being a constant reassuring presence,
considering one's child's every need, creating a stimulating environment exactly suited to its current developmental stage—all these take
up a great deal of time. Only with two children and a modernized
home can the demands of modern child-care theorists be comfortably
met. (p. 226)

It was in 1953, with demands for electrical power increasing
and with memories of the fuel crises in 1946–7 and 1950–1,
that the first British nuclear power station began to be built
(Robertson 1987); but in 1948 when the study children were
2 years old only 40 per cent of all the households in the nation
had vacuum cleaners, 4 per cent a washing machine, and 2 per
cent a refrigerator (Howarth 1985: 56–7). There was also at this
time still rationing of clothing (ended in 1954), tea and sugar
(ended in 1952), bread (rationed between 1946 and 1948), and
sweets (rationing ended in 1953 after a brief break in 1949). In
1948 the weekly allowance for each adult was 13 ounces of
meat, 1½ ounces of cheese, 6 ounces of butter and margarine, 1
ounce of cooking fat, 8 ounces of sugar, 2 pints of milk, and one
egg (Sissons and French 1986), although there were extra
allowances of milk, orange juice, and cod or halibut liver oil for
children. Amounts available on ration changed unfavourably
for those born in the immediate post-war years, and Burnett
(1989) noted that 'the post-1945 diet was more frugal than the
war-time ration, due principally to world shortages of

foodstuffs, poor harvests, and the ending of lend-lease'
(p. 303). In summer of the year in which study children were
born (1946), when school milk was first available at no cost

food was regarded as much the most pressing problem facing the
government. From the end of the war to the beginning of 1947, during
the Attlee government's tenure of office, the bacon ration had been
halved, as had the ration of margarine and cooking fat; the supply of
cheese had been reduced and bread rationing had been brought in. . . .
The only compensation for all these deprivations had been a
twopenny increase in the meat ration. The calorific value of food
consumed in working-class homes had fallen, young Dr Pyke of the
Ministry of Food calculated, from 102 per cent of what was necessary
to maintain physical efficiency at the beginning of 1945 to 93% by the
summer of 1946. And he noted that post-war children had lower
average body weight than war time children of the same age.
(Robertson 1987: 126)

By contrast with today relatively little entertainment was
provided, initially in part because of the fuel crisis in the post-
war years, which led to the cancellation of many mid-week
sporting fixtures. The Lord President's committee noted that
'the Saint Leger had cost the country some sixty or seventy
thousand tons of coal as large numbers of Yorkshire miners had
absented themselves from work to attend the race meeting at
Doncaster' (Robertson 1987: 119). For adults cinema-going
was very common (Marwick 1982) and television broad-
casting, which had restarted in 1946 but only in the London
area, was available to the 10 per cent of the population who
possessed a television set by the early 1950s. There were only
just over 2 million car owners in 1948 and petrol rationing,
which in 1946 permitted journeys of no more than 270 miles a
month, was not finally lifted until 1950.

Medicine was amongst the most powerful influences for
change in the everyday lives of mothers. Although by the
standards of today some fearsome childhood diseases were still
common (for example diphtheria, mastoiditis, lobar pneumonia) chances of survival for children were considerably
improved in comparison with the pre-war years, and the new
National Health Service, which began when the study children
were 2 years old, gave ready access to medical care. Medical
care was becoming increasingly better equipped, particularly

for the cure of infectious disease. But although penicillin had
first been manufactured in 1943, by 1951 the grip of serious
infections on the population had still in some respects not been
substantially released. The annual report of the Medical
Research Council for 1948–50 notes that

Although the death rate from tuberculosis continues to fall in this
country, the disease is still the main cause of death among men and
women of working age. The development in recent years of drugs
with an unequivocal effect against tuberculosis in experimental
animals and man, starting with streptomycin in 1944, has brought
new hopes to patient and physician. So far, however, the few agents in
this category have been only partially effective, and the complete cures
obtained by chemotherapy in certain other infections have not been
matched. . . . At present the greater part of the large group of chronic
pulmonary tuberculoses is virtually unaffected by chemotherapy.
(Medical Research Council 1951: 10–11)

This same report also refers to poliomyelitis, which had

flared-up in 1947 and gave rise to the largest outbreak in the history of
the country. The outbreak of 1949, though not so extensive as that of
1947, and the unusually high incidence of cases during the winter
months, made it likely that the disease had come to stay and a major
investigation to throw some light on the causes of its continued
prevalence became imperative. (p. 15)

In England and Wales in 1946 there had been 611 cases of
poliomyelitis notified, compared with 7,207 in 1947. In 1988 a
total of two cases of acute poliomyelitis were notified (Office of
Population Censuses and Surveys 1990).

Work was also proceeding on vaccines for the prevention of
whooping cough, because between 1946 and 1951

this disease has been responsible each year for more deaths than
measles, diphtheria and scarlet fever combined, and in the past ten
years over 10,000 deaths have been ascribed to it in England and
Wales. Moreover, it is often extremely distressing and disabling; in
over half of the affected children the cough lasts for more than eight
weeks, and in nearly a third for more than ten. (Medical Research
Council 1952: 15)

In everyday life by far the most important innovation of this
time was the introduction of the National Health Service. The
extent of its impact may be judged by Addison's (1985)

quotation from Dr Katharina Dalton, who qualified as a doctor on the day NHS began and went to work as an assistant general practitioner in a working class area.

I think what I remember most is two conditions that you don't see much now but you saw a tremendous amount in the first six months. One was low thyroid, hypothyroidism, and the women just got slower and duller and falling asleep in the evenings, and it was just accepted as their personality—and you know, you could suddenly change them. And then also the women with ulcers on their legs—they'd had varicose ulcers for twenty, thirty years and suddenly they could be treated . . . They had to pay before the health scheme and that was too much, too expensive. I mean, some of them were brought up with the idea that, you know, you never go to a solicitor, you never go to a doctor because it's always far too expensive. (p. 106)

## FINDINGS FROM THE NATIONAL SURVEY

Because the numbers of children studied at birth were relatively large (13,687) a sample was taken of a more manageable size, randomly stratified in order to be represent-ative of each social class. All the single, legitimate births were chosen from families whose fathers were non-manual or agricultural workers, since they formed a relatively small section of the population, together with a randomly selected one in four of all other single, legitimate births to make a total of 5,362 children. Multiple births were not included because they were thought to be too few for statistical analyses, and illegitimate births were not selected because of the impos-sibility of following a representative sample of which probably quite a large percentage would be adopted, and therefore impossible to follow up. A full description of the sample selection and its representativeness is given in Appendix 1.

New studies were carried out when members of the sample of children selected for follow-up were 2 years and 4 years old. Health visitors (community nurses) visited mothers at home to ask about the family's circumstances and the parent(s)' work, the child's health and development, habits, and use of nurseries (pre-school), and to weigh and measure each child; 94 per cent of mothers of all the selected children who were still alive and resident in England, Wales, or Scotland took part in the study at 2 years, and 96 per cent at 4 years.

## SURVIVAL

In 1946 the national death rate per thousand alive at age 4 years was 11.9; in 1984 the comparable rate was 2.3. The greatest change has come in the first year of life. In the exceptionally severe winter of 1946–7 the national death rate for all ages was 18 per cent higher in January to March than in the corresponding months in the previous winter, and death rates at all ages from chest diseases were 22 per cent higher (Robertson 1987).

Death amongst cohort children was most common in those from lowest social class families; it also occurred with greater frequency in boys. In 1981, although rates were much lower, social class differences in death rates in the first year of life in England and Wales were still large, ranging from 7.7 per thousand live births in social class I to 15.2 in social class V, and 15.2 for illegitimate births.

When deaths of light weight (under 2,500 g.) babies (which accounted for almost half the deaths in the first month of life) are excluded the social class differences in deaths in the first month of life are considerably reduced, and Douglas (1951) calculated that if 'the neo-natal death rates of the poorer classes could be reduced to the level of the well-to-do, some 4,000 lives could be saved each year'.

Deaths that occurred between the second month and the end of the second year of life continued to be much more common in children in lower social class families, especially before the age of 1 year, particularly as a result of pneumonia and gastroenteritis; in fact without these cases social class differences would hardly have existed. Douglas (1951) suggested that

these children may be over-warmly dressed and live in rooms that by middle-class standards, are under-ventilated. From an early age they may be taken in buses and trains, and contact with neighbours, friends and relatives is close and frequent. Thus they are more likely to meet infection than are the more cloistered children of the well-to-do.

Douglas also calculated that a reduction in death rates of children aged between four months and 1 year to the levels of those who were in professional and salaried class families would 'With a yearly total of 700,000 births . . . result in a saving of 6,300 lives'. He concluded that a continuing fall in infant mortality lay not altogether in medical technological advances, nor in the further development of health services, but would also be importantly influenced by improvements that could be brought about in the care that mothers provided for their children, and in living standards in what he called 'a more directly socio-medical approach' (Douglas 1951).

## ADMISSION TO HOSPITAL

During their first five years of life 958 of the study children were admitted to hospital, and of these one in five was admitted more than once. Almost half (47 per cent) of the children were in hospitals that did not permit visiting, but 16 per cent had no restrictions on visiting. Only three mothers were able to stay in hospital with their child. The average length of time spent in hospital was 21.3 days.

All these things have now changed. Visiting is now universally encouraged, average lengths of stay are very much shorter (8.2 days amongst the first born children of people in the study) and mothers are often able to stay in hospital with their children.

Nearly a fifth of all the days in hospital was accounted for by 16 study children with tuberculosis, who between them spent more than 4,000 days in hospital. This, too, is something rarely encountered now (156 cases, of all ages, of respiratory tuberculosis were notified in England and Wales in 1983), and cure is swift and virtually assured.

Because children from manual social class families were most at risk of illness, they were also more often admitted to hospital, but this social class difference was only found in admissions for infectious illness. In the more prosperous sections of the study population boys were more often admitted than girls, but in the poorer groups chances of admission were very similar for both boys and girls.

## ILLNESS

By the age of 5 years 127 children (26.3 per thousand) had experienced chronic physical illness which lasted three months or more or required them to be continuously in hospital for more than four weeks. These kinds of illnesses occurred in the study population at the same rates as were found in the general population with, for example, 24 deaf children, 11 with congenital heart defects, 11 with cerebral palsy, 4 who were blind, 3 with spina bifida, and 17 with epilepsy (Pless and Douglas 1971).

During the first two years of life 37 per cent of the children had caught an infectious illness (for example measles, mumps, german measles, whooping cough, scarlet fever, diphtheria, or chicken pox) and 8 per cent had had more than one. Social class differences in infectious illness were marked only in measles and whooping cough experienced during the first nine months of life, and in general the presence of a school child in the family increased chances of infection amongst this population of pre-school children, but over-crowding at home did not. Low maternal care scores in the more prosperous families were significantly associated with a greater risk of lower respiratory illness in children, and it was noted of the population in general that 'since 1921 there has been a widening rather than a narrowing of the gap between the social classes in deaths from respiratory infections' (Douglas and Blomfield 1958: 68).

The seriousness of illness may also be assessed by the extent of disruption to life that it causes, and in this study one useful, working definition of serious illness has been that which involved hospital admission for a minimum of twenty-eight consecutive days, including also at later ages school or work absence of three consecutive weeks or more, during a five-year period. During infancy, that is up to age 5 years, serious illness by this definition was experienced by 301 boys (11 per cent of all boys) and 224 girls (9 per cent of girls), and for boys, but not for girls, such illness was significantly more common amongst those from lower social groups, even when mental disorder, congenital problems, and injuries were excluded (Wadsworth 1986a).

During these first five years of life 27 per cent of boys and 21 per cent of girls were injured. Six died of their injuries, and 85 were treated in hospital as in-patients and 1,204 at hospital accident and emergency departments. It was not possible to differentiate non-accidental injury. None of the study information on home environment, social class, mother's work or numbers of siblings was found to be associated with injuries.

## LOW BIRTH WEIGHT

Particular attention was paid to children who had been of low birth weight because it was generally believed

that many of the survivors as a consequence of prematurity itself or of the antenatal conditions leading to it are sickly, stunted, or mentally retarded. It is probable that in the future we will be able to save the lives of more of these babies, and it is important to know how large a proportion will be handicapped in later life and what institutional or other special care they will need. (Douglas and Mogford 1953a)

The greater death rates amongst these children have already been described. They were also more inclined to stay longer in hospital after birth (39 per cent of low birth weight babies stayed for more than two weeks as compared with 11 per cent of matched controls, i.e. children who were of higher birth weights and from similar social circumstances), and more likely to be admitted again later (21 per cent of low birth weight children were admitted in the first four years of life compared with 15 per cent of the control group children), and for longer periods (all of the premature children spent between them a total of 1,269 days in hospital in the first two years of life, as compared with 359 days for the controls), but by the third and fourth years of life differences were quite small. These differences in health were not the result of social class differences, and Douglas and Mogford (1953a) concluded that 'premature children—after they have reached the age of two— appear to be as healthy as those born at term'. At the age of 4 years they were approximately two and a half pounds lighter and one inch shorter than their matched controls, but although 36 per cent had caught up with controls in weight and 44 per cent had done so in height (the smallest low birth weight children grew at the fastest rate), those who did not catch up in height were more likely to have shorter mothers than those of controls. In fact mother's height was found to be a reasonable predictor of the likely growth rate of the premature child (Douglas and Mogford 1953b).

## BREAST-FEEDING

By the end of their second month 53 per cent of cohort children were being breast-fed; this percentage then fell to 28 per cent at the end of the seventh month and finally to 0.3 per cent (9 babies) at the age of 2 years, reflecting the 'present-day opinion in Britain . . . that babies should be weaned from the breast between the sixth and ninth month' (Douglas 1950). Recent opinion is that if possible babies should be breast-fed for four to six months (Department of Health and Social Security 1983). In comparison with present day practice breast-feeding was much more usual in 1946, and was then at about a halfway point in a fall in prevalence from the 1920s until the early 1970s, when a striking new increase began (Whitehead and Paul 1987), which lasted until 1980; and between 1980 and 1985 there was little change (Martin and White 1988). Whereas 76 per cent of the 1946 study babies were being breast-fed at 2 weeks, the comparable figure for England and Wales in 1975 was 35 per cent (Martin 1978), for 1980 it was 54 per cent (Martin and Monk 1982), and for 1985 53 per cent (Martin and White 1988). By the age of four months 40 per cent of study babies were being breast-fed, compared with 13 per cent of babies of this age in 1975, and 27 per cent in 1980.

The average time of breast-feeding by those who successfully established lactation was five and a half months. Mothers from non-manual families were more successful in establishing breast-feeding and in maintaining lactation until the baby was aged seven months, but after that proportionately more manual class babies were breast-fed. This class difference in breast-feeding up to the seventh month was not accounted for by differences in the home environment, nor by the greater propensity of manual class mothers to wean earlier in order to return to work. But weaning was more likely if the baby had been taken to the infant welfare clinic where dried milk was readily available (Douglas 1950).

Then, as now, breast-feeding was thought to be a most important foundation for the continuing good health of the child. Truby King (who described himself as a New Zealand 'scientific farmer') had played an important part in establishing this belief through his discovery that fatal diarrhoeal disease in New Zealand calves (scouring) was eliminated by a system of rational, scientific artificial feeding for the calves, based on the percentage composition (and especially the protein ratio) of average cow's milk. As a result of this perfected feeding, the mortality from 'scouring' was entirely wiped out—better still the artificially-reared or so-called 'bucket-fed' calves attained the same weight as calves suckled by their mothers, and none died. (King 1934: 3)

Thus Truby King encouraged breast-feeding (which became 87 per cent successful under his influence—if it failed he encouraged the use of artificial milk), and infant death in Dunedin, New Zealand, for example from summer diarrhoea, fell from 25 per thousand in 1907 to 9 per thousand in 1912, to 4 per thousand in 1917, and to an annual average of less than one in the years 1918–22 (King 1934). Unfortunately, it is difficult to know, and it seems that Truby King did not reveal, the extent to which such marked improvements were the result of breast-feeding, or of improvements in the composition of artificial milk, or in hygiene in its preparation and in feeding the child.

In this British national study carried out twenty years later breast-feeding rates were much lower, and it was found that

bottle fed babies, if reared in poor surroundings, are less likely to survive than breast fed babies whereas, if their home conditions are good, their chances of survival are not impaired. Bottle fed babies are also more likely to suffer from measles and, during the early months of life, from lower respiratory infections and minor attacks of diarrhoea.

In spite of these findings it is not felt that any marked reduction in infant mortality or morbidity would be brought about solely by raising the incidence of breast feeding . . .

The main risk associated with artificial feeding would be avoided if mothers were more aware of the dangers of infection. . . . As well as encouraging breast feeding, therefore, every effort should be made to visit mothers in their homes and show them the best methods of preparing feeds, sterilising bottles and avoiding contamination of milk. Unfortunately shortages of health visitors are so acute that many mothers are not visited until several weeks after the midwife has left; consequently they evolve their own methods of preparing feeds and it may be difficult to re-educate them. (Douglas 1950)

## GROWTH

By the age of 4 years some important differences in growth rates were beginning to become clear. Children who lived in

the country were, on average, taller than those who lived in the
town, and those in the south-east taller than those in other
parts of Britain. But Douglas and Blomfield (1958) concluded
that

there is no reason to believe that rural life of itself favours the rapid
growth of children. The regional differences are explained by the fact
that the country areas contain a relatively high proportion of black-
coated and professional workers whose children were taller than
those in the other social groups. (pp. 56–7)

There was, however, at least in the immediately preceding
years, evidence of differences in nutrition between town and
country children. Titmuss (1943) quoted an article from the
*Lancet* of 1940 which revealed that

In large industrial centres, nutritional (iron-deficiency) anaemia
affects about two-thirds of the infant population in the 6–12 months
age period because of the absence during this time of iron-containing
foods in the diet. Rickets, albeit in a mild form, affects almost half the
same infant population. Its cause is well enough known. In the
presence of one or more of these conditions infection occurs and the
death is attributed to the infection. No mention is made, even by the
pathologist, of the part played by nutritional defects. (pp. 85–6)

Social class differences in height increased as the children grew
older, and the big social class differences that underlay the
observed geographical variations were associated with parental education, in that within each class the most educated
parents had the tallest children, and vice versa. Douglas and
Blomfield (1958) concluded that

The marked relation between the standard of maternal care and
growth in those families whose income, though not large, should be
sufficient—for example the black-coated workers, and the skilled
manual workers with small families—suggests that spending habits
are important. But the lack of such a relationship in the *large* families
of skilled manual workers, and in *all* families in the poorest groups,
suggests that below a certain level of income even the most careful
spending will not provide a diet fully adequate for growth. We should
estimate that approximately a quarter of all families in Great Britain
with children under five would suffer in this way. (p. 144)

Between the ages of 2 and 4 years height gain was greatest in
the upper social groups, and in the non-manual classes it was

significantly greater amongst girls than boys. Douglas and Blomfield (1958) noted

that in some important respects social group differences in growth are unlike those in illness. Whereas in illness these differences are greatest in the early years, in growth they increase as the child gets older. The standard of maternal care is important for both, but in illness exerts its greatest effect when home conditions are good, whereas in growth it has relatively little effect in the best homes as well as in the worst, and is most important when the main problem is how to spend a barely adequate income wisely. (p. 143)

Douglas (1969) concluded that the social class differences in achieved height, which were to persist into adult life, originated during the first two years, and cited the National Food Surveys of the late 1940s and early 1950s which showed a per capita decline in spending on food as family size increased, particularly in the poorer social classes. Gibbens (1947) advises mothers that

Most grownups of the poorer and middle classes live largely on these [tinned, dried or preserved] foods themselves, and since their growing years are over ill effects are less obvious. They see nothing wrong in taking these foods themselves, so they imagine they must be good for their children. 'He eats everything we have', a mother will say with pride: but that does not mean to say that tinned salmon, bread and margarine and strong tea are good for children.

  Cheap starchy foods (bread, porridge, potatoes, etc.) satisfy a child's appetite and often make him put on weight, to the mother's delight. But the weight is not healthy: it is not due to good muscle, but fat. . . . resistance to disease is lessened, and though perhaps the child may not fall ill, he is never really well. (p. 30)

## CHANGING OCCUPATION OF FATHERS

The years during which the study children were infants were a time of great social movement in Britain, in the sense that many people changed from wartime and immediate post-war work to settle into more stable peacetime occupations. It was also a time in Britain when the balance of occupations was beginning to change, so that there were, in the nation as a whole, fewer opportunities for manual work and more for clerical as time went on. In the long run this was to be an especially important shift that gradually prepared the groundwork for changes in attitudes and for future national prosperity, but which at this time, despite very low unemployment rates, was restrained by post-war 'austerity' and high levels of taxation (Thomson 1981).

Between 1946 and 1950, before the study children were aged 6, their fathers experienced a great amount of occupational change. There was considerable movement into professional occupations (which rose by 9 per cent during this period), into the status of employer (+15 per cent), into self-employment (+ 24 per cent), and into salaried non-manual work (+40 per cent), whilst skilled manual occupations experienced loss (–9 per cent) and so did the unskilled (–3 per cent). Douglas and Blomfield (1958) observed that in this study 'a man's chance of bettering himself seems to depend as much on his wife's education as upon his own and, if both have been to a secondary school, their chances are approximately twice as great' (p. 32).

## HOUSING

Nearly half the families had moved house before the study child was 4 years old. Most did so to escape from relatively poor conditions. Just how poor conditions may be illustrated by the fact that when the study children were 2 years old 49 per cent of families did not have running hot water, 43 per cent had no bathroom, and 18 per cent shared a kitchen or had no kitchen at all. In 1982, when cohort members were 36 years old, only 2 per cent no longer had running hot water, and fewer than 1 per cent shared a kitchen. More dramatic illustration is provided by health visitors' comments on the state of housing when children were 2 years old. For example

This dwelling is in a disgraceful state. There is no ventilation in the room at all—it is an old public house and is occupied by, I think, eight families. There is no garden or yard for the children to play in. The only washing facilities are one small bowl on a stand, and there are no cupboards at all. There is no kitchen, no bathroom, and hot water can only be obtained by boiling kettles. The family is crowded with three persons to a room and consists of three pre-school children, and one school child. The mother is pregnant. The father is a building labourer.

The house is in a good state of repair. No dampness. Good light, fair ventilation. Drinking and all water is conveyed here in open tanks on a trailer twice weekly. It is always warm in Summer. No drainage. Waste water thrown on garden. Elsan lavatory but cannot afford Elsanol, so contents buried by husband. In this house there was no kitchen, sink, or copper. An antiquated range was the only means of cooking and kettles the only means of heating water. This was a Council dwelling built before 1919. The family, which is crowded at one and a half persons per room, consists of three school children and one pre-school child. The father is a road scout. (Douglas and Blomfield 1958: 41–2)

Douglas and Blomfield (1958) divided families into those 34 per cent who lived in the best conditions (i.e. not overcrowded, and with three basic amenities, namely bathroom, kitchen, and running hot water), the 21 per cent who lived in the worst conditions (overcrowded—i.e. more than one and a half persons per room—and lacking one or more of the three amenities), and the 45 per cent in intermediate conditions (either overcrowded or lacking amenities, but not both). Using this classification it was found that 30 per cent of semi-skilled and of unskilled workers' families lived in the worst circumstances, as compared with 2 per cent of professional and salaried workers' families and 11 per cent of families of other non-manual workers. Conversely 74 per cent of highest socio-economic families lived in the best conditions as compared with 18 per cent of the unskilled.

For the children, overcrowding often meant sharing beds, and at the age of 4 years 26 per cent of study children in England and Wales and 51 per cent of those in Scotland did so, sometimes from habit, but very often from necessity; 12 per cent of Scottish children shared a bed with their parent(s) and so did 3 per cent of children in England and Wales.

Home ownership has also changed greatly, and whereas in 1982 75 per cent of cohort members at the age of 36 were buying their dwellings only 27 per cent of their parents were doing so in 1950. Most change has come in the private renting sector, in which 41 per cent were housed in 1950 compared with 3 per cent in 1982, closely followed by council housing down from 27 per cent in 1950 to 14 per cent in 1982. These figures are a rather colourless reflection of the acute shortage of housing and the poor state of housing that prevailed in the post-war period. Marwick (1982) notes more vividly that at that time 'over 70 per cent of the nation's dwellings dated back to the late 19th or early 20th century or earlier' (p. 22), and that only 806,000 houses were built during the six years 1945 and 1950, together with 157,000 prefabricated houses, compared with the 1953 total of over 300,000.

## SEPARATIONS

Separation of children and parents was an especially important topic at this time. Partly no doubt because of the all too recent experience of evacuation of city children to country districts to escape bombing raids, and because of fathers' absence in the armed forces (5 per cent of fathers were still in the forces when the study children were born, compared with 2 per cent in 1972), as well as the contemporary fears about the psychological effects of the separation of children from their parents (see Introduction to this chapter). Douglas and Blomfield (1958) noted that 'There is at present widespread uneasiness at the possible effects of lack of maternal care and affection in early childhood, and it is generally held that separation of a child from his mother at an early age may be followed by later emotional instability' (p. 110).

Separation was studied in three ways. First the separations caused by hospital admission, then those resulting from mother going out to work, and finally those caused by the permanent separation or divorce of parents or the death of a parent.

Hospital admissions have already been discussed, and findings about apparent long-term effects are described later, in Chapter 5.

Mothers who went out to work were said at the time to have 'latch key children', an emotive phrase which occurred frequently in Britain at this time in reports at magistrates' courts. But even then

attitudes towards the employment of mothers are conflicting. On the one hand it is felt that married women should have the right to choose for themselves whether or not they work outside their homes and that obstacles should be removed, even if special nurseries have to be opened and home helps provided. Moreover, the recruitment of women offers the best means of relieving the present shortage of labour. On the other hand it is generally accepted that mothers should look after their own children and that any substitute is only a second best (Ministry of Health 1946). While economic and social factors today are pushing more and more women, and particularly mothers of pre-school children, into employment, there is a general feeling that the price is being paid by their children and that present trends may result in permanent damage to the emotional development of a future generation. (World Health Organisation, 1951). (Douglas and Blomfield 1958: 117)

By the time the children were 4 years old 15 per cent of mothers worked regularly in paid employment, only 5 per cent full time or more than 35 hours a week. In comparison, in a national sample of children who were 5 years old in 1975, 33 per cent of mothers were working regularly in paid employment outside the home, and 6 per cent worked full time (Osborn, Butler, and Morris 1984).

Douglas and Blomfield (1958) compared matched pairs of children from similar social backgrounds and found amongst children whose mothers worked full time an excess of respiratory illness, and greatly increased chances of admission to hospital. The excess of respiratory illness was accounted for by the children who went to nursery schools, where they were at greater risk of catching infectious disease. The excess of hospital admissions occurred only during those periods when mothers were actually at work, and it seems therefore that these admissions were for social reasons and did not represent a heavier burden of serious illness. There were no differences between the two groups in habit behaviour (e.g. nail-biting and thumb-sucking) or in nightmares, and an excess of bed-wetting amongst children of working mothers was accounted for by the children whose mothers had also experienced divorce or separation.

Divorce and separation reached peak numbers in Great Britain during these years when the study children were aged 0–5 years, as figure 3.1 shows. During the mid-1930s the numbers of divorces in England and Wales averaged 4,500 a year. The Matrimonial Causes Act of 1937 eased the process, and then in 1939 annual numbers rose to 8,248, and this was

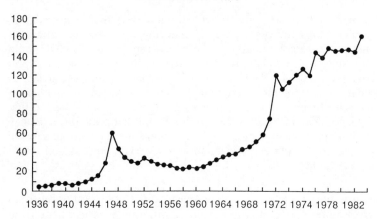

Fɪɢ. 3.1 Decrees nisi granted in England and Wales, 1936–1983
(in 000s)

believed to be because of the 'disposal of the cases which had
accumulated from previous years' (Registrar-General 1947).
But, as figure 3.1 shows, numbers then rose sharply. This was
to a great extent the result of wartime separations, when as
Minns (1980) points out 'exhausted wives and marital infi-
delity were just some of the situations that people had to cope
with as well as the housing shortage and rising prices' (p. 194).

In the study 142 children had experienced parental divorce
by the time they were 4 years old, and 40 fathers and 24
mothers had died. Compared with recent figures these children's experience of parental divorce and separation was
relatively low; by the age of 5 years 5 per cent of study children
born in 1946 had been separated from one or both parents, as
compared with 10 per cent of those born in 1970 (Osborn *et al.*
1984), a rise accounted for by divorce and separation, since
parental death rates have fallen considerably, but a comparison
complicated by the exclusion of illegitimately born children
from this study's population.

In the time immediately following such family disruption,
Rowntree (1955) and Douglas and Blomfield (1958) and
Douglas (1973*a*) found in this study that

When children from broken homes were compared with a control
group, they did not appear to be handicapped in either growth or
health. Nor was there any substantial evidence that they were

emotionally less stable. The only respect in which they differed significantly from their controls was in having a high incidence of bed wetting. (Douglas and Blomfield 1958: 116)

This is still frequently found today (Wallerstein and Kelly 1980).

## NURSERIES

Before the war there were relatively few nursery schools in Britain (104 day nurseries and 118 nursery schools, between them accommodating 13,795 children). They were then still thought of rather as a resource for the 'physical and medical nurture of the debilitated child' (Blackstone 1971), and relatively few mothers worked outside the home. But wartime demand for workers brought a very rapid change in the picture and by 1944, 106,000 children were receiving daytime nursery care (Minns 1980). After the war, as Minns (1980) summarizes,

With men returning from fighting needing jobs, suggestions from psychologists that mothers should be with their children full time in the early years, and a dramatic reduction in nursery schools after the war, it was thought that many women would be thrust back into their former positions in the home. (p. 200)

In the study's second book (*Children under Five*, 1958) Douglas and Blomfield pointed out that

In this country, the official attitude to the employment of women is that mothers of children under two should be discouraged from going into paid employment save in exceptional circumstances, but no special incentives are offered to them if they refrain from employment as is done, for example, in France, where mothers are given increased allowances if they are not at work (Watson 1954). In Scandinavia and America, on the other hand, the employment of mothers is actively encouraged by providing nurseries, creches and meals for the children of those who want to work (ILO 1955). During the war years when national needs made it essential that mothers, even if they had young children, should be at work, day nurseries were set up in this country. Since 1945 many of these have been closed, the scale of charges has been greatly raised and restrictions have been imposed on their acceptance of children. As a result, the number of children under the age of two has been halved and the number of older children also much reduced. In spite of this official policy, the continuing need for nurseries is shown by the fact that the number provided by factories and private bodies is increasing each year. (pp. 123–4)

Thus, the study's children were born at a time of declining resources and of conflict between official, expert views and public ideas about what was required, and only 648 (13 per cent) attended any kind of nursery school and a further 59 (1 per cent) were looked after by a nanny or 'daily minder' at home. There was great concern about the supposed effect of separation of child and mother that nursery school entailed. But this study could find no evidence that there was any ill effect, other than the increase in respiratory illness already described (see 'Separations' above), and increased chances of getting whooping cough, measles, and other infections (Douglas and Blomfield 1958), as would be expected amongst children attending any kind of school for the first time. Much more positive effects of nursery school experience were found in the next generation amongst the offspring of the study children (Wadsworth 1986*b*), and the evidence for this and the discussion of why it may be is given in Chapter 7.


CONCLUSION

By the time the visit to 4-year-olds had been completed the important medical question of the infant outcomes of low birth weight could be examined, by comparison of low weight births with other births to families in similar social circumstances; it was clear that in these years of life the survivors of low birth weight did not differ markedly in terms of health, and had made great gains in catching up in height. The social class differences in growth rates and breast-feeding, and the evidence that maternal care was of much greater relevance to infant health than the state of the home physical environment, were also important findings. Undoubtedly a very pressing social question at this time was the matter of mothers who went out to work, and here too the study was able to provide clear and objective evidence that at least up until the children were 4 years old this did not seem to be disadvantageous.

In the much longer term many other aspects of the information collected in 1948 and 1950, when the study children were infants, turned out to be of great interest and influence on their later lives, and these long-term links are described in the succeeding chapters.

At the time, the value of the study was also to be found in the evidence, for instance, that not only were children in lower social class families most at risk of death in their first year of life, they continued also to be at greater risk of illness, and particularly of serious illness, during infancy. Titmuss (1943) showed that infant death rates were not universally taken to be a problem, by quoting from an article published in the *Lancet* in 1940 and written by the President of the Royal College of Physicians of London:

'One cannot help wondering, indeed, whether the stinting production and careful saving of infant lives today is really, biologically speaking, as wholesome as the massive production and lavish scrapping of the last century'.

In retrospect this study of infancy is striking for the very considerable differences it reveals between life and home circumstances of forty years ago and the circumstances of today. Also striking is the extent to which change has not occurred, for example in the continuation of concern about the possible effects of parental divorce, and in social inequalities in health and survival, despite massive overall improvements in services and in medical methods.

On the basis of the findings described in this chapter, it was concluded that great improvements in child health could be made by improved working methods in local authority medical services, and in particular by home visiting (Douglas and Blomfield 1958). However, others at the time took a very different view.

In 1952 Professor Banks, when discussing the future of local authority health services said, 'an infant mortality rate of 26 and a maternal mortality rate of 0.7 show that the years of endeavour have at last borne fruit. They also show that, having defeated the enemy, the great army of workers could now be demobilised, retaining only a highly skilled skeleton staff . . . the time has come to merge the maternal and infant welfare services with the hospital, obstetric and paediatric services.' (Banks 1952) The findings we have just described do not support these suggestions. (Douglas and Blomfield 1958: 142)

It was concluded in the study's second book (*Children Under*

*Five*, Douglas and Blomfield 1958) that 'the social and educational approach is still of primary importance in the saving of infant life' (p. 142).

The gulf between this view and that of Banks (1952), quoted above, represents a difference of opinion that was to be a continuing source of tension in health service planning and research in Britain for many future years.

# 4
## *From 5 to 11 Years*

### INTRODUCTION

Between the time when children in the study were 5 years old, in 1951, and first at school, until their eleventh birthdays in 1957, they lived through a time of immense change. In 1951 Britain was still in the age of post-war austerity. Shortages of all kinds were encountered in everyday life, including rationing of fuel and power, clothes and food; butter, cheese, margarine, cooking fats, and meat were finally derationed in 1954 when study children were 8 years old. But by 1957 the country was in the midst of a consumer spending boom. During these six years from 1951 to 1957 there was a great flourishing in the sciences and arts, as well as the beginnings of some fundamental changes in values, aspirations, and behaviour.

Although in the general election of 1951 the first Labour government, which had been in power since 1945, was replaced by a considerable Tory majority, the experience of Labour rule, of practically full employment and the assured benefits of free medical care, national insurance, family and maternity allowances had given a great boost of confidence to the working class (Marwick 1982). This confidence was complemented by the increasing purchasing power of individuals and families (Pinto-Duschinsky 1970) helped in 1955 by the reduction in the standard rate of income tax by six old pence in the pound, and assisted too by rising numbers of gainfully employed women. Thomson (1981) summarizes this change in discussing the government's domestic policy in 1955.

Britain from 1947 onwards was becoming a nation with a very large intermediate income range of lower middle class and well-paid working-class. The Hulton Readership Survey for 1955 showed that since 1947 these two groups had risen from 75 to 81 per cent of the whole. However contestable the figures, they reflect one consequence

of the Welfare State and of a spell of full employment. The statistics of
small savings and building society deposits tell the same story. The
centre of gravity of Britain, whether for the commercial advertisers
utilizing the Hulton Survey or for political party headquarters
contemplating electioneering appeals, was the well-to-do working
class and the lower middle class. (pp. 247–8)

Indicators of such change were visible in many aspects of
everyday life. For example, the period 1952–6 saw an enormous acceleration in the rate of building of new houses
compared with earlier times, rising from an annual average of
65,000 between the end of the war and 1947, to 181,000 in the
years 1948–51, 266,000 in the years 1952–4, 283,000 in 1955,
and 269,000 in 1956. At the same time home ownership
increased, in line with the Conservative government's intention to create a 'property-owning democracy' (Thomson 1981:
247). These new houses were built in housing estates as
additions to existing towns and in new towns, and Marwick
(1982) notes, for example, that Basildon, Bracknell, Hemel
Hempstead, Hatfield, Stevenage, Harlow, Welwyn Garden
City, and Crawley were all expanding at the rate of 9,000
houses a year by 1956. The new young families that tended to
get priority for housing in such areas were inclined to feel cut
off from their parents and older relations, like Mrs Harper in
Young and Willmott's study of Bethnal Green families who
moved to a new town. Her husband still returned to Bethnal
Green to work each day, and she disliked the loneliness of the
new town and the 'quietness' which she thinks will in time
'send people off their heads' (Young and Willmott 1962: 132).
In fact a comparative study of general practice in a new town
and in other areas at the time showed no variation in
consultations about feelings of depression and discontent
(Taylor and Chave 1964). At the same time some traditional
spare-time activities, such as cricket and football, experienced a
decline in spectator attendances, and television viewing rose
spectacularly from an estimated audience of 0.2 per cent of
adults in 1947 to 40 per cent in 1955 (Carr-Saunders *et al.*
1958), following the year in which the Independent Television
Authority first operated commercial television. With petrol
rationing at an end increasing numbers of vehicles took to the
roads, more than doubling between 1951 (4.3 million) and

1961 (9.5 million), although the first motorway, part of the M1, was not opened until 1959. The number of vehicles licensed in 1988 was 23.3 million (*Social Trends* 1990). A comparison of consumer expenditure in 1938 and 1956 found that there had been an increase of 6–7 per cent 'and when it is remembered that this figure does not take account of the growth of free health services, free education and other state provision, the measure of our considerably improved living standards is revealed' (Carr-Saunders *et al.* 1958: 159).

As well as the visible signs of change important shifts in values were also taking place, many of them initiated during the war. Costello (1985) describes how 'The urgency and excitement of wartime soon eroded moral restraints' (p. 23), and although there had been many calls for a return to pre-war standards of behaviour other kinds of contemporary social change were already loosening the family bonds that had helped to maintain earlier values and styles of behaviour. Prominent amongst these changes was the annually increasing numbers of married women going out to work. During the war many women had come to enjoy the various benefits of going out to work, and afterwards were anxious to continue to do so (Minns 1980). The controversy over whether mothers who went out to work were as a result seriously neglecting their children has already been described (in Chapter 3). But for women who went out to work considerable changes in attitudes were necessary and inevitable, whereas those who stayed at home had a rather different view of life. For example, in her study of tradition and change in an English town, carried out in 1950, Stacey (1960) describes how for women the role of keeping the family together

spills over into their attitudes in wider fields, for they have been shown in previous chapters to be more traditional on balance than men. They are more religious and more conservative in politics. Maintenance of the institution of the family apparently leads them to show more concern about maintaining established institutions generally. (p. 136)

Family links were also loosened as more of those of working age had to move away from their parents' homes to find appropriate occupation and a sizeable proportion emigrated, mostly to Canada, Australia, New Zealand, and South Africa; in fact 276 (5 per cent) children who were members of this study had by the age of 11 years emigrated with their families, most of them in infancy (see Appendix 1). In the first nine months of 1947 46,502 people left Britain to live in the Dominions, and they were estimated to be only one-tenth of those who wanted to go (Robertson 1987). By 1958 it was suggested that since the end of the Second World War 'the United Kingdom has resumed its additional role as a country of emigration' (Carr-Saunders *et al.* 1958: 17). More recently it has been shown that 'return migration of British citizens is at an all-time high' (Coleman 1988: 101).

Other signs of changes in values are to be found in educational expansion, in declining church attendance, and in the arts. The greater educational opportunities which the 1944 Education Act had initiated helped to speed this process of change, although its implementation was scarcely even across the divides of class and sex. For example, the proportion of young people in full-time education between ages 15 and 19 years had more than doubled in the thirty years between 1921 and 1951, rising from 62 per thousand to 142 per thousand of this age. Yet in 1955–6 when 26 per cent of men admitted to English universities were from manual social class families (at that time almost three-quarters of the labour force was in manual employment (Halsey 1987)) the proportion from this class admitted to Cambridge was 9 per cent, compared with 13 per cent to Oxford, 21 per cent to London, and an average of 31 per cent at the other English universities. Only 25 per cent of full-time students were women (Carr-Saunders *et al.* 1958).

Changes may also be seen in the arts. It has been argued that at the beginning of the period discussed in this chapter (i.e. 1951), 'the novels of the time . . . perhaps have a national even parochial quality' (Marwick 1982), but by the end of this time (1957) the 'angry young men' had arrived with such works as John Osborne's *Look Back in Anger*, first staged in 1956, and John Braine's *Room at the Top*, published in 1957. Those interested in the arts discussed whether it was 'essential for the preservation of the culture of the minority that it should continue to be a "minority" culture' (T. S. Eliot quoted by Sissons and French 1986), and the general dismay of the observant post-war bourgeois that their culture had declined into nullity, and could only be resurrected by observing the old social forms. . . . Mr Eliot too wanted the family to propagate the traditional culture, and, the better placed the family, the higher the culture, so that an elite was formed. A carefully regulated attitude to marriage must be at the centre of such an existence. (Sissons and French 1986: 216)

There were, of course, others who held comparable views about social change, and not necessarily only about the arts. The speed of change must have been much too great, for example, for those 1.2 per cent of all private households who still in 1951 maintained resident domestic servants, and perhaps the decline from the 1931 proportion of 4.8 per cent was seen as the writing on the wall (Carr-Saunders *et al.* 1958).

In the medical sciences these years were a time of great progress. Vaccines were developed and brought into use for tuberculosis (in 1953), poliomyelitis (in 1956), and whooping cough (also in 1956), and the crippling effects of the second of these and the high death rates from the third (there were over ten thousand deaths from whooping cough in England and Wales between 1941 and 1951) were practically eliminated. The research that had been carried out on these viruses led to work on the measles virus and on carcinogenic viruses and their immunology (Medical Research Council 1958). Also during this time experiments in tissue grafting were preparing the ground work that made possible the transplant operations of all kinds which began a decade or more later. Research was also taking place on the harmful effects of work environments, for example work in exceptionally dusty atmospheres was investigated in the study of pneumoconiosis, and led eventually to improved industrial compensation, and work on the effects of pesticides later led to strict controls on their use, particularly of DDT. Important discoveries were made in genetics, molecular biology, and biophysics, the most well known being those in proteins and peptides, particularly deoxyribonucleic acid (DNA). Interferon was discovered in 1957 and this led to important improvements in antibiotics.

However, the Medical Research Council's Annual Report for 1952–3 observed that since the advent of antibiotics which have greatly reduced mortality from infections, diseases affecting the middle-aged and elderly, particularly cancer and certain diseases of the heart and blood vessels, have become increasingly important causes of disability and death. (Medical Research Council 1953)

Lung cancer deaths had more than doubled from 188 deaths per million of the population in 1945 to 388 per million in 1955, and in 1956 the definitive work that demonstrated the association of lung cancer with smoking was published (Doll and Hill 1956). Deaths from leukaemia had also risen from 17 per million persons in 1931 to 50 per million in 1955, the third greatest rise following those from lung cancer and coronary thrombosis. The suspicion that radiation was involved in these deaths from leukaemia was confirmed by Stewart and her colleagues, who found that babies of mothers who had had abdominal x-rays during pregnancy were those most at risk of leukaemia (Stewart *et al.* 1956). The 'widespread social cata-strophe' (Medical Research Council 1954) of the steep rise in blindness in the newborn (retrolental fibroplasia), first noted in 1942, was in 1954 traced to the use of high concentrations of oxygen in the care of premature babies; practice was changed and the number of new cases immediately fell sharply. The effects of antibiotics on the prevailing pattern of disease on a population in which the proportion of elderly persons was steadily increasing was also found in the rising prevalence of heart disease. Between 1951 and 1963 the proportion of all deaths in England and Wales that were caused by coronary artery disease rose from 10.5 per cent to 18.5 per cent.

By the end of the time considered in this chapter (1957) the optimism of Beveridge and others had lessened, partly because the anticipated fall in the rates of illness that had taken place in infectious disease had been offset by corresponding increases in other conditions, and partly because of the apparently ever increasing costs of the National Health Service. However, the government-appointed Guillebaud Committee reported in 1956 that the cost of the service as a proportion of the annual gross national product, had in fact, slightly declined (Marshall 1965). The Willinck Committee was also optimistic in its report in 1957 on the future national medical manpower require-ments. It concluded that a reduced annual number of newly qualified doctors would suffice during the years 1961 to 1970, and speculated that in 1980–5 the annual requirement would be of the order of 1,670. In fact in 1956 the number of new medical graduates in Great Britain was 2,032 (University Grants Committee 1957), but in 1984 it had risen to 4,693 (University Grants Committee 1986).

The most notable legislation for disease prevention passed during the time study children were aged 5–11 years (1951–7) was the Clean Air Act of 1956. The scale of its achievement may be seen in the fact that smoke emissions in England and Wales which had been measured at 2.36 million metric tons a year in 1951, had been reduced to 1.62 million by 1961, and were as low as 0.84 million in 1969. Consequently the average daily hours of winter sunshine measured at the London Weather Centre showed an increase of 56 per cent between 1944 and 1964 (*Social Trends* 1971). Also during this period the regulations that forbade midwives, working without a doctor present, to adminster any form of pain relief during childbirth, a problem which this study had identified in the investigation of birth (see Chapter 2), were amended to permit them to do so.

Changes in the rates and types of scientific discovery were hard to anticipate and thus to use in developing workable, effective, and acceptable policies for the National Health Service. Planners of education services had to contend with the pressure of population change and increased expectations of education. Lowndes (1969) wrote that at the time of the Education Act of 1944

No one could foresee that the 4½ million school population of 1944 would by 1955 have risen to nearly 7 million, or that the cost of secondary school building, assumed during the debates to be likely to be 34 per cent higher than in 1939, would in fact increase by more than 400 per cent . . . . In the twenty one years (up to 1965) during which the local finance of public education has concentrated in the hands of the county and county borough councils, the country has witnessed the building of 7,500 new schools providing places for 3,750,000 children at a cost of some £1,300 millions. (pp. 244, 249)

Thus, in many ways this was a time of change, of questioning of the received wisdom, and of much more widely felt concern about the nature of society and its effects on the individual.

During these years, when the study children first began

full-time school at the age of 5 and on until they were 11 years old, they and their families were contacted at regular intervals. Mothers agreed to answer questions when the children were 6, 7, 8, 9 and 11 years old, and they consented to have the survey child medically examined at school at ages 6, 7, and 11 years. In addition, when the children were 7 and 10 years old teachers made assessments of their attitudes to work, of their parents' concern for their school progress, and teachers also described the school and gave information about class sizes and whether children were taught in groups according to attainment (streaming). By the end of this period contact was still maintained successfully with 89 per cent of the children.


## HEALTH AND GROWTH

### (a) Survival

Infancy is a time of relative vulnerability to death, when deaths occur largely because of infectious disease and because of the effects of birth injury and problems with which babies are born. In this study 232 (4 per cent) of the 5,362 children died before their fifth birthday, and in fact 92 per cent of all deaths before age 16 years had occurred by the age 5, and 83 per cent before the first birthday (see Appendix 1). Whilst they were aged 5 to 11 years only a further 15 of the study children died, and during these ages the proportion of children who died was essentially the same (0.2 per cent) in each social group.


### (b) Air pollution and respiratory illness

Each child's exposure to atmospheric pollution was calculated for the first 11 years of life using national data on domestic coal consumption, and during these years 22 per cent of children lived in relatively highly polluted areas, that is with domestic coal consumption of seven thousand tons or more per square mile per year. Children who lived in the most polluted districts were found to have the greatest amount of chest illness by the age of 11, including admissions to hospital for bronchitis and pneumonia, and signs of chest illness recorded at school medical examinations. They also had significantly more time off school because of illness. This important effect was in due course found to be long term, and Douglas and Waller (1966) concluded in their report at this stage of the investigation that 'Boys and girls were similarly affected, and no difference was found between children in middle class and working class families.'

However, far more children from lower social class families lived in the areas of high atmospheric pollution.

More recent analyses of this early life information showed the importance of parental chest illness and of poor home circumstances in the development of risk of chest disease in early childhood (Mann *et al.* forthcoming). The effects of poor home circumstances were thought perhaps to be the result of poor nutrition likely in many such families (Douglas 1969), poor housing, and delay in getting medical care in the years before the National Health Service. The powerful influence of parental chest illness may be explained by smoking, which was far more prevalent at that time than today.

### (c) *Chronic illness*

Serious, persisting, or chronic illness in the study children was mostly (80 per cent of the children who had chronic illness) evident by the age of 11 years (Pless and Douglas 1971), by which time 422 children (8 per cent of all the study children) had been diagnosed as having 'a physical, usually non-fatal condition which lasted three months in a given year or necessitated a period of continuous hospitalization of more than one month' (Pless and Douglas 1971). Such a definition, of course, includes relatively minor problems like squint (229 children) and eczema (206 children) as well as conditions of further reaching effect such as asthma (99 children), blindness (4 children), and congenital heart disease (11 children). However, only a third (35 per cent) of these chronically sick children were assessed as having a temporary condition and another third (34 per cent) were thought to have illness of moderate severity, whilst 12 per cent were regarded as severely ill.

There were no differences in rates of chronic illness in the various social groups, but the chances of death amongst those with chronic illness was very much greater in children from manual social group families, as figures 6.2*a* and 6.2*b* show (Pless *et al.* 1989).

When the definition of chronic illness was altered to include only those more serious conditions which needed hospital admission of a minimum of 28 consecutive days, or school absence of three consecutive weeks or more altogether, then significantly more boys from lower social group families were found to have been chronically ill, but there were no significant class differences amongst girls (Wadsworth 1986*a*).

### (d) Low birth weight

A particular study was made of the educational attainment of children who had survived relatively low birth weight (2,500 g. or less); 26 per cent of these children had died by age 11 years. Although in comparison with controls they under-achieved in the tests at 8 years, and were less likely to have gained grammar school places, these differences were attribut-able to their poor home circumstances and the low level of parental interest in their school progress, rather than to any attribute of low birth weight (Douglas 1960).

### (e) Growth

Children were measured by school doctors or nurses at the ages of 7 and 11 years, and each time the average (mean) height of boys and girls from upper social group families was greater than the average for those from lower social groups (Douglas and Simpson 1964). It was also clear that amongst all the girls, and the boys in the lower middle and the manual social groups, those who were only children were of greater average height than those within the same social group who had brothers or sisters. Serious childhood illness had the effect of slowing down growth in the manual class children, so that they were significantly shorter than their healthy counterparts, but non-manual class children who were seriously ill did not experi-ence this to a significant extent (Wadsworth 1986*a*).

Few children were obese by today's standards, in fact only 1 per cent at 7 years and 4 per cent at 11 years (Braddon *et al.* 1986). When measured a generation later at 8 years, a sample of first born offspring of the study children were much more inclined to be obese (2.5 per cent were obese), and 2 per cent of the children in the 1958 cohort of birth were obese at 7 years (Peckham *et al.* 1983), reflecting the tendency for children to be of greater body mass now than in the immediate post-war years. This may well be associated with food rationing experienced by the children born in 1946 as discussed in Chapter 3.

Although information on diet was not collected in childhood, replies to a question on what each child ate during the previous day, asked of mothers when their children were 10 years old in 1956, refer frequently to toast and dripping, as well as to the ubiquitous stew and milk puddings. Drummond and Wilbraham (1959) reported that between 1947 and the late 1950s the fat content of diets had on average increased by 30 per cent since the pre-war years. Sugar consumption rose very sharply in post-war years and until 1960, but by comparison with the pre-war years intakes of calcium, iron, and vitamins were greatly improved (Burnett 1989). A study of eating habits in 1958 found that they were still 'traditional'; the big change to a 'lighter and less bulky' diet did not begin until the 1960s (Burnett 1989).

### (f) Emotional problems

By the time that they are 5 or 6 years old most children have stopped wetting the bed, and those who continue to do so with any regularity may be thought to have some kind of emotional or physical problem. In the early 1950s there was concern about the rate of rejection of men for compulsory military training because of bed-wetting (Bransby *et al.* 1955), and there had been a joint committee of the British Medical Association and the Magistrates' Association to consider the problem (Joint Committee(*b*) 1948).

Bed-wetting was more a problem in this study amongst boys than girls, at any age, and was more often experienced by manual class children than others (Blomfield and Douglas

1956). At age 7 years 3 per cent of study children wet the bed regularly, and a further 4 per cent did so occasionally. From the age of 6 up until 15 years the highest percentage of children who wet the bed was found among those who had experienced, before they were 6 years old, the death of their mother, followed by those whose parents had been divorced or separated. Even at 15 years, when bed-wetting was reported only by 2 per cent of the population, 8 per cent of children whose mothers had died nine years earlier still wet the bed, compared with 5 per cent of those whose parents had separated or divorced at that time, and 2 per cent of those who lived with both parents at least until they were 6 years old. Death of the father was not associated with this problem (Douglas 1973a). It was found that 'the greatest excess of enuresis [bed-wetting] is recorded for children who were fostered or in institutions, and the least for those who remained with their mothers and did not have a stepfather' (Douglas 1973a).

In addition to bed-wetting other potential signs of emotional problems were found in mothers' reports to health visitors and school doctors of stammering, nail-biting, unexplained vomiting, abdominal pain, night terrors, and other difficulties. All together 5 per cent of boys and 4 per cent of girls were reported to have three or more of these habits. There was some degree of association of these habits with other indicators of problems. For example, amongst those who had three or more of these habits 5 per cent had been to child guidance clinics, as compared with only 0.1 per cent of those with no reported habits. There was a higher rate of habits amongst children who had been severely scarred or disfigured (Douglas and Mulligan 1961). The association of these habits with educational attainment is discussed later in this chapter and in Chapter 5, and their association with adult emotional health is discussed in Chapter 6.

## HOME CIRCUMSTANCES AND SOCIAL CLASS CHANGE

Improvements in living standards were considerable during the first eleven years of the life of the study child, but differences between social classes were not eliminated. By 1957 the home amenities of running hot water and the use of a bath were still enjoyed only by 30 per cent of those in the manual class, and 22 per cent of manual families still either shared such amenities or had no running hot water. The threshold for overcrowding was taken to be two or more persons to each living room, and by these standards, when the children were 11 years old, 3 per cent of non-manual families lived in overcrowded circumstances and so did 13 per cent of manual families.

During the period 1946–57 a great deal of occupational change or social mobility took place in the study population, as many fathers changed their jobs. This was not exceptional for the time, partly because those leaving the armed forces did not always at first get the most appropriate occupation or level of occupation for their skills, and partly because the nature of available occupations was changing. Using a nine-point ranking of occupations Douglas (1964) found that during these eleven years 43 per cent of families changed their social class, and that the greatest amount of change was amongst those in manual class occupations. However, although 'The main direction of change is upward, . . . there is a semi-permeable barrier between the non-manual and the manual groups across which, in the whole eleven years, only 5 per cent moved up and 3 per cent down' (Douglas 1964: 40). Accordingly a stable measure of social position was constructed to take account of parents' education and the social class of their families when they were growing up (Douglas 1964, Douglas *et al.* 1968, and see Chapter 7 and Appendix 2). More extensive discussion of social class change is given in Chapter 7.

Unemployment of the study children's fathers during this time was at its maximum of 3 per cent in 1957.

## EDUCATION

Education has very often been regarded as a source of opportunity. Parents have seen it as the basic means of access for children to eventual adult financial independence and broad occupational choice, and as a means of upward social mobility (Jackson and Marsden 1962); philosophers have seen it as the fundamental method of bringing equality and tolerance to society (Russell 1926); and politicians have used it as a way to attempt to

provide both equality of opportunity and the skills necessary for
the maintenance of a buoyant economy (Halsey *et al.* 1980,
Goldthorpe 1980). It is no coincidence that the great Parliament-
ary Acts of educational reform were passed (in 1902, 1918, and
1944) in times of renewed aspiration and desire for regeneration
immediately after wars (Thomson 1981: 281). By these means,
and through pressure from the population, change has come
about, but sometimes painfully slowly. For example in 1926 the
report of the Hadow Committee recommended that the school-
leaving age should be raised to 15 years, and eventually the
Education Act of 1936 legislated for this, but implementation of
the Act was postponed until after the war (Barnett 1986: 232–3).
Equality of educational opportunity has also been slow to
progress. Since Hogben wrote in 1938 that 'more than half the
gifted children did not get beyond the elementary school, and one
child in five was given a standard of education to which he was
unsuited; a standard more often too low than too high' (Douglas
1964: 14), equality of opportunity has continued to be a problem,
even though educational services have changed considerably and
have expanded greatly since the 1940s (Halsey *et al.* 1980).

Within education psychological research had been concerned
with how children acquire skills and the best means to
translate such knowledge into educational practice. There was
also concern amongst psychologists about what were called
'over zealous' or 'problem parents' (Lawrence 1970), and about
the nature of affection in relationships between children and
parents (Burlingham and Freud 1965) since,

The practice of the best infant schools would be better understood and
more appreciated, where it is realised that the task of these years is not
just to teach children to read and write, important as these skills are,
but to help them to feel accepted, loved and secure, confident to try
new experiences, stable enough to face failure and frustration, able to
talk and to think for themselves. These needs met, the learning of
skills follows. (Lawrence 1970: 368)

Concern about the role of parents in the process of education
had been strikingly described in 1931 in the *Report of the
Consultative Committee on the Primary School* (Board of Education
1931).

In the poor home it is the linguistic and literary side of the child's mental equipment that suffers most. His vocabulary is limited; his general knowledge is narrow; he has little opportunity for reading, and his power of expressing himself in good English is inadequate. In the household where the family is small and means are adequate the child usually enters school with the foundations of education already well laid. Before he comes to the infant department, he has been encouraged to teach himself to read; and at an early stage he is expected to write little letters to his relatives. As he grows older, he will acquire almost as much general knowledge in the home as he does in the school, and glean almost as much information about the world and its way during leisure hours as he does from the formal lessons in the classroom. For many young children from the poorest home all this is reversed. Their parents know very little of any life except their own, and have neither the time nor the leisure to impart what little they know. The vocabulary that the child picks up is restricted to a few hundred words, most of them inaccurate, uncouth and mispronounced, and a good many unfit for reproduction in the classroom. There is no literature that deserves the title, and the pictures are equally unworthy of their name. His universe is closed in and circumscribed by walls of brick and a pall of smoke. From one end of the year to the other he may go no further than the nearest shops or the neighbouring recreation-ground. The country or the seaside are mere words to him, dimly suggesting some place to which cripples are sent after an accident. (pp. 56–7)

This Consultative Committee, aware of the impossibility of a rapid redress of what it saw as the root of the problem, namely the poverty of many families' social and environmental circumstances, made instead recommendations on what it felt was the next best thing it could do, which was to stimulate parents' interests in their child's progress at primary school. Sadly, 34 years later, Young (1965) observed that it was still rarely recognized that 'it should, for the sake of the child, be part of the function of the school to stimulate parental interest' (p. 73).

This present study of children born in 1946 showed the importance for children's attainment of home circumstances, and particularly parents' interest in their child's education. By following the progress of the children on through secondary schools and into adult life it has been possible to see how far equality of opportunity was realized. Measures of attainment as well as records of exam success enabled the study not only to compare the earlier life circumstances of those who did well in education with those of others, but also to assess how many of the apparently capable children did not succeed in examinations, and to describe what happened to them in terms of careers, in later life.

Whilst they were between 5 and 8 years old the children went to infant schools, and from 8 to 11 years they were at junior schools. Some went to independent or fee-paying schools (7 per cent), but most were at state schools. At the end of the period they spent in these types of schools, when they were 8 years old, the children took tests of attainment, administered by their teachers on behalf of the study; the tests were of reading, vocabulary, sentence completion, and picture intelligence, and they are described in Appendix 2. These tests were not designed to be measures of innate ability, but were intended to measure the level of achievement in school subjects, so that the influences of home, school, and the children themselves on these measures of attainment could be unravelled and understood.

### (a) 8 years old

The relationship of family circumstances with the child's average score on the attainment tests taken at this age was striking, as tables 4.1a and 4.1b show, for three reasons; the sex

TABLE 4.1a   *The influence of parental interest on 8-year-old boys' and girls' reading average scores*[a]

| Parental interest | Non-manual families | | Manual families | |
|---|---|---|---|---|
| | Boys | Girls | Boys | Girls |
| Lowest quarter | 50.5 | 52.6 | 47.1 | 48.5 |
| Second quarter | 53.3 | 55.3 | 48.1 | 48.7 |
| Third quarter | 54.5 | 55.6 | 49.5 | 52.0 |
| Highest or greatest interest | 58.3 | 58.2 | 54.4 | 55.5 |
| Average score for all interest levels | 54.7 | 56.0 | 48.5 | 50.0 |

[a] See Appendix 2 for details of these tests.

TABLE 4.1b  *The influence of parental interest on 8-year-old boys' and girls' picture intelligence average scores*[a]

| Parental interest | Non-manual families | | Manual families | |
|---|---|---|---|---|
| | Boys | Girls | Boys | Girls |
| Lowest quarter | 52.7 | 51.2 | 48.2 | 47.4 |
| Second quarter | 53.2 | 53.3 | 49.3 | 49.0 |
| Third quarter | 53.4 | 53.0 | 50.4 | 52.3 |
| Highest or greatest interest | 56.3 | 56.6 | 54.4 | 53.2 |
| Average score for all interest levels | 54.1 | 54.0 | 49.5 | 49.6 |

[a] See Appendix 2 for details of these tests.

differences, the social group differences, and the overriding influence of parental interest in the child's education.

Parental interest was assessed when the children were 6 years old and again at age 10 years using teachers' and parents' reports of mothers' and fathers' visits to the schools for discussion about their child's progress. Although middle class parents took more interest in education compared with those in the manual class (e.g. 32 per cent of middle class fathers visited their child's school compared with 12 per cent of manual class fathers), children of interested parents scored higher than others, in all social groups as tables 4.1a and 4.1b show. It was found, for example, that 'In the upper middle class . . . children of very interested parents make scores that are 3.7 points higher on the average than those made by the children of uninterested parents. In the lower manual working class they make scores that are 9.2 points higher' (Douglas 1964: 55).

Parents' own experience of education was strongly associated with their level of interest in their child's progress, and there were other indications earlier in the child's life of this differentiation of interest. Douglas (1964) found that 'Within each social class . . . the parents who give their children the most encouragement in their school work also give them the best care in infancy' (p. 54). Parents' aspirations may perhaps also be seen in their own socio-economic advancement, and children of fathers who moved up the socio-economic scale achieved scores on these attainment tests that were more closely akin to those of the class they joined than to the class they left. Conversely, children from especially poor circumstances achieved on average relatively low scores; for example, those whose homes were in the most crowded and worst conditions did not on average score highly, and neither did those few whose fathers were unemployed (3 per cent of fathers when the children were 11 years old and only 1 per cent of fathers when the children were 4 years old). But almost all prolonged unemployment of fathers was a result of their illness, and Douglas (1964) speculated that perhaps the key to the relatively low scores of children of these fathers lay 'in worries and anxieties at home' (p. 41)

At the age of 8, only children did not achieve significantly higher scores than others on these attainment tests, nor did those who were first born, but children in families with five or more children altogether were inclined to achieve lower test scores. Living in a large family may often be associated with other kinds of difficulties, such as poor housing and relatively low parental interest, but even when the effects of such disadvantages were taken into account an influence of family size on test score still remained.

Parents were inclined to be more interested in the school progress of girls rather than boys at this age, and there were differences in teachers' assessments of boys' and girls' interests in and concentration on school work, and this is discussed below.

The junior schools which children attended at the age of 8 years were inclined to be old; 48 per cent of the children were at schools built in the nineteenth century, and nearly half of such schools had not been modernized during the ten years which had elapsed since the end of the war. Consequently necessities like electric lights, hot running water, efficient sanitation, and adequate playgrounds, dining halls, assembly halls, or even a study for the head teacher were lacking in many. In fact 16 per cent of the children went to schools which lacked four or more of these amenities, and only 24 per cent were at schools which had them all. Classes were often large, and when they were 11 years old 45 per cent of children were being taught in classes of forty or more.

When the children were 10 class teachers assessed their attitude to work, and girls were then more often than boys reported as hard working and better able to concentrate and to submit to discipline. Douglas (1964) noted that

These judgements are made mostly by women, and might have been different if they had been made by men. Upper middle class children appear to be better behaved at school than lower manual working class children, but the upper middle class boys are picked out as being lazier and more difficult than the upper middle class girls, just as the lower manual working class boys are picked out as being lazier and more difficult than the lower manual working class girls. There is constant criticism of the boys; for example, though the behaviour of school children is much more favourably reported on when their parents show great interest in their work, the boys still get nearly twice as much criticism as the girls. (p. 73)

In assessing attitudes to school work teachers rated 26 per cent of upper middle and 17 per cent of lower middle children as hard workers, compared with 11 per cent of upper manual and 7 per cent of lower manual.

Choice of school also revealed, as it still does, differences in social backgrounds and parental interest. Nearly three times the proportion of middle class parents (44 per cent) sent their children to primary schools which had good records of achieving grammar school places for their pupils (the criterion used was 31 per cent or more of the pupils), when compared with manual class parents (16 per cent). But on the other hand educationally ambitious working class parents were more selective in their choice of schools, although this must also have been influenced by their ability to pay for the child to travel to a school other than the local primary, or to move house to live within a particular school's catchment area, or to persuade Education Authority officials of the need for a child to be educated at a school other than that locally available.

In order to assess the relative strength of these various influences on the children's school experience and their measured attainment, a statistical analysis was carried out which took account of the combined effect of parental interest, standard of the home environment, family size, and the primary school's academic record; this was designed to show which was the most important of these elements. (Full details of these analyses of variance are given in Douglas 1964.) In each of the four social groups parental interest was the influence most powerfully associated with test scores at the age of 8 years.


### (b) 11 years old

Before the children took the secondary school selection examination and when they were 11 years old, class teachers once again gave them four attainment tests. These were tests of verbal and non-verbal ability, of arithmetic, of reading, and of vocabulary, and examples from each test are given in Appendix 2. During the time since they had first taken an attainment test at 8 years more information had been collected about the children from their mothers by school nurses and from their teachers, and a particular interest was now to see how far the children's environment at home and at school continued to affect attainment and the likelihood of achieving a place at grammar or other form of selective school.

Again, as at the age of 8 years, mean scores that girls achieved on the attainment tests were higher than those of boys, even within each social class. However, there were already signs of a pulling apart in terms of sex and social class.

In the middle classes, the boys improve their scores between eight and eleven years; they start by doing less well than the girls but have nearly caught them up by the time they are eleven. In contrast the boys from the manual working classes are as far behind the girls at eleven as they are at eight. (Douglas 1964: 71)

Class differences in scores were greater at 11 years than at 8, so that the 'backward manual working class child shows less improvement between eight and eleven years than the backward middle class child' (Douglas 1964: 47). The greatest divergence between the social classes was in the non-verbal test scores (Douglas *et al.* 1968), and this was attributed to the greater familiarity of non-manual social class children with such tests in their preparation for the entry examinations to secondary schools. The differences in average scores between 8 and 11 years were very little associated with parental interest, and were far more strongly correlated with the children's adjudged attitude to work: 'The hard working children improve their scores on the average between eight and eleven years whether their parents encourage them or not, and the poor workers and lazy children deteriorate in performance whatever their parents' attitude' (Douglas 1964: 63).

Also at this age mothers were asked about bed-wetting, nightmares, and abdominal pain, recurrent vomiting, nail-biting, thumb-sucking, and other habits that were then thought to indicate some form of disturbance in the child which would probably be a source of worry to the mother. At this age the more of these habits the children had, the worse their average attainment test score in comparison with children with no such problems. These problems were somewhat more common in boys than in girls, but they were inclined to be of greater severity in girls.

The most powerful school influence on attainment test score at 11 years, and on the differences between scores achieved at 8 and 11 years, was the school's record in achieving grammar school places for its pupils. This was more influential than the mix of social classes of pupils, or the school's size, amenities, or locality, and it was particularly advantageous for middle class children and for those who scored in the lower half or even the lower sixth of scores achieved at 8 years. But, of course, such successful schools attracted children whose predominantly middle class parents were particularly interested in their educational attainment. In some schools the influence of streaming, that is of teaching children grouped according to ability, was stimulating for children in the upper attainment streams, but in the lower streams Douglas (1964) concluded that 'the relatively bright children are handicapped either by unsuitable teaching or lack of competition . . . once allocated, the children tend to take on the characteristics expected of them and the forecasts of ability made at the point of streaming are to this extent self-fulfilling' (p. 115).

In fact, and in summary,

streaming by ability reinforces the process of social selection . . . Children who come from well-kept homes and who are themselves clean, well clothed and shod, stand a greater chance of being put in the upper streams than their measured ability would seem to justify. Once there they are likely to stay and to improve in performance in succeeding years. This is in striking contrast to the deterioration noticed in those children of similar initial measured ability who were placed in the lower streams. In this way the validity of the initial selection appears to be confirmed by the subsequent performance of the children, and an element of rigidity is introduced early into the primary school system. (Douglas 1964: 118)

### (c) Selection for secondary school

Douglas (1964) quotes the Spens report on secondary education, published in 1938, which noted that 'the existing arrangements for the whole-time higher education of boys and girls above the age of 11 in England and Wales (had) ceased to correspond with the actual structure of modern society and with the economic facts of the situation', and Douglas (1964) continues that

The expressed aim of the 1944 Education Act was to remedy this situation and to provide all children with the type of secondary education best matched to their abilities. A primary, or preparatory school system should be available for all children up to the age of 11+, followed by varying forms of secondary education corresponding to their different talents and capacities after that age. (p. 14)

By 1957 a few local education authorities selected children using non-competitive methods, but Douglas (1964) noted that 'most authorities use combinations of mental tests, teachers' reports, written examinations and interviews' (p. 15). When tests were abandoned in one area the proportion of manual class boys who gained grammar school places fell, whilst that of non-manual boys rose (Floud and Halsey 1957).

   In this study parents were already very aware of the selection process even when the study children were 8 years old, and by then most mothers had decided on the actual or the type of secondary school they wanted their child to attend. At that time 62 per cent wanted a grammar school place for their child. Only 2 per cent of mothers said that they would refuse grammar school places offered, but nearly half the mothers who hoped for a grammar school place intended their child to leave at the earliest school-leaving age. In practice 19 per cent of study children gained grammar school places; most of those who failed to do so went to secondary modern schools, 5 per cent went to independent schools, and 5 per cent to technical schools.

Awards of grammar school places accorded well with scores the children obtained on the study's tests of attainment taken a few weeks before the secondary school selection procedures. The average test score of those who gained grammar school places was 60.98, compared with 47.05 obtained by those who went to secondary modern schools. But other influences were at work on the selection procedure.

Children who scored in the lowest parts of the range of scores achieved by those who gained grammar school places were far more likely to have gained a place if their parents had shown interest in their educational progress and aspirations for the child to go to grammar school. Higher proportions of the children who had interested and aspiring parents went to grammar school (42 per cent) compared with those with similar test scores but with parents who were undecided about the value of a grammar school place for this child (21 per cent of such children obtained a grammar school place). Amongst those who obtained similar scores but whose parents originally had said they would be happy for this child to go to secondary modern school only 8 per cent gained a grammar school place. Teachers' assessments were in accord with this.

The teachers' assessments of the ability of children to benefit from a grammar school education agree with these figures in suggesting that there is a particularly high wastage in the selection examinations among those who are expected by their parents to go to secondary modern schools. These children get less than half the grammar school places they deserve according to their teachers, who see a much greater wastage among them than among those whose parents are more ambitious for their educational success. (Douglas 1964: 22)

Children who were fortunate enough to go to good primary schools where the standard of teaching (assessed in terms of the school's record in gaining grammar school places) made up for deficiencies in parental concern did as well in gaining places as children of parents with high interest and aspirations.

There were considerable regional inequalities in the availability of grammar school places, and the biggest inequalities were found among children whose relatively low test scores gave them a reduced chance of getting into grammar school.

High scoring children's chances did not vary much across
regions. Sex differences were slight (20 per cent of girls went to
grammar school compared with 18 per cent of boys), but social
class differences were considerable especially, as table 4.2
shows, amongst those in the lowest bands of scores attained on
the tests which the children took for the study at age 11.

TABLE 4.2    *Social group[a] by level of attainment at age 11 years; percentage of*
*15-year-old children attending grammar schools*

| Test score at 11 years | Middle class | | Manual working class | |
| --- | --- | --- | --- | --- |
| | Upper | Lower | Upper | Lower |
| 49–51 | 16.7 | 2.5 | 3.3 | 3.5 |
| 52–4 | 27.4 | 18.4 | 13.1 | 7.2 |
| 55–7 | 59.3 | 39.0 | 25.0 | 26.6 |
| 58–60 | 63.3 | 59.7 | 46.1 | 51.8 |
| 61–3 | 94.0 | 86.5 | 97.9 | 79.7 |
| 64–6 | 94.0 | 87.7 | 80.0 | 89.0 |
| 67 and over | 100.0 | 92.9 | 97.8 | 100.0 |

[a] See Appendix 2.

Douglas (1964) concluded that

much potential ability is wasted during the primary school years and
misdirected at the point of secondary selection ... (p.119)

It seems that a substantial proportion of the potentially clever children
are today not reaching the selective secondary schools. When ability is
judged by the eleven year test score, 26.8 per cent of children with
scores of 55 or over, and 5.0 per cent with scores of 60 or over, go to
secondary modern schools; when ability is judged by the eight year
scores the equivalent percentages rise to 33.1 per cent and 16.6 per
cent.... (p. 123)

Over a period of three years in the primary schools, there is a
substantial loss of ability in the manual working class children which
could be prevented, it seems, by better teaching, even if the attitude of
working class parents towards education does not change. If our aim
is to preserve the pool of talent it may be more important to improve
the level of teaching in the primary than in the secondary schools. The

problem goes beyond this, however, for it is likely that in the pre-school years the mental development of many children is stunted by the intellectual poverty of their surroundings. (p. 128)

## CONCLUSION

From this study's work with information collected whilst the children were aged between 5 and 11 years it is evident that health status and educational attainments were both heavily influenced by the family's social class and by parents' concern for their child's education.

The study's findings on education were described by the educational correspondent of the *Observer* (9 February 1964) as building up 'A picture of a nation, educationally, slopping about the house in broken-down bedroom slippers . . . It is a story of wastage'. The *Evening Standard's* correspondent felt that 'The chief lesson is that education begins at home' (10 February); and in the *New Statesman* (14 February) Micheal Young wrote that

The main finding is that working class children were doubly handicapped . . . [the research] may even influence teachers, by showing again how limited they are in what they can do with children unless they have, or go out and secure, the co-operation of the whole family.

Although it was clear that threats to the child's educational attainment posed by a low level of parental interest and aspiration might be counterbalanced by good teaching, it is important to ask why some parents were apparently not especially concerned with their child's educational progress, and apparently not particularly anxious for him or her to go to grammar school. Parents of the study children were not asked about their own school experience, but one small set of information is available from another study about girls who went to grammar schools in two working class areas of London in the five years immediately before the war, when many of the mothers of study children were also at school. Young and Willmott (1962) interviewed these girls when they had grown up, and found that they felt they had

lost the friends who had formerly been their classmates; there was probably no one else in the whole street going to the same grammar school. When they came home in the afternoon they were supposed to do homework instead of rushing into the street to play. They became different, lonely, 'sort of reserved', regarded as 'someone apart'. 'Oh, look at her,' the other girls shouted after one of them. The uniform was a special trial—a mark of superior status detested because it made them feel inferior. (p. 176)

Clearly such recollection would deter those who could not in their generation correct these problems of social difference and increase their child's chances of going to a grammar school, for instance, by living in an area where a high proportion of children went to grammar school. There is also contemporary evidence from the Banbury study of 1950, of 'parents' anxiety as to whether their grammar-school-educated children will be ashamed of them' (Stacey 1960: 140). Parents with such anxieties might well have been concerned about their children going to grammar school, and perhaps the low regard for 'book learning' felt by many in Britain added to the reasons why some parents were not particularly concerned that their study child should go to an academically inclined secondary school.

Health of the study children varied with social class and social circumstances, most strikingly in the greater risk of chest illness and of poor growth among children who lived in the poorest circumstances. The effects of such problems in childhood were to prove difficult to escape in adult life. These were, however, years of gradual improvement in many of the circumstances which put children's health at risk. They were also times of great development in the technical aspects of medicine, and of the beginnings of important changes in the prevailing pattern of disease and in relationships between medical care professionals and the lay public. In the 1950s the public attitude was generally one characterized by Titmuss (1958) of 'acceptance and submission' (p. 196), perhaps associated with the authoritative tones of the Ministry of Health's Annual Report of 1953 which noted that 'continued fecklessness on the part of the public is shown by the steady increase in the annual numbers of children accidentally poisoned by drugs', and in the Ministry's reference to public health inspectors, health visitors, and social workers as the Public

Health Department's 'outdoor staff' (Ministry of Health 1953). Titmuss (1958) noticed, however,

a tendency for more people to adopt a questioning and critical attitude to medical care. The advertising of drugs, the prestige of science in medicine, the use of television and radio for 'health education', the spread of middle class attitudes and patterns of behaviour, and a long public health campaign for the early detection and prevention of disease all evoke a more questioning attitude. (pp. 196–7)

Titmuss and others feared what he called 'a new authoritarianism in medicine', which was likely to be increased in effect by advances in scientific, medical, and biological knowledge and the consequent demand for increasing specialization, which Titmuss (1958) summarized with a quotation from a letter published in the *Lancet* in 1952: 'Medicine can never become fully scientific unless it becomes completely inhuman' (p. 202).

# 5

## From 11 to 18 Years

### INTRODUCTION

During the years 1957 to 1964, while the children grew from 11 to 18 years, those changes in many aspects of life which had begun in the mid–1950s continued, and accelerated faster in the 1960s than at any time since the Second World War.

The social revolution of 1945, though profound, took ten years to show its effect on spending. For nearly twenty years London's skyline, broken by bomb damage, remained almost unchanged. Newspapers rationed their newsprint. The BBC was unchallenged. . . . Then, within two years, the credit squeeze ended, skyscrapers rushed up, supermarkets spread over cities, newspapers became fatter or died, commercial television began making millions, shops, airlines, even coal and banks had to fight for their lives. . . . Only now [the early 1960s] is Britain becoming *visually* aware of living in a state of perpetual and perilous change. (Sampson 1962: 636–7)

Material changes were everywhere visible in daily life, particularly with the great expansion of popular culture, including the arrival of the Beatles' first mass sale records in 1962 and the rapid rise in record sales. The first Habitat shop opened in London in 1964 with, Marwick (1982) notes, the comment from its founder that it provided a 'predigested shopping programme' (p. 143). The increasing purchasing power and freedom to choose from a wide range of things to buy are revealed by the continuous rise in sales of clothes, refrigerators, washing machines, televisions, and cars, and by Sampson's (1962) note that 'taking the 1947 average as 100 wages have risen to 230 in 1960 and prices to only 170' (p. 574).

Teenagers spent their new-found wealth (the consequences of full employment and the well-paid youthful labour force it produced) on long-playing records of 'pop' singers, on transistor radio sets, scooters, and cosmetics. (Thomson 1981: 274)

There was expansion too in the arts (fifteen new art galleries opened in London in 1961 (Sampson 1962: 578)), in ambitions for holidays, and in travel (Toland 1980), and the increasing use of cars and road transport brought the expansion of the motorway system.

By contrast a comparison of Ministry of Labour information on poverty in the United Kingdom in 1953–4 and in 1960 'contradicts the commonly held view that a trend towards greater equality has accompanied the trend towards greater affluence' (Abel-Smith and Townsend 1965: 66). It showed that the proportion of the population living at less than 40 per cent above the National Assistance scale increased from 7.8 to 14.2 per cent between 1953–4 and 1960, accounted for to some extent by increases in the proportion of the retired and of those in large families. It was estimated that about 2¼ million children lived in low income households in 1960, and the authors concluded that 'the problem of poverty among children is more than two-thirds of the size of poverty among the aged. . . . it is also worth observing that there were substantially more children in poverty than adults of working age' (p. 65).

Such extensive changes, and the end of thirteen years of Conservative government in 1964 with the election of a Labour administration, could be interpreted as the beginnings of fundamental change in the social structure of the country. But, in practice, for many people, things were much the same. The social structure had changed remarkably little. The public schools flourished, Oxford and Cambridge Universities, attended by less than 1 per cent of the population, still provided

87 per cent of permanent secretaries, 72 per cent of the cabinet, nearly 40 per cent of members of parliament and 71 per cent of the vice-chancellors of other universities. In 1959 Oxford and Cambridge provided all but one of the successful candidates (by examination and interview) for the Senior Civil Service and Foreign Service. (Sampson 1962: 198)

Sampson (1962) summarized by saying that after all the immediate post-war desire for change, and the official reports, including the Beveridge Report, 'each with their insistence on social change and mobility, the post-war years have had a sense of tragic bathos. . . . the social ferment has subsided, the public schools have prospered as never before, and Oxford and

Cambridge have refashioned their gilded cages. The professions have become more separate and self-absorbed' (p. 634).

Besides the apparent lack of this kind of structural change there was not much perception of social as compared with material change in everyday life at work, as seen through the eyes of ordinary people. Marwick (1982) reviewed the findings of opinion polls and studies of class throughout the 1960s, and concluded that

Certainly, the British people were under no illusion as to the disappearance of class boundaries. . . . To be working-class in the sixties, then, despite the occasional instance of rapid upward mobility, meant a 'life sentence' of hard manual work where, by an implicit irony, the attainment of middle-class living standards was only possible through expending, on overtime, even more excessive amounts of energy in a traditionally working-class way. (pp. 158, 161)

Although the social structure seemed in these respects to have changed relatively little, attitudes to some kinds of behaviour were beginning to relax, as contemporary legal changes and victories reveal. In 1957 the Wolfenden Committee recommended that male homosexual acts between consenting adults in private should no longer be illegal. The Betting and Gaming Act of 1960 legalized various types of betting, including bingo. The attempt to suppress the publication of D. H. Lawrence's novel *Lady Chatterley's Lover* under the terms of the Obscene Publications Act failed in 1959, and Mrs Mary Whitehouse's campaign to 'Clean Up TV', from what she saw as the worst excesses of permissiveness, began in 1964. The sexual behaviour of young people was of great concern because of the introduction of the oral contraceptive, which became widely available in the late 1960s, and because the incidence of sexually transmitted diseases and the percentage of illegitimate births to girls under 21 years were rising. Schofield's (1968) study of sexual behaviour in boys and girls aged 15 to 19 years, carried out in the early 1960s, revealed how a representative sample of teenagers had received little sex education, and showed that the desire for independence from adults and conformity to the developing 'teenage culture' was associated with greater sexual experience. The growing desire for independence earlier in life was also to be seen in the increasing

numbers of early marriages and of divorces, which continued
to rise throughout the 1960s and on into the next decades.
Attitudes to other aspects of behaviour were also changing, and
Thomson (1981) observed that the enthusiasm for the Campaign for Nuclear Disarmanent and for Voluntary Service
Overseas showed that there was certainly no 'indifference to
the deepest spiritual problems of the age' (p. 278).

During these years, in the late 1950s and early 1960s, there
was a growing awareness of changes in the structure of the
population in terms particularly of births, marriages, and the
increasing proportion of the elderly. The average age at
marriage was falling, and at the same time in Great Britain the
birth rate had risen from 15.5 (per thousand persons of all ages)
in 1951 to 17.6 in 1961. In 1967 Morris wrote that

The growing numbers of over 75s, and the conditions under which
many of them live, must sooner or later present a winter 'emergency'.
Will there be a crisis in nursing, teaching and social work from the
disappearance of the young unmarried woman? (Morris 1967: 41–2)

The nature of employment was also changing quickly, with
increasing numbers of jobs in clerical work and the service
industries, and fewer in manual occupations; whereas in 1951
in Great Britain 72 per cent of men in the labour force and 64
per cent of women had been employed in manual jobs these
proportions had fallen to 62 per cent and 53 per cent by 1971
(Halsey 1987), and to 48 per cent and 29 per cent in 1981 (Price
and Bain 1988). This change required greater numbers of better
trained and educated persons to fill the new vacancies, and had
the health implication that the proportion of sedentary workers
in the employed population must therefore be rising.

Planning for education and health in such changing circumstances was difficult. There was acute awareness of the need for
both expansion and change in education, especially in the light
of demonstrable inequalities of opportunity. The Crowther
Committee had reported in 1959 that armed forces recruits had
evidently not benefited fully from their recently completed
years of education, since there were many of high ability who
had left school early, especially amongst the sons of manual
workers. It recommended, amongst other things, raising the
school-leaving age to 16 years, but this was rejected by the

government. In 1963 the Newsom Report on secondary
education and the Robbins Report on higher education each
recommended expansion. Between 1957 and 1960 six technical
colleges were improved to the status of college of advanced
technology, to make a national total of nine, and between 1960
and 1965 seven new universities were built in England, to add
to the existing twenty-three. But still, as Sampson (1962)
pointed out, compared with other countries both in Europe and
the United States, Britain was far behind in its provision of
opportunities for university education; even when teacher-
training and technical college numbers were added to the total
of university places, still only 8 per cent of children then
had the opportunity to go on to higher education, compared
with 30 per cent in the United States. In 1983–4 13 per cent of
the British population of 18–19 year-olds became new students
on higher education courses (Halsey 1988). In 1963 the
Plowden Committee was set up to 'consider primary education
in all its aspects'. It reported in 1967 that a programme to
encourage parent and teacher contact would do much to reduce
the kind of wastage from the population pool of ability that the
Crowther Report (1959) had described, since it was evident
from the work of this study (i.e. the longitudinal study
described in this book), and others, that in many respects the
problems originated during the pre-school and the primary
school years. The Plowden Committee concluded that their
wide range of recommendations was justified since

*Paragraph 1174*   Good primary education will help to equip children
to live and work in a rapidly changing economy. Unlike the economy
of the nineteenth century our present society does not require a small
number of highly qualified men supported by an army of workers
with routine skills owing little to education. It requires a highly
adaptable labour force, which is not only more skilled, but is better
able to learn new skills, to tackle new jobs and face new problems.
Workers change their job and their homes frequently. The educational
assumptions that were appropriate for the economy of the nineteenth
century have been largely superseded.

*Paragraph 1175*   The qualities needed in a modern economy extend far
beyond skills such as accurate spelling and arithmetic. They include
greater curiosity and adaptability, a high level of aspiration, and
others which are difficult to measure. To assess these yields from

primary education would require long term study of the effects of different systems and different approaches to the education of younger children. (Plowden Report 1967: 432–3)

The need to raise standards and to contend with inequalities of educational opportunity was tackled in 1965 by the Labour government circular requesting local authorities to submit proposals for the establishment of comprehensive schools. Young (1965) described the intentions at that time.

Douglas shows that in the lower streams of primary schools, children become discouraged and deteriorate in ability [i.e. in the findings of this study—see Chapter 4], and the same thing is only too liable to happen in the secondary modern school [the Newsom Report 1963]. Teachers expect children to do badly, and the children conform to the expectation. The comprehensive reform will not end streaming inside individual schools, but it should end the division of children of different ability into completely different schools. At the same time, the reforms should make it easier, at any age and any stage of schooling, for children from the working or any other class to change over to more academic studies if that is where their inclination and talent lie. (pp. 78–9)

In topics other than education changes were just as difficult, since improvements in standards of living had not simply brought a reduction in social and health problems, as many had anticipated. Thomson (1981) quotes a government report published in 1959:

It is a disquieting feature of our society that, in the years since the war, rising standards of material prosperity, education, and social welfare have brought no decrease in the high rate of crime during the war: on the contrary, crime has increased and is still increasing. (p. 276)

In the following year the Report of the Committee on Children and Young Persons (1960) noted that 'It is not always so clearly recognized what a complete change there has been in social and personal relationships (between classes, between the sexes and between individuals) and also in the basic assumptions which regulate behaviour.'

In health the picture was equally confusing, but even more complicated.

Scientific discovery was booming. Rapid progress in biochemistry and in techniques such as electron microscopy increased the scope of work on genetics and the chemistry of living systems. There were consequent advances in vaccine development, in drug resistance, in the chemical control of ovarian function, which was associated with the development of the contraceptive pill, in blood chemistry, which led to developments in the chemotherapeutic treatment of cancers, as well as to greater understanding of blood lipids and their association with heart disease (Medical Research Council 1957, 1958). Research on chemical transmission in the central nervous system was associated with the growth of bioengineering, with the development of a range of drugs that included the antidepressants (Medical Research Council 1961). In addition to laboratory work, concern was already developing for research into the mental disorders of old age (Medical Research Council 1961), and the developments in biochemistry were beginning to be used in practice in screening for illnesses that could be detected in their early stages, before symptoms developed. This was, in part, a stimulus to debate about where to draw the thresholds in biological measures which indicate where illness begins, for example, in the normal population distributions of urine and blood sugar measures, and in blood pressure (Pickering 1955, Butterfield 1968). These were discussions with very far reaching implications about the role of the National Health Service and the stage at which intervention should take place.

Despite this harvest of discovery there was confusion about the delivery of its fruits to the general public. Great and increasing investment was made in the National Health Service, particularly in hospital medicine, yet a strategy for the future of 'front-line' care was not at all evident. A particularly vivid picture of the problem of equitable delivery of new knowledge was given by a study of obstetric care and survival in early infancy carried out in 1958. An investigation of all the births that occurred in England, Wales, and Scotland in one week in March 1958 found that, compared with earlier times and despite great improvement in survival rates during the first week of life, babies born to wives of manual workers were still at far greater risk of death than those born into non-manual families, and those born illegitimately were at greatest risk of all (Butler and Bonham 1963). There were also considerable regional differences in chances of survival, with the best chances being in London and the south-east and the worst in the north of England and Scotland. In fact, despite the overall improvement in chances of survival for all babies, the differences between the social classes had scarcely changed when compared with findings from this present study of children born twelve years before, in 1946. Explanations suggested for the findings included technical errors made by staff with insufficient up-to-date knowledge, lack of modern equipment, failure of mothers to ask for antenatal care early in pregnancy, and a legacy of poor physique among lower social class women as a result of poor nutrition in their childhood. Thus, it seemed that only some part of the benefit anticipated from the National Health Service had been achieved.

Evidently, therefore, new ideas were necessary about the working of health services. On the one hand there were those who saw a model for future health service development in the success of the mobile chest x-ray units (Mass Miniature Radiography Service) which every adult was encouraged to use, and which played an important part in the drastic reduction of tuberculosis incidence through wide population coverage and early detection of the disease. The proponents of this idea believed that technological advances in biochemistry and in laboratory automation could be used to extend screening techniques to other conditions, in order to 'nip them in the bud', and thus reduce the cost and the work of the NHS (Butterfield 1968). This could help to reduce the 'iceberg of disease' which it was feared lurked beneath the surface of what was treated (Morris 1967), much of which might be detected in presymptomatic form. On the other hand, many of the chronic diseases, sometimes referred to as the diseases of affluence (e.g. varicose veins, diabetes), and conditions that predispose to them (e.g. obesity), which had replaced infection as medicine's chief concern, were thought to be largely self-inflicted in one way or another; these were seen to offer the possibility of reduction of National Health Service load through health education.

There was also considerable debate about the amount of 'trivial' problems taken to general practitioners (Cartwright 1967, Cartwright and Anderson 1981); was this simply increased expectation by patients, and if so was it engendered chiefly by the ready availability of the service, or by the increased effectiveness of the treatments provided and the range of problems that they could tackle?

The health, education, and family circumstances of the children in this study continued to be investigated whilst they were aged 11 to 18 years (1957–64), partly through health visitors and school nurses interviewing mothers when the children were 11 and 15 years old, through medical examinations carried out by school doctors at the same ages, through questionnaires to schools at 11 years, 13 years, and 15 years, and through questionnaires to study members at ages 13,15,16, and 17 years. Study members completed tests of verbal and non-verbal ability, reading, and mathematics when they were 11 and 15 years old, and these tests are described in Appendix 2. At age 16½ years careers officers, then called youth employment officers, interviewed those who had left school at 15 years.

During the time whilst the children were aged 11 to 18 years the rate of response from those who were still resident in England, Wales, or Scotland ranged from 86 per cent to 89 per cent.

## HEALTH

During adolescence death and illness rates are relatively low (only 16 study boys and 7 study girls died at these ages), most disabilities which begin early in life have been discovered already, and serious illnesses have not apparently yet begun. Nevertheless important biological changes are taking place. Full height is attained only during the later part of this time, which has begun for many with the spurt in height growth which precedes the achievement of physical maturity. Many of the habits which will be associated with health later on in life are either begun or become more entrenched during these years, for instance smoking, eating habits, alcohol drinking, and physical exercise.

If health is considered as a stock of potential, inherited and developed in childhood for use throughout later life, then it is useful to consider adolescence as a time when measures may be made of that potential and its development by looking, for instance, at the rate of height gain by this age. This is an indicator of skeletal growth which may reflect the development of other organs, and which may well have long-term implications. For example, in the national study of infant survival carried out in 1958 (Butler and Bonham 1963) mothers' height was found to be an important predictive factor, and babies born to shorter mothers were at greater risk of problems. Illsley and Kincaid (1963) concluded that 'the biological mechanism through which early social experience is translated into later reproductive functioning is by no means clear, but there is a strong implication that physical growth and development are related to later obstetric performance'. Emanuel (1986) has also found this in studies of mothers' health before first pregnancy.

Risks to individuals' health potential may also be seen in such indicators as overweight, as well as in such health related habits as smoking. In fact some studies have shown that health deterioration is already taking place at this age. Berenson (1986) and his colleagues found in a clinical follow-up of children living in Bogalusa, just outside New Orleans, that study populations of apparently healthy children were differentiated by their wide range of values on measures of biochemical and physiological risks of heart and blood vessel disease. Whatever the causes of this surprising range, its existence implied an early life beginning of such biological differences, and it may be that as age increases and blood pressure rises in all members of the population those with relatively high blood pressure in childhood will tend to continue to have relatively high blood pressure (de Swiet 1986). It may also be that differences in childhood blood pressure are the result of differences in development before birth (Barker *et al.* 1990, Bock and Whelan 1991).

Information on some of the visible risk factors, such as shape, is available in this study, but not on the biochemical aspects of risk. For this study the important question is whether risks to health can be discerned before illness begins.

### (a) Health related habits

Smoking was the only health related habit studied during the teenage years, and 973 males (50 per cent of those asked) and

541 (29 per cent) females reported when they were 20 that they
had already started to smoke by age 16. In subsequent years
nationally representative surveys found that fewer men were
smoking, but that there was little or no change amongst
women. Numbers of cigarettes smoked by those who continued to do so were hardly reduced (Toland 1980). Cherry and
Kiernan (1976) found that in this study those who were the
first to smoke had the highest neuroticism and extraversion
scores on the measure of personality (the short Maudsley
Personality Inventory) completed at age 16 years. The relationship of smoking with risk of chest illness is described in the
section on illness.

### (b) Growth and development

Children from upper social class families continued during these
ages to grow taller at a significantly greater rate than other
children (Douglas 1962, Douglas and Simpson 1964). Those who
were tallest were the first to reach puberty, and girls reached
puberty on average two years earlier than boys; earliest maturing
boys and girls were also those who were tallest at earlier ages,
even at age 2 years (Douglas *et al.* 1968). These early maturing
children came on average from smaller families than others.

   Since the turn of the century there has been a steady trend
towards earlier achievement of puberty by both boys and girls
(Tanner 1962), thought to be the result of improvements in
home circumstances and in nutrition, and this was believed to
have implications for education in the sense that the 'trend
towards earlier puberty, if it continues, will lead to a more
mature and physically more uniform sixth form' (Douglas *et al.*
1968: 136).

   These were also years of weight gain (Stark *et al.* 1981), and
the numbers of obese (relative weight index >130) children
rose from 33 (1 per cent) at age 7 years to 155 (4 per cent) at age
11 years, and remained very little changed at 14 years (Braddon
*et al.* 1986). Earlier life breast-feeding and weaning were not
associated with later body shape (Crisp *et al.* 1970).

   The medical examination at 15 years found that 78 per cent of
the children had normal vision, 12 per cent had at least one eye
with good or fair, but not perfect vision, and the remaining 10

per cent had various eye defects, the most common of which was short sight. Short-sighted children were significantly more inclined to be from upper middle class families, to have parents who were very interested in their educational attainment and who were themselves relatively well educated, to have interests which were rather more bookish than sporting, to be good educational achievers, even at earlier ages before their short sight was first detected, and to have ambitions for occupations of high socio-economic status. Since their scores on the non-verbal tests did not differ significantly from those of others it was concluded that the greater educational attainment of the short-sighted was most likely to have originated in their intense application to school work, rather than being in some inherent way associated with greater academic ability. Douglas *et al.* (1967, 1968) ascribed these findings to genetic origins, speculating that perhaps

owing to the greater ease with which their eyes can accommodate to near work, there have grown up over the generations, attitudes to education and employment that differentiate families with a persistent history of short sight from those in which short sight is rarely found. (Douglas *et al.* 1968: 161)

### (c) *Illness*

The study has been especially concerned with respiratory illness both because it is a widespread problem and also because children born in the late 1940s and early 1950s spent the first ten years of their lives in the relatively polluted atmosphere that prevailed before the Clean Air Act of 1956. An indicator of the exposure of study children to atmospheric pollution was made using national information on domestic coal consumption in each area when the children were age 5–6 years (Douglas and Waller 1966). Investigation of the 81 per cent of children who remained in areas of the same degree of air pollution throughout the first eleven years of their lives showed that 22 per cent of them lived in the most highly polluted districts. These 705 children had no greater incidence of colds or ear, nose, or throat troubles up to age 7 years, but they were much more inclined than others to suffer from such chest illnesses as bronchitis or pneumonia during their first two years of life, and began to do so at an earlier age when compared with others, whatever their social class. Chest illness in early life was associated with increased risk of lower respiratory problems in adolescence and early adult life (Mann *et al.* forthcoming). Doctors who examined all the study children at ages 6, 7, 11, and 15 years heard significantly more chest rattles at each of these ages in the children who lived in the most highly polluted areas (Douglas and Waller 1966).

This was the peak time of popularity of the operation to remove childrens' tonsils, and 26 per cent of study children had had their tonsils removed by the age of 11 years, compared with 20 per cent of children born twelve years later, who became 11 years old in 1969 (Calnan *et al.* 1978). Removal of tonsils was most frequent in the upper social classes (31 per cent of children in non-manual families had their tonsils out) and fell with falling social class to 23 per cent of children from families in the semi- and unskilled manual classes. The children who had their tonsils out were afterwards less often absent from school because of ear, nose, or throat problems or coughs or colds, but were also after this operation more inclined than others to put on weight (Douglas 1973*b*).

Another operation which may be a matter of choice, namely circumcision in boys, was also more common among study children from upper (30 per cent were operated on) rather than the lower social classes (20 per cent). Like tonsillectomy, circumcision became much less common over the twelve years between this study of children born in 1946 and the study of those born in 1958, falling from 23 per cent to 11 per cent (Calnan *et al.* 1978).

Illnesses were classified as serious if they involved hospital admission of a minimum of twenty-eight consecutive days, or absence from school of three consecutive weeks or more. Those who were this ill were on average significantly shorter than others, possibly as a result of their illness, and seriously ill boys scored significantly lower than others on the tests of attainment taken at age 15 years, but there were no such differences among girls (Wadsworth 1986*a*).

## (d) Hospital admission

Between ages 11 and 18 years 24 per cent of the children were admitted to hospital, as compared with 26 per cent during the pre-school years, and 11 per cent between ages 6 and 10 years.

In the immediate post-war years children spent many days in hospital for such conditions as tuberculosis or poliomyelitis. There was concern about the psychological effect of this experience (Edelston 1943), and this led in due course to the inquiry into the welfare of children in hospital (Platt Report 1959). Douglas (1975) looked at the adolescent behaviour and early work experience of all those who had been in hospital by the age of 5 years. Those admitted for long periods (more than one consecutive week) or on several occasions were significantly more inclined, in adolescence, to have behaviour problems, to be relatively poor readers, and later to have a history of many job changes, whatever the social class or size of their family. Douglas (1975) concluded that such long-term adolescent problems following early life hospital admissions were most likely in children who were emotionally insecure at the time of admission because, for example, of great dependence on their mother, or because they were not used to being looked after by others, or had recently had a disturbing experience, or were in strong competition with an older brother or sister.

Using detailed psychiatric assessments on two other populations of children aged 10 years Quinton and Rutter (1976) also found that repeated hospital admissions experienced before the age of 5 were associated with later signs of disturbance. These findings were particularly important because they were from a study of children admitted to hospital in the mid-1960s when conditions for the care of children in hospital had begun to improve. Since children who were admitted to hospital for long periods in both of these studies were more likely than others to have come from disadvantaged homes, family circumstances may have played an important part in the links found in both investigations between long hospital admissions and later disturbance, but neither study had enough information to make further exploration of this possibility. Quinton and Rutter (1976) felt that it was now clear from the evidence of several studies that 'particular care is needed in the hospital admission of children from unhappy, disrupted or deprived homes'.


## EDUCATION

Educational attainment at secondary schools was measured by scores on the study's tests of reading, maths, and verbal and non-verbal attainment taken at 15 years (see Appendix 2), and by the extent of success in the General Certificate of Education Ordinary (O) level public examination taken at 16 years.

Between 8 and 11 years average attainment test scores of children from non-manual social class families had increased to a greater extent than averages of those from manual families (see Chapter 4), and between 11 and 15 years this divergence continued in reading and in maths; in non-verbal and verbal attainment, however, average scores tended to converge (Douglas *et al.* 1968).


### (a) Home and individual influences on attainment

Influences of home and family life on educational attainment were still of evident importance whilst the children were aged between 11 and 15 years. Parents who had at earlier times shown a lively interest in their child's education were very likely to continue to do so, and to be encouraging during the secondary school years. Children who enjoyed this benefit were considerably more likely than others to score high marks in the attainment tests (Ross and Simpson 1971), and to do better in the O level examinations. Only children or those in small families, who could receive most parental interest, tended to do better than others, and those in families where parental concern had to be more thinly spread were inclined to lower educational attainment. Only children and those with one sibling had the best O level results and were more inclined than others to stay on at school. They had the highest average scores in the tests taken at age 15 years, as they had at 8 and 11 years, and in the vocabulary tests at age 15 years those who were only children scored on average eight points higher than those who had three or more brothers or sisters. Longer intervals between children were associated with higher educational attainment. Conversely, however, children who experienced disruption of family life were significantly less likely to do well in educational terms. This was found in children whose family life was disrupted through the long illness of a parent, particularly if the father had been unemployed as a result (Douglas *et al.* 1968), or if parents had divorced or separated (Maclean and Wadsworth 1988). This is discussed in more detail in the section on 'family disruption' later in this chapter.

Parents' attitudes were associated with sex differences in attainment and aspiration. Whereas at the ages of 8 and 11 years girls achieved rather higher scores than boys on all the tests, the position was reversed by 15 years. Then boys had higher average scores than girls in maths and in non-verbal intelligence, and girls were ahead only in verbal scores; these differences were found in each social class. At 15 years amongst children of high ability 62 per cent of boys compared with 54 per cent of girls wanted to go on to further or higher education, and this kind of sex difference in favour of boys was found also at this age in parents' and teachers' aspirations for the later education of boys and girls. These differences were particularly marked amongst middle class children (Douglas *et al.* 1968).

The influence of the family's social class and the parents' education are more difficult to understand than other influences already discussed, but they remained very strongly associated with childrens' educational attainment at this as at earlier ages (Ross and Simpson 1971). Table 5.1 shows that 'good' O level results were much more likely to be gained by children in upper middle social groups than by others, whatever their achievement on the study's tests of attainment; this was also so, but to a lesser extent, among those gaining any O level passes.

Information on emotional adjustment was collected about the children during the secondary school years. Secondary school teachers assessed the children's behaviour, the children themselves completed a self-assessment form about personality at age 13 years (Douglas and Mulligan 1961), and mothers were asked about habits in study children which may have been associated with behaviour disturbance. Children assessed

TABLE 5.1   *Percentages of children who achieved O level examination passes, in relation to the social group of their family and their attainment tests score at age 15 years*

| Attainment tests score band | Percentage gaining 'good' O level passes[a] | | | | Percentage gaining any O level pass | | | |
|---|---|---|---|---|---|---|---|---|
| | Middle class | | Manual working class | | Middle class | | Manual working class | |
| | Upper | Lower | Upper | Lower | Upper | Lower | Upper | Lower |
| 60 and over | 77 | 60 | 53 | 37 | 94 | 87 | 86 | 69 |
| 55–9 | 33 | 18 | 15 | 9 | 79 | 59 | 45 | 31 |
| 50–4 | 11 | 6 | 2 | 3 | 54 | 38 | 17 | 12 |
| 45–9 | 4 | — | 1 | — | 27 | 13 | 5 | 2 |
| 44 and below | — | — | — | — | 20 | 1 | — | — |

[a] Passes in at least 4 subjects, with 3 or more in the fields English language, a science subject, mathematics, and a foreign language.

*Note:* Social groups are described in Appendix 2.

by their teachers as nervous or aggressive achieved relatively low test scores and had been inclined to do so at earlier ages. Those assessed as troublesome in class or having little interest in school work or persistently having had such habits or problems as nail-biting, thumb-sucking, or stammering had on the other hand a deterioration in attainment between 8 and 15 years. The self-rated personality scores of those whose behaviour was adversely rated by their teachers also show them to be high on the measure of neuroticism. It seemed therefore that there was a continuous gradient in these signs of emotional adjustment, such that the more adverse the reports the lower was the performance in school.

Educational attainment was also related to achievement of puberty. Children who achieved physical maturity early, from whatever social class they came, were highest educational achievers, both before puberty (in the 8-year tests) and afterwards. These children who came relatively early to physical maturity tended to come from smaller families, and it was this fact that accounted for their higher achievement rather than any direct relationship between physical maturity and intellectual ability (Douglas *et al.* 1968).

### (b) School influences on attainment

Table 5.2 shows the types of schools children attended, and the relatively small sex differences between the types.

Selective schools (grammar, direct grant, and technical schools) were considered in three groups, according to the proportion of graduate members of their teaching staff. Those with less than 70 per cent graduates were regarded as low, and 80 per cent or more as high. Whichever of these types of selective school was attended there was an increase in the educational attainment of children from non-manual social class homes compared with that of other children, as measured by the difference in attainment test scores at ages 11 and 15 years. However, in terms of O levels achieved the proportion of graduate teachers in the school attended was also important. Children from manual social class families, although still lower achievers in these terms than other children, achieved better O level results when the proportion of graduate teachers was

*From 11 to 18 Years*

TABLE 5.2    *Types of schools attended by girls and boys at age 15 years*

|                      | Girls (%) | Boys (%) |
|----------------------|-----------|----------|
| Grammar              | 19        | 18       |
| Direct grant         | 2         | 2        |
| Technical            | 3         | 4        |
| Secondary modern     | 57        | 59       |
| Comprehensive        | 12        | 10       |
| Independent          | 6         | 4        |
| Special and approved | 2         | 3        |

high. Douglas *et al.* (1968) concluded that this was not necessarily only a result of better standards of teaching, but possibly also a more rigorous selection procedure at age 11 years. At selective schools girls were less likely than boys to be taught by graduates.

Secondary modern schools were categorized according to the percentage of pupils who stayed on after the school-leaving age, ranging from those with the poorest record (less than 10 per cent of pupils stayed on) to those with a good record (20 per cent or more stayed on). The good record schools were also most likely to have attractive and well-equipped buildings, medium sized classes, and a relatively high proportion of graduate staff. At 11 years children who went to good record schools had significantly higher test scores than other children, and this difference was found in their reading and maths scores four years later. Data collected in this follow-up study of children whilst they were at secondary school (1957 to 1962) included only a relatively narrow range of measures of the school's atmosphere and omitted such things as norms of behaviour, acceptance of those norms, activities pupils and staff did together. But of the data collected on school environment the academic record of schools was most strongly associated with the educational attainment of study children, as Rutter *et al.* (1979) later found in an appropriately wide-ranging study of secondary schools and their effects.

In terms of O level achievements children in this study who

were at good record secondary modern schools were eight times as likely as others to gain an examination pass. These differences were, however, rather more accounted for by social class than by the type of school, but it was concluded that

although the lower manual working class pupils are at a disadvantage relative to the middle class (in secondary modern schools, whatever their record in proportions of children staying on after the school leaving age) those at schools with a good record are far less handicapped.

Thus the secondary modern schools can do something to make up for the deficiencies of the homes, even more so perhaps than the selective schools, though here again problems of selection are relevant. *The Home and the School* (Douglas 1964) showed that good teaching compensates in part for lack of parental interest in the earlier years—and this appears to be also true at the secondary stage. (Douglas *et al.* 1968: 48)

The small percentages of children in private secondary education (4 per cent of boys and 6 per cent of girls) attended schools with a very wide variety of facilities, and themselves represented a wider cross-section of ability than pupils at selective schools. In fact 19 per cent of those at such fee-paying schools had failed to obtain a place at a selective school. Girls in particular at fee-paying schools on average achieved fewer O level passes than those who were at selective schools. At fee-paying schools 74 per cent of girls with high attainment test scores (scoring 60 or over in the aggregate test scores) at 15 years obtained one or more passes at O level, compared with 92 per cent of high attaining girls at selective schools. Among boys the differences were much smaller but of the same kind. In general, attainment of O level results was worse at fee-paying schools which were not ranked as public schools (that is those whose headteachers were members of the Headmasters Conference or the Association of Headmistresses) than at grammar schools, particularly so in girls.

Co-education was most common in Scotland, and more common in Wales than in England, and lowest of all in south-east England. Almost half the study children (46 per cent at age 13 years and 49 per cent at age 15) were taught in co-educational circumstances, and this was more common amongst manual class pupils; more than half of these pupils

were at co-educational schools compared with 2 out of 5 of
those from lower middle social group families, or 1 in 4 from
upper middle social group families (see Appendix 2 for the
definition of social group). Sex-segregated selective schools,
whether for boys or girls, had on average smaller class sizes
than others, and a higher proportion of graduate teachers and of
middle class pupils. Non-manual class boys who attended
these kinds of schools achieved highest scores in the attainment tests and had increased chances of attaining good O level
results. But girls from non-manual class families who went to
mixed-sex selective schools achieved higher educational standards than those who went to single-sex schools. The educational achievements of manual class boys and girls who went
to single-sex selective schools did not differ significantly.

Secondary school teachers made assessments of attitudes to
school work when the children were 13 and 15 years old.
Agreement between these and the assessments made by
primary school teachers when the children were 8 years old
(see Chapter 4) was high, and the rating of attitude to work
was closely associated with the parents' level of interest in the
child's education. Children of parents with a low level of
interest in their education were four times as likely to have
deteriorated, in terms of these teachers' assessments, between
primary and secondary school, whilst those with high parental
interest were twice as likely to have improved. Before the O
level examinations were taken, when the children were 15
years old, teachers made assessments of the children's ability to
benefit from higher education. Among the 16 per cent of
children who scored highest on the attainment tests (scores of
60 or more) teachers thought that 91 per cent of those from the
upper middle class social groups were likely to benefit from
going on to higher education compared with 69 per cent of
those from lower manual social group families (Douglas *et al.*
1968).

Scottish pupils scored on average higher in the attainment
tests than those in England or Wales at the age of 8. By 11 years
this difference was narrowed in reading, reversed in vocabulary, but very little changed in arithmetic. At 15 years Scottish
children were still ahead in mathematics, but no longer so in
other subjects.

There was proportionately a slight excess of English and

Welsh children gaining one or more O level passes (33 per cent) compared with their Scottish counterparts (30 per cent), but the proportions gaining a good O level result (passes in at least four subjects including three or more in English language, maths, a science subject, and a foreign language) were the same (16 per cent). Numbers of Welsh pupils (184) were too few for such comparisons. Within England, however, there were considerable differences in attainment amongst those living north of a line from the Bristol Channel to the Wash compared with those in the south, in part, no doubt, because 18 per cent of study families who lived north of the line were middle class as compared with 30 per cent in the south. Essentially similar proportions of children went to grammar schools in the north as in the south, but in the south 4 per cent more went to technical or independent schools, which were in more plentiful supply. Children in the south scored higher in the attainment tests and did better in the O level examinations, but within social classes there were no north/south differences, except in reading which was better in the south. At each level of attainment test score southern pupils got better O level results than those in the north. Areas which provided relatively high proportions of pupils with selective school places (24 per cent or more) were more common in the south, but in both the north and the south these tended to be in urban areas with a high proportion of middle class families, whereas in working class districts and rural areas the supply of places was less. Parental interest in their children's education, which was found in this study to be strongly associated with the child's educational achievements, was higher in areas which were relatively well provided with selective school places, whether parents were from non-manual or manual social backgrounds, and it was speculated that 'education itself is infectious and the more places that are supplied the more parents become aware of the importance of learning' (Douglas *et al.* 1968: 78). Where the availability of selective school places was proportionately high, girls' test scores and O level results were nearly the same as those of boys, but where places were in relatively short supply girls' achievements were lower. A greater supply of places at selective schools was associated with relatively high attainment by the manual class children.

### (c) *School-leaving*

About half of the children (47 per cent of boys and 51 per cent of girls) left school at the earliest opportunity, which was then at age 15 years, and a further 27 per cent of boys and 24 per cent of girls left at the end of the school year. Few pupils (19 per cent) stayed on at school in areas where there were relatively few selective school places, but in areas with the highest proportions of selective school places 30 per cent of children stayed on. These differences were greatest for those from manual class homes, especially girls; only 12 per cent of girls stayed on in areas with few selective places compared with 21 per cent in areas with better facilities. Those at grammar or independent schools were much more likely than others to stay on at school, and because of the increases in post-war provision of secondary school places Halsey *et al.* (1980) found that during this time

Grammar-school places doubled, but the numbers entering the sixth forms (i.e. staying on at school) more than trebled, and the numbers staying on to complete a sixth-form course rose fourfold. We have here an example of a general characteristic of educational expansion in advanced industrial countries since the Second World War; the higher the educational level the faster the rate of growth. (p. 109)

The children who stayed on at school after age 15 years were more than twice as likely to be from non-manual families, whatever their scores on the study's attainment tests, and they much more often had parents with a high level of interest in their education who had themselves received some further education after leaving school. Amongst those who scored 60 or more in the attainment tests (the top 16 per cent) the proportions of children who left at age 15 years were 10 per cent from the upper middle class, 22 per cent from the lower middle, 33 per cent from the upper manual families, and 50 per cent of the lower manual group. It was concluded that

The social class inequalities in opportunity observed in the primary schools have increased in the secondary and extend, in a way which was not evident at the time of secondary selection, even to the highest levels of ability. It seems that the able boys and girls from manual working class families, although encountering no obstacles at entry to the selective secondary schools, have been heavily handicapped in their later secondary school careers through relatively early leaving and poor examination results. (Douglas *et al.* 1968: 27–8)

These results were disappointingly similar to those reported from another study carried out eleven years earlier (Central Advisory Council for Education 1954), but they represent an improvement on the pre-war figures (Marwick 1982). In a longer-term context Halsey *et al.* (1980) showed in their study of men that since the end of the Second World War the trend has been for an increasing proportion of pupils from non-manual class families to stay on at school after the leaving age; a similar trend was found in the manual classes, but since increases in proportions staying on at school began after those in the non-manual classes a narrowing of social class differences seems likely to take a long time to be achieved.

(*d*) *Education and qualifications after school-leaving age (15 years)*

The greater rates of drop-out from education and of falling behind in attainment found among children from manual social class families, despite their potential as assessed by the study's tests, continued after age 16 years, and as table 5.3 shows these young persons' chances of going to university were much lower than those of others. As already discussed, the social class differences were in some part because in the early 1960s further and higher education was regarded by many working class families not only as the key to a wide range of job and other opportunities, but also as carrying a greater risk of alienation from the family of origin. Staying on for further or higher education also involved expense and loss of potential additional household income, as well as a great deal of homework, which may have been particularly difficult for working class children to achieve because of crowded home circumstances and pressures from other young people outside the family (Douglas *et al.* 1968).

In this study, as in others, it was found that neither manual social class children nor girls who stayed on at school were at a disadvantage in terms of likelihood of examination success at the advanced (A) level general school certificate examinations (Douglas and Cherry 1977), and as Halsey *et al.* (1980) described in

TABLE 5.3    *The association of educational attainment at 8 years with educational outcome*

|  | Social class of family of origin (%) | |
| --- | --- | --- |
|  | Non-manual | Manual |
| *Top fifth of test scores at 8 years[a]* | | |
| Higher school-leaving exams | | |
| (A levels) and equivalents | 44 | 26 |
| University | 25 | 6 |
| *Middle two-fifths of test scores at 8 years[a]* | | |
| Higher school-leaving exams | | |
| (A levels) and equivalents | 40 | 16 |
| University | 7 | 1 |
| *Lowest two-fifths of test scores at 8 years[a]* | | |
| Higher school-leaving exams | | |
| (A levels) and equivalents | 19 | 4 |
| University | 0.5 | — |

[a] Scores in tests of verbal and non-verbal attainment taken at 8 years.

their study 'the differentials in exam success can almost wholly be explained by the differentials in staying on at secondary school' (p. 141). Similarly, sex and social class differences in gaining university level qualifications reflected contemporary attitudes to education and, for girls, the relatively small provision of university places.

Parental influence was still discernible in the form of parents' own education; the higher their attainment the greater the likelihood of offspring going on to gain qualifications after leaving school, as the Robbins Committee on Higher Education (1963) also reported. Table 5.4 shows this association in the present study population, and reveals striking sex differences in the level of attainment by age 26 years. Whatever the level of parental qualifications young women were more inclined than young men to achieve qualifications up to school-leaving age examinations, but much less likely to do so at higher levels. At higher levels the greater the parents' qualifications the greater the likelihood of their offspring gaining similar qualifications, but sex differences were very great, and no young women at all had achieved qualifications equivalent to those of a university doctorate by their mid-20s.

The mood of the time was predominantly against women entering the professions and gaining higher qualifications.

Reasons for sex differences in educational attainment were sought in interviews with those study members who were then (1964–7) second-year university students. Explanations offered were either in terms of circumstances at school or of individual differences in learning which were taken to be 'innate'. Schools were seen as less inclined to offer girls good quality specialist teaching in the final years, particularly in science, or good advice about choice of university, subject, or subsequent career. Sex differences in learning were described in a variety of ways. Girls tended to see themselves as less ambitious about careers and, because of their earlier attainment of physical maturity, to be more distracted by the opposite sex; one woman undergraduate said the girls liked to think of boys as 'cleverer and more responsible'. Girls were also described by themselves and by boys as more inclined to learn in a parrot fashion, in order to overcome tension in examinations, and to be less logical than boys and with less common sense. One undergraduate felt that there was a 'great danger' amongst boys from single-sex schools 'of thinking that girls are inferior and that you can't honestly expect a girl to argue'. A women undergraduate replied that

Girls in tutorials expect the boys to do better if they, the girls, come from a single sex school. If we give in an essay, they just assume the boys are going to get better marks, whereas, we from mixed schools see that the girls are better anyway.

In many ways these comments seem now to have come from another era. Specialist teaching for girls has since become far more common, and so has advice about choice of universities, courses, and careers. The lack of substance in the notion of 'innate' sex differences is clear both from the evidence in this study, and in what has happened in the educational attainment of girls and women in subsequent years. At the ages of 8 and 11 years the study girls achieved higher average attainment scores than boys (see Chapter 4), but by 15 years, when girls' average scores were lower than those of boys, parents, teachers, and the girls themselves had lower expectations of their chances of continuing in further and higher education. Nowadays the proportion of women undergraduate students resident in Great Britain and entering British universities for their first year has risen to 42 per cent (University Grants Committee 1986), but this proportion took a long time to achieve. In 1919–20, when

TABLE 5.4   *The relationship between parents' and children's qualifications*

| Parents' highest level of education and training | Sex of study members | Study member's highest level of education and equivalents[a] (%) | | |
|---|---|---|---|---|
| | | No quali-fications | Below school leaving exam (O level) qualifications | School leaving (O level) qualifications |
| *Minimum time at school and no qualifications* | Male | 60.2 | 7.2 | 12.3 |
| | Female | 57.3 | 13.5 | 19.8 |
| *More than minimum time at school but no qualifications* | Male | 37.2 | 5.5 | 16.4 |
| | Female | 36.4 | 10.6 | 27.8 |
| *More than minimum time at school and below degree and professional level qualifications* | Male | 20.8 | 5.7 | 19.5 |
| | Female | 20.5 | 5.9 | 33.5 |
| *More than minimum time at school and degree and/or professional qualifications* | Male | 4.3 | 1.1 | 13.3 |
| | Female | 7.4 | 2.3 | 14.9 |

[a] Equivalent training and professional qualifications were coded using the Burnham Further Education Committee's *Grading of Courses* (Burnham Further Education Committee, 1980).

| Higher school leaving (A level) qualifications | University first degree and equivalents | University higher degree and equivalents | Total (=100%) |
|---|---|---|---|
| 17.3 | 2.4 | 0.6 | 984 |
| 8.8 | 0.6 | — | 936 |
| 30.7 | 9.0 | 1.2 | 323 |
| 22.8 | 2.0 | 0.3 | 302 |
| 33.9 | 17.9 | 2.2 | 548 |
| 31.6 | 7.7 | 0.8 | 478 |
| 35.8 | 39.6 | 5.9 | 187 |
| 50.3 | 24.6 | 0.6 | 175 |

the total number of students in all English, Welsh, and Scottish universities was only 33,951, women comprised 27 per cent of that population. Numbers of students rose to 50,002 in 1938–9 (23 per cent were women), to 80,602 in 1953–4 (25 per cent were women), to 169,486 in 1965–6 (26 per cent women) and to 317,572 in 1988–9 (42 per cent women) (Universities Funding Council 1990).

Thus although explanations for sex differences in educational attainment had been offered in terms of school differences by study members who were undergraduate students in the mid-1960s, these were clearly not inevitable and nor were the individual 'innate' differences. These explanations ignored effects of evident pressures from parents and teachers, among whom expectations for girls' attainments had clearly been lower than those for boys. Reasons for the changes that have since come about are discussed in the last two chapters.

### (e) Parents' aspirations for their children's employment, pupils' ambitions, and teachers' assessments

Parents' aspirations about the level of occupation for their children were related to their own social class. For example, among parents of boys with the highest scores on the attainment tests, 79 per cent of those in the upper middle social group (defined in Appendix 2) had aspirations for their sons to enter one of the professions, compared with 39 per cent of parents from the lower manual social group. As children's attainment scores fell so the social group gap in parental aspirations widened. Comparable associations were found with parental level of education.

At age 15 years boys' and girls' own aspirations for the level of their future employment were usually in accord with those of their parents, and only 13 per cent of boys and 9 per cent of girls had aspirations which differed from those of their parents. Children's aspirations were also strongly associated with their parents' achieved educational levels, and Douglas and his colleagues were left

in no doubt that there is a large group of young men and women who, though potentially capable of entering one of the professions, choose manual work. The reason for this lies partly perhaps in the fact that they are unable to see themselves as following a way of life that is radically different from that of their parents and the rest of their family and friends. If their expectations are fulfilled the new generation of manual workers will contain many of high ability; 18 per cent will, it seems, be in the top third of measured ability and 5 per cent in the top sixth. (Douglas *et al.* 1968: 100)

On the other hand if the aspirations of parents for their children to be professional workers were fulfilled then the balance of class of origin of professional workers would change considerably. Whereas one in five of study fathers who were in the professional classes came from a manual class family of origin this proportion would be expected to be one in two in their children's generation. These kinds of generation differences are discussed in Chapter 7.

Pupils' own ambitions for their future occupation were also assessed using an interest-scoring system (Miller 1968). At 15 years they arranged lists of job titles in order of preference, and from this Cherry (1974*a*) developed a score of ambition. These scores were found to be associated with social class, with parental interest in the study member's education, and with type of secondary school attended. Pupils from middle class families had significantly higher ambitions, according to this assessment, those whose parents were most interested in their education were more ambitious than those whose parents showed relatively little concern, and those at selective schools were significantly more ambitious than those at other kinds. Ambitions of those at non-selective schools were associated with the social class composition of the school. Where the majority of pupils were middle class, ambition scores were significantly higher than at schools classified as of mixed social class and, in turn, ambitions at these mixed class schools were significantly higher than those of children at predominantly working class schools. Cherry (1974*a*) concluded that 'Children from working class homes in schools with mainly working class pupils appeared to have less interest in breaking with working class occupational traditions than do similar children mixing with pupils from more varied home backgrounds.'

## EARLIEST OPPORTUNITY SCHOOL-LEAVERS

### (a) First employment

Young men and women who left school at 15 years, the earliest opportunity, were most likely to begin working in semi-skilled jobs (61 per cent of men and 81 per cent of women); only 13 per cent of men and 5 per cent of women first started in unskilled jobs, and a quarter (26 per cent) of men and 14 per cent of women started in skilled occupations. By the end of their first six months of work one in four had left this first job, and such early job leaving was characteristic of those who had not taken the Youth Employment Service Careers Officer's advice about first job at the time of leaving school (Cherry 1974b).

By the time they were 18 years old occupational change since the first job tended to achieve a better fit between the skill level of the job and the score on the attainment tests taken during the final year at school (Cherry 1974b). Higher test scorers tended to change jobs up to higher skill levels, and relatively lower test scorers changed jobs down to lower levels of skill. Those young men (44 per cent) and women (37 per cent) who had stayed in their first job from age 15 to age 18 years were those who reported greatest interest in their work (Cherry 1974b).

At 18 years a group was identified as occupationally unstable. These young men and women had had four or more jobs during their first three years of work, each with an average length of less than eight months. They were inclined already to have had poor records of school attendance, punctuality, obedience, and discipline, low test scores, and, if they were boys they were more likely to be the fourth or later born in the family. Information on length of time in the first job and on reason for leaving it also added to the prediction of having four or more job changes between ages 15 and 18 (Cherry 1976).

### (b) Further education

Cherry (1978) found that one in three of those who left school at the end of the school year in which they were 15 years old then enrolled for a part-time training course at a college.

Those who did so were significantly more likely than others who left school at this earliest opportunity to have scored at an average level or above (and at low levels too for girls) in the 15-year-old attainment tests, and their fathers were most likely to be in skilled or non-manual occupations. Parents of such boys usually had a high interest in their sons' education, and the boys themselves were most likely to have been to a school of mixed social class composition; girls tended to have relatively high job ambitions.

## MARRIAGE AND CHILDREN

Teenage marriage, that is before the twentieth birthday, was far more common among women (25 per cent) than among men (7 per cent). Those who married at these ages were most likely to have come from families of low social class and have parents with relatively poor educational achievement, who had themselves married early in life. Educational attainments of these teenage wives and husbands were low, and they had tended to leave school at the earliest possible age. Women who married at these ages were more likely than those who married later already to be pregnant, and one-third were pregnant at the time of marriage (Kiernan and Diamond 1983, Kiernan 1986). During the years before their twentieth birthday 4 per cent of men and 13 per cent of women had become parents.

## FAMILY DISRUPTION

Parental divorce or separation had been experienced by 217 (4 per cent) of the children before their eleventh birthday, and by age 15 years a further 110 (making a total of 6 per cent) were to experience this kind of family disruption. Maternal death was the least likely, and had been experienced by 67 children (1 per cent) by their eleventh birthday, and by a further 41 by age 15 years. Death of father was experienced by 150 children by their eleventh birthday, and by a further 69 by age 15.

At whatever age children experience the disruption of family life through parental divorce or death it is likely to be distressing. For some children this kind of distress may be relatively short lived, but in this study it was beginning to be clear when the children were teenagers that amongst those who had had this experience in their pre-school years, or before the age of 6, there were still some who had a particularly high rate of behaviour problems. For instance, at age 15 years bed-wetting was reported in only 2 per cent of the children who had lived all their lives with both parents, but it was higher (8 per cent) among those whose parents had died nine years or more earlier, and in those whose parents had divorced or separated at that time (5 per cent). After such an experience 'The greatest excess of enuresis [bed-wetting] is recorded for the children who were fostered or in institutions, and the least for those who remained with their mothers and did not have a stepfather' (Douglas 1970).

Educational achievement was also apparently affected by the experience of parental divorce, and to some extent, but rather less so, by parental death, as table 5.5 shows. The relatively high rates of A level examination passes and university places gained by children from manual class families who had experienced parental death may be the result of 'compensatory' hard work and application by these children. Only children were the exception to the apparent effects shown in table 5.5, and the experience of parental death or divorce did not seem to affect their educational achievements. The relatively poor educational attainments of children who experienced parental divorce or separation may be partly the results of emotional disturbance, and may also be associated with a fall in income and changes of home circumstances which usually take place after a family break of this kind (Eekalaar and Maclean 1986, Wadsworth *et al.* 1990). Remarriage of the widowed parent after a death was associated with relatively good educational achievements by the children, but remarriage after either of these kinds of family disruption did not restore the educational chances of children to the level of those who had not had such disruption (Wadsworth and Maclean 1986).

Since there is no information in this study on families' emotional circumstances, it is possible only to hypothesize that the disruptive effect of parental divorce and separation may be associated with the longer periods of family disturbance likely to precede parents' decision to live apart. By contrast the majority of parental deaths happened suddenly; they were

TABLE 5.5 *Educational attainment of boys and girls from different social backgrounds, according to their experience of parental divorce or death whilst 0–15 years*

| Social class | Educational attainment by age 26 years | | | | Total (=100%) |
|---|---|---|---|---|---|
| | None | Up to and including O level | A level and equivalents | University | |
| *Non-manual* | | | | | |
| No loss | 16.9 | 28.7 | 35.2 | 19.2 | 1,471 |
| Parental divorce | 42.9 | 20.4 | 25.5 | 11.2 | 98 |
| Parental death | 22.0 | 34.9 | 33.0 | 10.1 | 109 |
| *Manual* | | | | | |
| No loss | 53.2 | 27.6 | 16.6 | 2.6 | 1,936 |
| Parental divorce | 67.9 | 24.2 | 7.3 | 0.6 | 165 |
| Parental death | 61.1 | 22.2 | 13.0 | 3.8 | 185 |

$X^2$ for non-manual families = 47.29 with 6 d.f. p<.001.
$X^2$ for manual families = 20.61 with 4 d.f. (adding cols. 3 and 4) p<.001.

perhaps also more readily 'explained' to and 'understood' by a child (Wallerstein and Kelly 1980). There is, in addition, evidence that the risk of long-term problems is greater if the parental divorce or death occurs during the child's pre-school years, and further evidence of this is presented in the following chapter.

## CONCLUSIONS

There is no doubt that for the study members' generation grammar school greatly broadened the opportunities in education for those children from lower non-manual and manual social class families who were educated there (Halsey *et al.* 1980). At first sight this looked like a change towards the equality of educational opportunity which had been hoped for at the time of the 1944 Education Act, by giving the ablest children, from whatever social background, the opportunity to 'get on in the world':

> the most significant tributary is the stream of grammar school boys, and a thin river . . . of boys going from grammar schools to universities: for it is this breakthrough which is beginning to change Britain's elite. The grammar schools provide what has come to be known as the 'meritocracy'—the new caste of men owing nothing to family influence or money, sifted out by intelligence tests, separated from the rest, and groomed for positions of influence. (Sampson 1962: 185)

But this ignores the absence of change in educational opportunities for women, and could not at that time have taken into account the effect of expansion of universities, which increased the numbers of available undergraduate places but did little to change the difference between social classes in rates of admission (Halsey *et al.* 1980, Murphy 1990). Halsey and his colleagues (Halsey *et al.* 1980) studied four cohorts of men born between 1913 and 1922, 1923–32, 1933–42, and 1943–52. They found a rise in proportions going to university from 2 per cent in the earliest born group to 8 per cent in the most recently born. Although the fastest rates of increase were among students from working class families, the difference between the classes was nevertheless still wide; 7 per cent of highest social class men from the oldest group went to university, compared with 1 per cent of working class men, and in the most recently born cohort the comparable proportions were 26 per cent of the highest class but only 3 per cent of the lowest.

In this study 'able' lower social class children, in comparison with 'able' middle class children, did not enjoy equality of opportunity in getting to grammar school, nor an equal chance of staying on at school after 15 years, nor of going on to a university. Far fewer girls than boys stayed on at school, or went into further or higher education, whatever their earlier educational experience and attainments, or family circumstances. This was described as waste of talent, particularly of the talents and potential of women from all kinds of social background as well as those of men and women from working class homes.

To take advantage of secondary school educational opportunities required not only more grammar school places and better geographical spread of such places, but also a broader appreciation of all that was required to encourage the 'able' child. To take the opportunities the child had to be intellectually capable, well motivated by parental encouragement and by schools' high expectations, and working class children and girls from all social classes had to be able to withstand contemporary pressures to leave school at the earliest opportunity, not to take A levels, and not to go on to university. Children of poor parents may also have had to resist pressures to become earners, as well as coping with homework in crowded home circumstances. For parents to encourage their children in sixth form and higher education required agreement to forgo for a number of years the extra income the child could bring to the household, and needed a foundation of parental self-confidence and some knowledge of and familiarity with the education system, increasingly so as the child grew older. These things were not readily available in a generation of parents who had themselves received relatively little education. Only 6 per cent of parents had university degrees or equivalents, and only 11 per cent had any kind of educational qualifications; by comparison 9 per cent of study members achieved university degrees or equivalents, and 60 per cent had some kind of qualification. Parents had been at school in the very different system of the war and pre-war years, when educational expectations were very much lower, particularly for girls. Even parents with most educational qualifications, who generally had the highest degree of concern for education, had daughters whose qualifications were much lower than those of their sons; and women university students' views about appropriateness of higher education for women were similar to those of the prevailing contemporary public attitude. The educational ambitions which parents had for their study children came from an earlier time when the views of those who had the minimum of education were deeply divided about the value of further and higher education into those who saw it as a way of 'getting on' and those who believed it was no concern of theirs. Those who did not see any particular value in higher education were not only from manual social class families; Murphy (1990) suggests that they were those whose notions of success and satisfaction in adult life simply did not require education beyond school-leaving age.

Seen in broader terms than university places there is no doubt that the expansion of education for those aged 11 years and over offered opportunities to many more than in pre-war years. Nevertheless this present study of men and women born in 1946 showed that many working class boys and girls could, in terms of attainment scores, have benefited from a university education which would, in turn, have been of benefit to the community, as subsequent chapters show.

The view that girls were less adept than boys at logical thinking, expressed by some undergraduate study members, was associated with another revealing attitude of that time. In 1959 C. P. Snow described his idea of the divide between the two 'cultures' of science and the humanities. An important part of Snow's characterization of the divide was that the humanities had ignored the 'scientific revolution', and that its students were devoid of the logic of science and the attributes of a trained mind, attributes described by undergraduates in this study as peculiar mainly to scientists and to men. Such attitudes may well have reflected and influenced the relatively slow progression of change in girls' education. In 1967, for example, 23 per cent of boys stayed on at school after the leaving age, compared to 30 per cent in 1983; but for girls comparable proportions were 21 per cent in 1967 and 22 per cent in 1983 (Halsey 1988). And although numbers of girls taking A levels and numbers going on to university have now greatly increased, 'almost the whole of the short-fall in science/ technology [in terms of Robbins Report targets for 1980] is attributable to the absence of women students who had been hoped for' (Halsey 1988: 278).

Commentaries on the educational findings of this study concentrated particularly on the notion of 'waste of talent' and Denis Marsden, for instance, wrote in *Tribune* that the analyses showed 'how the educational system is wasting the country's brains'. Some, however, noticed that the findings supported the recommendations of the Plowden Committee on Children and their Primary School (Plowden Report 1967), and felt that they confirmed

to the hilt the arguments of the Plowden Report in favour of spending extra money and effort on the education of very young children, . . . to counteract the depressing spectacle of an ever-widening gap between the performance of the better-off and worse-off children throughout their whole time at school. (*The Economist* 1968)

Few commentators remarked that, compared with earlier times, proportionately more manual social class children now stayed on at school after the leaving age, and continued into higher and further education. However, one reviewer suggested that readers should

spare a passing thought on the activities and attitudes of some of those who have benefited, academically at least, from the opportunities afforded; and they might wonder if 'never had it so good' always implies 'never valued it so little'. . . . The expansion of higher education has brought in large numbers of students who do not merely rebel against an Establishment they are soon to join: they reject it. (*Tablet* 1968)

Carr (1964) anticipated that the corollary of expanding higher education would be increasing numbers of people emerging 'into social and political consciousness' (p. 149).

In health, the fall in demand for care that the designers of the NHS felt sure would follow the clearance of the backlog of illness waiting to be treated was obviously, by the mid-1960s, not going to occur; nor was the changing age structure of the population likely to be associated with anything but increasing demands. Social inequalities in health were evident, in the sense that the nation's death and illness rates, despite spectacular improvements, were still far higher in the lower social classes than in other sections of the population (Townsend and Davidson 1982). Despite the flourishing of research in medicine there was evidently a problem in delivering its benefits in the form of improved medical care for the general public, and in the continuing reluctance among some influential professionals to see medicine as anything but a necessarily rather impersonal service. Social aspects of medical care tended to be categorized as medical social work or described only in terms of the fecklessness of patients who failed to turn up for appointments, or who came too frequently, failed to take the medicine, continued to smoke, or did not take enough exercise. This may have occurred because social aspects of patient care were considered only at the appropriate level for everyday clinical work. Later the concept was broadened to include factors beyond the patient's influence, such as the nature of work, and the aetiological significance of social factors came to be seriously considered (Illsley and Kincaid 1963, Morris 1967). The concept of self-inflicted illness (see introduction to this chapter) contained the germ of the idea, of particular interest to the social scientists who were beginning to work in medicine at this time, that human behaviour was influenced not only by personal and assumed rational choice but also by opportunity, custom, expectation, and social context. The basic geographical and generation differences revealed by the 1958 study of births (Butler and Bonham 1963, Illsley and Kincaid 1963), and described in the introduction to this chapter, were a powerful incentive to expand ideas about the origins of ill health in childhood to include a wider range of environmental and social factors.

Health problems during the secondary school years were relatively few, but some significant effects of earlier illnesses and health risks were detectable, and the risks associated with smoking began to be acquired. Respiratory problems were greatest in those who had had chest illness before age 2 years, and smoking added to the risk. Height growth continued to be significantly greater in those from the most favourable family circumstances. Those who had been in hospital for a relatively long time before age 5 years were at greatest risk during adolescence of behaviour problems and poor reading attainment.

The difference between the childhood of these children born in 1946 and the childhood of their parents was very great in terms of environmental circumstances, of health, of education, of culture, and of expectation of what opportunities could be available in life. This study showed how appropriate the notions of many educational theorists had been in concluding that influences which had their effect in childhood were especially powerful, and would continue to influence the life course of the individual; this was clear, for instance, in the findings on the long-term influence of parents' concern for their child's education, and of health and family circumstances in early life. Society should be seen as comprising not only people of many ages and social classes, but also as a series of age groups or cohorts each carrying the imprint of the time of their childhood.

# 6
## Adulthood

### INTRODUCTION

By the time the men and women in the study were adults
Britain had in many ways 'broken out of the straitjacket of
dullness and conformity which had pinioned it since Victorian
times' (Marwick 1982: 156). The beginnings of this change had
become most evident in everyday life in the late 1960s in the
great upsurge in popular music and in popular fashions for
young people; the Beatles, the Rolling Stones, and the first
striking differences in fashions between young people and the
rest of the adult population promoted a colourful and vividly
expressed image of youth, and emphasized the differences
between the generations. During these years public attitudes
became in some respects more relaxed, as reflected in the
abandonment of theatre censorship in 1968 and in the Abortion
Law Reform Act of 1967, the NHS Family Planning Act of 1967,
which allowed local authorities to provide clinics to offer
contraceptive advice, the Sexual Offences Act, which permitted
homosexual acts between consenting adults in private, and the
Divorce Law Reform Act of 1969. Of course a change in
legislation did not amount to approval of a particular kind of
behaviour in everyday life (Thomson 1981), as attitudes
towards homosexuality have shown.

There was also a gradual rise in the real value of incomes.
Marwick (1982) noted that

average weekly earnings rose 34 per cent between 1955 and 1960, and
130 per cent between 1955 and 1969. This last figure was almost
exactly matched by the average earnings of middle-class salaried
employees, which rose 127 per cent between 1955 and 1969. While
prices of food and other necessities were steadily rising, the prices of
small cars, in relation to earning power, were falling, and the many
products of new technology, such as television sets and washing
machines were, despite inflation, actually costing less. (p. 118)

. . . a manual worker with average earnings would have had to work thirty-four minutes to buy a pint of beer in 1950, but only eighteen minutes in 1977. (p. 242)

In 1987 the average time a manual worker needed to work to buy a pint of beer was about 14 minutes. This change in purchasing power and the introduction of credit cards provided easier access for many people to a wide range of goods and services.

There were other signs that a redistribution of incomes was taking place. Between 1971 and 1987 there was a modest decrease in the percentage of wealth owned by the most wealthy. There was also, between 1976 and 1984, a decrease in household disposable income of those in the bottom three-fifths of the distribution of household incomes, particularly so amongst those in the bottom fifth, and some increase in incomes of those in the top fifth (Halsey 1988). Relative poverty (the constant relative poverty level, as indicated by proportion of personal disposable income) in households under pensionable age rose from 6.7 per cent of households in 1973 to 17.2 per cent in 1983, and 'among couples with one or more children the proportion below the constant relative poverty level rose from 2.9 per cent in 1975 to 12.4 per cent in 1983' (Piachaud 1988).

An increasing proportion of jobs were in non-manual work (44 per cent in 1981), and a growing proportion of women had paid occupations; 39 per cent of the labour force were women by 1981 (Price and Bain 1988). Between 1961 and 1985 the proportion of all married women who were economically active rose from 38 per cent to 52 per cent. However, the problem of unemployment grew. The proportion of the United Kingdom population of working age who were unemployed rose from 6.1 per cent in 1978 to 13.1 per cent in 1984 (Price and Bain 1988), and was still at least 8 per cent in 1988 (Central Statistical Office 1990) following a change in the definition of the unemployment statistics.

Increases in purchasing power brought considerable changes in living standards for many. Home ownership rose from 49 per cent of all British households in 1971 to 65 per cent in 1988, but numbers of homeless households rose from 112,000 in 1986 to 122,600 in 1988. The percentage of homes with some form of central heating rose from 35 per cent in 1971 to 73 per cent in 1987, numbers of private cars and light goods vehicles licensed increased from 6.3 million in 1961 to 12.1 million in 1971 and 20.4 million in 1988, and annual numbers of holidays taken abroad rose from 7 million in 1971 to 21 million in 1988 (*Social Trends* 1990).

Such changes in living standards and purchasing power were all part of the increase in the concepts and the actuality of individual choice and opportunity which were found, for example, in increasing opportunities to travel, to vote at an earlier age than before, to own property, to be free from illness for most of the time, particularly infection, to be able to control birth spacing and numbers of births, and in the growing demand for private health insurance. However, the latter, like many other aspects of this kind of change, including particularly changes in purchasing power, was by no means equally distributed across the social classes. In 1987, for instance, 27 per cent of men and women in the professional classes had private medical insurance, compared with 23 per cent of those in managerial and employer classes, 3 per cent in skilled manual classes, 2 per cent in semi-skilled classes, and 1 per cent of those in unskilled classes. The proportion of the British population with private medical insurance rose from 7 to 9 per cent between 1982 and 1987 (Office of Population Censuses and Surveys 1989). There was a continuing demand for fee-paying education, particularly in the years of preparation for further and higher education. In 1986 7 per cent of secondary school pupils aged 11–15 years were in independent schools, and so were 18 per cent of those aged 16 years and over. Between 1970 and 1987 active membership of Anglican, Nonconformist, Roman Catholic, and other Trinitarian churches fell from 16 per cent of the United Kingdom population to 12 per cent.

At the same time opportunities and choice were in many respects increasing. Signs of greater awareness of the need for equality of the sexes were to be found in the continuing campaigns for women's liberation and in legislation in the form, for example, of the Equal Pay and the Sex Discrimination Acts, both of 1975, and the Matrimonial Property Act of 1970. Other signs of a new sense of concern included, for example, the inauguration in 1969 of the British Society for Social Responsibility in Science, and of the Child Poverty Action Group in 1965, and in the 1960s Oxfam, which had begun in 1942, inaugurated its programmes of aid for development, rather than contending only with disasters. Anthony Sampson (1971) noted that 'at the beginning of the sixties such words as environment, ecology, participation, permissiveness, feedback —let alone the four-letter words—were hardly muttered in polite society'.

These increases in opportunities for choice in individual behaviour also brought other forms of change. New cases of sexually transmitted diseases more than doubled in women during the fourteen years from 1971 to 1985, and rose by more than a third in men. Divorce rates rose steeply as figure 3.1 shows. The proportion of lone parents with dependent children rose from 2 per cent in 1961 to 4 per cent in 1987 (*Social Trends* 1990). In general, crime rates rose by approximately 4.5 per cent a year during the 1980s. Between 1971 and 1984 admissions to hospital for the care of drug misuse problems more than doubled in men and almost doubled in women. In 1984 reported alcohol consumption was greatest in the youngest age groups, and 34 per cent of men and 5 per cent of women aged 18–24 years were classified as 'heavier' drinkers, that is those who consumed seven or more standard units of alcohol (a standard unit is for example half a pint of beer or an English single measure of spirits) three or four times a week (*Social Trends* 1987). And although the percentages of cigarette smokers fell from 52 per cent of men and 41 per cent of women in 1972 to 36 per cent of men and 32 per cent of women in 1984, average weekly consumption of cigarettes per smoker during the same period fell only from 120 to 115 in men, but rose from 87 to 96 in women (*Social Trends* 1987). But there has been a rising proportion of reported non-smokers at ages 11–15 years (*Social Trends* 1990).

Ideas changed, too, about the origins of good health and the beginnings of illness. Concepts of environmental health risks broadened to include not only more chemicals used in industry and agriculture, but also some things once believed in the lifetime of many to have been largely beneficial, such as sunlight and cigarette smoking (see Chapter 1), and a number of everyday foods including butter and creamy milk. In most instances damage to health from such environmental agents was usually thought to take a relatively long time, and it is unclear whether these agents, together with such other aspects of behaviour as insufficient physical exercise and sustained psychological distress, should be regarded as causal, or as sources of increased susceptibility. These new ideas required a different concept of the time illness took to develop, and studies were begun to see how early in life the origins of risk of some serious and highly prevalent adult illness might be detected. Amongst these has been the work of this study on blood pressure (Wadsworth *et al.* 1985) and on respiratory problems (Mann *et al.* forthcoming), and that of Berenson and his colleagues (Berenson 1986), who were concerned particularly with differences in blood pressure and blood chemistry in populations of children. Barker and Osmond have found associations between environment in childhood and some common causes of death in adult life (Barker and Osmond 1986*a*, 1986*b*, 1987, Barker *et al.* 1989, 1990).

These new ideas about the origins of some important illnesses raised questions about responsibility for their cause, both in terms of environment and of personal responsibility. In terms of personal responsibility there was during the 1970s a tendency to refer to some conditions as self-inflicted if their development was thought to involve behaviour, such as smoking, excess alcohol drinking, and poor choice of foods, which tended to be regarded as simply a matter of self-control, except in the instance of pathological addictions. In opposition to this view it was strongly argued that the powerful pressures of advertising and the ready availability and relatively low cost of cigarettes and alcohol made them an obvious choice of comfort in stressful and tedious circumstances at home and at work (Graham 1984). It is also true that smoking and alcohol drinking were in the earlier part of this period scarcely frowned upon at all in everyday life, but widely seen as important props of social life; they were also habits, like those of food choice, which tended to be established in childhood and adolescence (Braddon *et al.* 1988; Cox *et al.* 1987). In these circumstances the relevance of health education grew, and studies of public acceptance of advice, for example about smoking (*General Household Survey* 1984), diet (Whitehead 1987), and exercise (*General Household Survey* 1977 and 1983, Marmot *et al*. 1984), showed that the non-manual social classes were quickest to alter their behaviour in accordance with the latest advice.

Also during these years there was a growing awareness that the social class differences in health, which had been expected to diminish under the influences of the National Health Service and of the rapid improvements in medicines and diagnoses, were not doing so. Despite immense reductions in death rates, social class differences in the risk of death had changed very little. Signs of this problem were published by Titmuss (1943) and in this national study (Joint Committee (*a*) 1948), and then in the national study of births carried out in 1958 (Butler and Bonham 1963), which was described in the introduction to Chapter 5. They were found again in another national study of births which took place in 1970 (Chamberlain *et al*. 1975). Evidence of poorer health and greater risk of ill health and death earlier in life for those in the manual social classes was brought together in the Black Report (Townsend and Davidson 1982) and brought up to date in *The Health Divide* (Whitehead 1987), which summarized the circumstances in the 1980s in these terms:

All the major killer diseases now affect the poor more than the rich (and so do most of the less common ones too). The less favoured occupational classes also experience higher rates of chronic sickness and their children tend to have lower birth weight, shorter stature and other indicators suggesting poorer health status. (Whitehead 1987: 1)

It is, however, not clear to what extent these social class differences had their origins in the various ways of life of people in the very broad and ill-defined groups which constitute social class, rather than in social class differences in the use of and attitudes towards medical care (Whitehead 1987), or in some far longer-term influences which begin to have their effects during the early years of life and in previous generations (Barker and Osmond 1986*a*, 1986*b*, Berenson 1986, Wadsworth 1988).

During these years the proportion of the elderly in the national population continued to grow. By 1987 20 per cent of the British population was aged 60 years and over, compared with 8 per cent at the turn of the century. In future the proportion aged 75 years and over is going to grow particularly quickly, and is projected to reach 8 per cent of the population in twenty years' time, as compared with 6 per cent in 1985 and 1 per cent in 1901. This presents a number of problems. There is still much to be discovered about the early natural history and the origins of the most prevalent disorders of old age, particularly problems with bones and those, like arthritis, that impede activity, as well as those of memory and cognition. It has been estimated that

Half a million people in the UK suffer from dementia—destruction of their intellect—and about half of these have Alzheimer's disease, which affects one person in 20 aged over 65 and as many as one in four of people in their eighties. Clinically the disease is (usually) characterized in its early stages by impairment of memory, in particular an unusual forgetfulness for things that happened recently. Later sufferers develop dyspraxia—difficulty in performing complicated actions such as tying shoelaces, and then deterioration of social behaviour. Because the disease destroys the mind without killing the patient—who may take several years to die—an enormous burden is placed on the families of sufferers and on the Health and Social Services. (Medical Research Council 1986)

In the over-70s the risks of all kinds of illness are relatively high compared with the risks for other age groups, and recovery from such problems and coping with them are usually slow and may well require considerable amounts of home visiting. Reduced mobility, loneliness, low morale, memory loss, and confusion all exacerbate the problems of recovery and of remaining healthy, and are themselves risk factors for such further problems as falls, poor nutrition, infections, and failure to maintain medication programmes. The cost of medical care of the elderly is also considerable. In 1984 the annual NHS costs per person were highest for those aged 75 years and over; for men they were £945, and the next nearest cost for males was £578 for those aged under 1 year. For women aged 75 years and over the costs were £1,159, and the next nearest cost for females was £472 for those aged under 1 year.

Good care of the very old, the prevention of chronic, serious illness, and the achievement of equitable opportunities for good health are all problem topics for health care planners. In these circumstances a prospective and long-term study which has observed the health and social circumstances of its participants is a source of information and ideas.

During their adult life, from age 19 years onwards, members of the study population have so far been contacted five times by post and have been interviewed four times at home at ages 19, 26, 36, and 43 years, and measured at the last three ages. At this last visit 85 per cent of those who were still resident in England, Wales, or Scotland and willing to continue to take part in the study, were contacted (see Appendix 1). In this chapter information collected up to 36 years is used.

## DEATH

Age differences in national death rates after the first year of life and up to 34 years are now really very similar and much closer together than they have been since the turn of the century, especially since death rates at ages 1 to 4 years have been so dramatically reduced since the Second World War. Even now it is difficult to show death rates under 1 year of age on the same scale, since in 1980 the English rates for males, for example, were 13 per thousand live births, as compared with 0.6 deaths per thousand population at ages 1–4 years.

Significant social class differences in death rates are evident in men in this study population at these relatively young ages, as figure 6.1 shows. Figure 6.2*a* shows how, even after account is taken of the death rates in men who suffered chronic illness (as defined in 'Chronic Illness' in Chapter 4), there was still a substantial social class difference in death rates amongst men. Figures 6.2*a* and 6.2*b* also show the increased risks of death in chronically ill men and women who had been brought up in manual social class families. Men and women with long-term or chronic illness who were alive at 36 years were in a relatively vulnerable position in terms of housing and income, and this is discussed later in this chapter.

## HEALTH AND ILLNESS

There is no doubt that, as with premature death, illness at all stages in adult life is more common in the manual classes than the non-manual. It is therefore particularly appropriate to ask

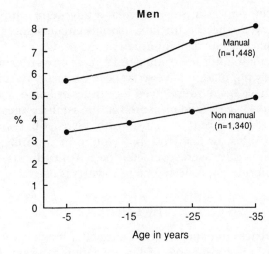

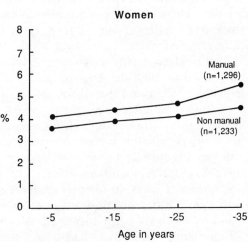

FIG. 6.1 Cumulative death rates from birth to 35 years in men and women according to the social class of their family of origin

in a long-term follow-up study how far back in life the origins of illness may be traced, and to see whether the risk factors for illness in later life differ between the sexes and the social classes. Answers to such questions would be useful in understanding the development of illness, as well as in planning most effective ways for health services to work.

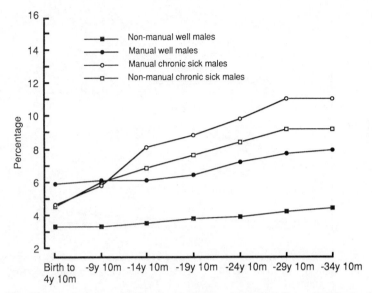

Fɪɢ. 6.2*a* Cumulative death rates in men, comparing the social class of the family of origin, and those with and without chronic illness in childhood

(*a*) *Long-term illness: the example of epilepsy that began in childhood*

The important questions of how individuals with long-term illness manage in everyday life, and how such illness affects the life chances of sufferers have both been examined in this study.

Epilepsy provides an interesting example of the problems of coping with a long-term, serious illness, since it not only brings some restriction in choice of lifestyle and career, but also anxiety about heritability of the condition, worries about having a seizure in public, concern about what others may think, and whether or not they will treat you differently because of this illness. These last aspects have for many years been lumped together, rather unsatisfactorily, in the portmanteau term 'stigma' when, as more recent observers have pointed out, it is at least necessary to differentiate the sufferer's feelings about having epilepsy from the way that those with epilepsy are treated in daily life (Scambler 1982).

By the time they were 26 years old 9.5 per thousand study

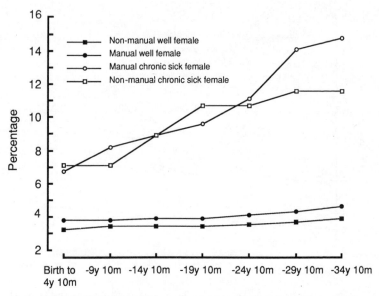

FIG. 6.2*b* Cumulative death rates in women, comparing the social class of the family of origin, and those with and without chronic illness in childhood

members were diagnosed as having epilepsy, two-thirds of them having uncomplicated epilepsy (6.4 per thousand) and one-third (3.1 per thousand) epilepsy complicated with other conditions, such as Down's syndrome or other congenital problems (Britten *et al.* 1986).

Teachers' reports of pupils' behaviour and chances of educational achievement were compared between those with epilepsy and those without any long-term illness, comparing with two sets of study children from similar social and family backgrounds. There were practically no differences in teachers' reports and expectations, except that rather more attention-seeking and aggressive behaviour was reported amongst those with epilepsy. There was a tendency for children with epilepsy to be more neurotic, perhaps as a result of their physical illness. There was little difference between sufferers and others in rates of marriage and becoming parents. By 36 years, however, there was some evidence of worse socio-economic circumstances amongst sufferers, together with higher levels of discontent about their working lives and about the fact that life had not been good to them. It was concluded therefore that perhaps the self-concepts of sufferers had undergone a change by this age, moving away from the neurotic and attention-seeking style of adolescence to a more introspective style in adult life (Britten *et al.* 1986).

### (b) Long-term illness and life chances

There is now a very great deal of evidence to show that ill health and premature death are disproportionately experienced by people in lower social classes (Townsend and Davidson 1982, Whitehead 1987), but it is not at all clear how far this is a result of known class differentials in the uptake of care and advice (Blaxter 1981, Pill and Stott 1982, Calnan 1982), or exposure to harmful substances (McQueen and Siegrist 1982), nor yet how and when this process begins (Illsley 1980). There is evidence from this study that social class differences in illness in adult life may in part originate in childhood. This can be seen first in the study of those who were seriously ill in childhood, and then in the study of health habits.

If serious illness is taken to be that which kept a child in hospital for a minimum of twenty-eight consecutive days or away from school for three consecutive weeks or more, then 388 men (15 per cent of men whose health histories were known up to 26 years) and 311 women (13 per cent of women with known health histories) had had serious illness by the time they were 10 years old. These people who had been seriously ill as children were twice as likely as others to be seriously ill in early adult life, up to age 26 years. Their chances of educational achievement were reduced if they were male (Chapter 5), and by age 26 years men's social class position achieved through their occupation, was less likely to be higher and more likely to be lower than their father's if they had been seriously ill in childhood. This was especially marked in those from manual social class families of origin (Wadsworth 1986*a*).

By 36 years it was clear that the seriously ill child who had continued to be seriously ill up to 25 years was significantly less likely than others to marry and, if a woman, less likely to have children (Pless *et al.* 1989). This group of 160 persons (31 per thousand in this cohort, and likely to be greater in later born groups as survivors of serious illness in childhood increase in number) who were seriously ill both as children and in early adult life seemed especially vulnerable at 36 years, because their comparatively high rates of renting rather than buying their homes, their relatively low chances of marriage, and their higher rates of parental death meant that they had much less fundamental social support, although they were arguably amongst those in greatest need (Pless *et al.* 1989).

### (c) *Respiratory illness*

Chest illness (lower respiratory disease) and reports of chronic cough in adult life up to 36 years were significantly more common among those who had experienced bronchitis, pneumonia, or a similar chest illness before two years (Colley *et al.* 1973, Kiernan *et al.* 1976, Britten *et al.* 1987, Mann *et al.* forthcoming). This risk was increased by cigarette smoking, which was also a source of risk for those who had not had chest illness in infancy. Other childhood risks for adult chest illness were parental bronchitis, living in an area of high atmospheric pollution from coal burning sources, and, strongest of all, living in overcrowded and poor home circumstances (Mann *et al.* forthcoming). Among those who had never had chest disease parental bronchitis and overcrowded home circumstances in early childhood were associated with a relatively poor performance on a measure of respiratory function (peak expiratory flow rate) at 36 years. It was concluded that such long-term associations of childhood illness and home circumstances with adult risk of illness might be accounted for by the damage caused to the developing respiratory system by infant chest illness, by the chance of repeated infection as a result of living in poor and crowded circumstances with bronchitic parents, and with possible exacerbating effects from poor nutrition and parental smoking. There was no doubt about the increased risk associated with the study members' own cigarette smoking (Mann *et al.* forthcoming).

These findings of a long-term association between early childhood illness and similar problems in adult life have been strengthened by Barker and Osmond's (1986*a*) review of national data which showed that generations or cohorts of children who grew up during times of high rates of infant death from bronchitis and pneumonia, and who survived into adult life, then had in their adult years high rates of death from bronchitis or emphysema; and as the infant death rates from these causes fell, from 1900 onwards, so the corresponding adult rates fell, from 1940 onwards.

Not all childhood respiratory problems were associated with long-term respiratory difficulties. Whooping cough, experienced by over half (57 per cent) of the study population in childhood was not found to have significant respiratory consequences by age 36 years (Britten and Wadsworth 1986).

### (d) Obesity

Obesity is also a condition thought to be more common in adult life amongst those who were overweight in childhood. In this study there was evidently an increased risk of adult obesity amongst those who had been obese or overweight as children. But these individuals amounted only to one in five (21 per cent) of those who were obese at 36 years, and the remaining four out of five first became overweight in adult life. It was concluded that preventive care should include advice in childhood, so that patterns of healthy eating would be established as early as possible (Braddon *et al.* 1986) when, it was known from the studies of diet in these same men and women, habits tended to be established (Braddon *et al.* 1988). Good health care advice was evidently necessary in adult life too, since by 36 years 43 per cent of men were overweight (including 5 per cent obese) and so were 33 per cent of women, 8 per cent of whom were obese. Being overweight or obese at 36 years was a much greater risk for those from manual social class families of origin than for others.

Later born children who did not live through a period of national food rationing were at much greater risk of obesity. Comparisons of obesity in the study population and their own first born offspring at ages 7–8 years showed a greatly increased risk of obesity in the offspring (Wadsworth 1985) and in a national study of children born in 1958 the risk of being overweight was twice as great at age 7 years, but considerably less, and then only in boys, at age 11 (Peckham *et al.* 1983). These indicators of increase in the proportion of the population who are overweight are a cause for concern, since obesity is known to be a risk factor in a number of serious adult conditions, including high blood pressure.

### (e) Blood pressure

Blood pressure was first measured in these men and women at age 36 years, and 79 per thousand men and 40 per thousand women were found to have high blood pressure. Only 12 per cent of men with high blood pressure were receiving treatment, compared with 22 per cent of women. In an investigation of the association of obesity, smoking, and social and family factors with blood pressure at this age, it was found that current obesity (body mass), low birth weight, and father's death from a blood pressure related disorder, all of which were far more characteristic of those from manual class families of origin, were most strongly associated with high blood pressure; smoking was also associated, but less strongly, and only in men (Wadsworth *et al.* 1985). The association with cause of paternal death may reflect both genetic and shared environmental effects, and the strong association with obesity is of particular concern when it seems that obesity may well be increasing in prevalence. In this study most obesity had been acquired in early adult life (see section (*d*) above).

The association of high blood pressure with low birth weight may be because such small babies grew rapidly to catch up with other children by age 2 years (Douglas and Mogford 1953*a*, 1953*b*), and Ounstead *et al.* (1985) found that such rapid growth was associated with an increase in blood pressure. Since it looks as if the individual's blood pressure level may be established before (de Swiet 1986) the beginning of the gradual rise that occurs in the adult blood pressure of practically all members of populations in Western urbanized countries (Marmot 1986), then the relatively high blood pressure in those of low birth weight may simply be the result of its early establishment at a relatively high level. On the other hand the relationship of low birth weight with the risk of high adult blood pressure may be associated with relatively poor foetal growth. Barker *et al.* (1990) found that the adult blood pressure of those who had not grown well *in utero* (who had been small babies with large placentas) was significantly higher than that of others, and suggested that 'such discordance between placental and foetal size may lead to circulatory adaptation in the foetus, altered arterial structure in the child, and hypertension in the adult'. It was concluded that

The decrease in mortality from stroke in Britain during the past forty years is consistent with past improvements in maternal physique and health (Barker and Osmond 1987). Reducing blood pressure in a population may partly depend on improving the environment of girls and women, including improving their nutrition. (Barker *et al.* 1990)

This is an area of great and continuing controversy, and questions about the extent to which such long-term associations are mediated by experience in the intervening years, by environmental factors in adulthood, and by genetic predisposition still remain to be fully investigated.

### (f) Emotional problems

In adult life study members reported their experience of emotional difficulties between ages 15 and 26 years, and at 36 years the short version of the Present State Examination was given by specially trained nurses. This is a standardized rating of symptoms of anxiety, depression, and phobias experienced in the previous month (Rodgers and Mann 1986).

Just over a third (39 per cent) of study members reported having emotional difficulties at some time between ages 15 and 26 years; 1 per cent had treatment for such problems in hospital out-patient clinics, and a further 2 per cent were admitted to hospital for care of such problems during this time. Findings which use this information are described later in this chapter in the section on strain at work.

Use of the Present State Examination found 4 per cent of men and 9 per cent of women to have a score indicating that at that time their emotional state would be appropriate for them to have clinical care, and indeed 51 per cent had visited a doctor with such problems in the previous twelve months (Rodgers and Mann 1986). Close in time to emotional problems at 36 years sufferers had been more at risk than others of poor home circumstances, insecurity of housing and financial support, divorce or separation, and, for men, employment problems (Rodgers 1989). Over a longer period sufferers had also experienced more serious physical illness in adult life than others, they had been more neurotic, had more behaviour problems at school and in childhood, and they had had more problems with sleeping and bed-wetting, ill health and poor emotional well-being of parents, death of a parent, and prolonged absence from parents (Rodgers 1989, 1990a, 1990b, 1990c). Many of these earlier life problems were correlated with one another.

How could these earlier life factors be associated with emotional problems at 36 years? Since the risk factors listed above were not common to all those who had later problems, there are likely to be many ways in which links between childhood and adolescent problems and later adult emotional difficulties were established (Robins and Rutter 1990).

It is possible that emotional maturity and coping systems were not well founded because of damage to the child's psyche during a sensitive period of development. There is no information in this study, however, to show whether or not this could be true, but since childhood adversity was not a necessary precursor of adult emotional problems this is unlikely to be the only explanation, even if it were true.

It is more likely that a series or a chain of problems was experienced because one precipitated another, and because social and family circumstances and self-esteem were not strong enough to support the individual at such times. Wallerstein and Kelly (1980) found, for example, that before the age of 5 or 6 children were inclined to be frightened and confused by parental divorce, and in looking for an explanation of the family disruption even blamed themselves. At later ages children were increasingly open about their feelings, and better able to express them. Older children were less inclined to feel responsible for what had happened, but more inclined to feel ashamed and embarrassed by their parents' behaviour, with increasing likelihood of feelings of loneliness, detachment, and rejection. If such emotional confusion and low self-esteem continued or was perpetuated by changes in such material circumstances as a move to worse housing conditions (Eekelaar and Maclean 1986), or by the attitudes of others (Wadsworth *et al.* 1990) then school work and attainment and behaviour would be likely to be at risk, as was found in this study (Douglas 1970, 1973*a*, 1975, Cherry 1976, Rodgers 1990*b*, 1990*c*, 1990*d*, Wadsworth and Maclean 1986). The risks to job prospects brought by this relative lack of educational qualifications became clear in adult life. Incomes of men who had experienced parental divorce or separation during the years before they left school were significantly lower than those of others at ages 26 and 36 years, and their risks of unemployment were greater at 36 years, since at this time (1982) of increasing unemployment those with no qualifications were at greatest risk of losing their jobs (Maclean and Wadsworth 1988). Significantly smaller proportions of women from families in which parents had divorced were in jobs in the top two social classes at age 36 years (Kuh and Maclean 1990).

Thus, adult vulnerability to emotional difficulties may be the current end point of many earlier experiences of problems, some a matter of bad luck, some a question of poor self-regard, and others a problem of poor social support; the many interrelationships found between these factors add to the likelihood of strong links perpetuating the chain over many years (Rodgers 1989).

For those who may be emotionally vulnerable because of childhood adversity the risks of adult emotional and coping problems may be reduced through the effect of a supportive marriage or other relationship (Brown and Harris 1978), and this may strengthen resolve against future difficulties (Hetherington 1988). But additional vulnerability to adult problems can be caused by such potentially stressful experiences as the death of a close friend, or by financial hardship or the lack of an escape from poor home or difficult family circumstances that may be provided by a job (Rodgers 1990*d*).

Because emotional problems usually involve the interaction of psychological factors with current social circumstances and attitudes to what may be seen as problem behaviour, it can be difficult to know how to interpret associations between factors which may change over time. Attitudes to divorce, for example, have changed greatly since the late 1940s and 1950s, when parental separation was seen as a serious risk to the 'moral fibre' of the developing child, and teachers and health visitors who collected information for this study were very pessimistic about the future life of children from such families (Wadsworth *et al.* 1990). However, it is unlikely that the emotional circumstances of childhood adversities have lessened in their impact on the child, and there is evidence from more recent studies to show that the risks arising from a reduction in income at the time of family separation are still as great as ever (Eekalaar and Maclean 1986).

## HABITS ASSOCIATED WITH HEALTH

### (a) Smoking

When they were 20 years old just over half the men (53 per cent) and a little more than one-third of women (38 per cent) reported that they were regular smokers. Sixteen years later, at 36 years, the proportion of men and women who smoked had dropped to 34 per cent of each sex. By this age more men than women smoked heavily (12 per cent of men and 5 per cent of women smoked more than 20 cigarettes a day), and women were much more likely to have been lifetime non-smokers (29 per cent of women) compared with men (19 per cent). Those who said they were regular smokers at 20 years were more likely to have come from manual social class families of origin, but occasional smokers were most usually from non-manual families. At 36 years it was those then in the manual social classes and those who had achieved only the lowest levels of educational attainment who were the heaviest smokers, and heaviest smokers from such backgrounds were most inclined to select cigarettes with the highest contents of tar, carbon monoxide, and nicotine.

Effects of smoking on the risk of chest illness were discussed earlier in this chapter.

## (b) Diet

Information on diet was first collected at 36 years, when study members kept seven-day diaries of everything consumed. But although there is no information on childhood diet there is information on breast-feeding. This is of particular interest because American studies have found that fatty deposits on artery walls (atheroma) can be present in children and in young people who are apparently exceptionally fit (Berenson 1986). Theories to account for this implicate genetic predetermination and infant diet, and it has been suggested that perhaps breast-feeding may retard the process of acquiring atheroma. A study of 172 study members when they were 32 years old found that those who had been breast-fed, particularly women, were indeed more inclined to have low plasma cholesterol levels in comparison with those who were not breast-fed (Marmot *et al.* 1980).

The findings on diet of the study members at 36 years show, like those on smoking, that those in manual social class families and those with the lowest educational levels seemed to have the least health conscious habits (Braddon *et al.* 1988). Iron, calcium, fibre, and vitamin C were on average consumed in significantly smaller amounts each week by the least educated compared with others, and by those in manual classes compared with those in non-manual classes. Just over half the women did not achieve the recommended daily intake of iron, and well over half the population were below the recommended level of fibre intake. The difficulties of maintaining a healthy dietary balance were well illustrated by the women who had achieved a high level of educational qualifications (A levels or above) and who came from a manual class family of origin; although they ate, for the most part, a diet consistent with recommended intakes, their diets were still not as healthy as those of women from non-manual families with similar qualifications, and they had the highest average alcohol intake amongst all women from manual class backgrounds (Braddon *et al.* 1988).

## OCCUPATION

In many ways occupation and income were associated with education and with the circumstances of the family of origin. In a society which has sought to change and to improve educational opportunities (see Chapter 1) achievements in occupation and income will show how far such policies have been successful in this study population's experience. Information on these topics will also show whether there has been an associated cost in any such achievements in terms of the loosening of family ties, as Stacey (1960) and others had feared (see conclusions of Chapter 4). Findings on occupation and income by 36 years, and their relationship with educational attainment and income are described in this and the following section. Comparisons of occupational achievement in the generation of study members with those of their parents, and the extent of contacts between the generations are described in Chapter 7.

Although the population of study members in professional, salaried, or clerical jobs was more than half made up of those from manual social class family backgrounds, the chances of the individual working in these kinds of occupations did not by any means favour women or those from working class origins. Tables 6.1*a* and 6.1*b* show that even with a high educational test score at 8 years, or a place at a selective or fee-paying secondary school, or a father in professional or salaried employment, women were far less likely than men to have achieved high employment status by 36 years. In both sexes, but particularly in men, the experience of the selective school or fee-paying education after 11 years conferred much greater likelihood of getting a high social class occupation at 36 years, when compared with the chances of those who had gone to non-selective schools. Similarly, whatever type of school had been attended a distinct career advantage was conferred by an upbringing in a family in which the father was employed in a non-manual class job. Yet although those with relatively poor attainment scores in childhood, or who went to non-selective state schools, had much less chance of gaining higher educational qualifications, and were least well represented in higher social class occupations, they were not by any means unable to

TABLE 6.1a  *Employment of men (and women, in brackets) who scored in the top third on attainment tests at 8 years, and the home and school routes to employment* (Weighted data—see Appendix 1)

| | Percentage of total population at these schools | Percentage in each social class of those employed at 36 years | | | | Total (=100%) | Percentage not employed at 36 years |
|---|---|---|---|---|---|---|---|
| | | I and II | III non manual | III manual | IV and V | | |
| *Non-manual family of origin* | | | | | | | |
| Grammar or other selective state school | 64 (67) | 83 (53) | 9 (39) | 8 ( 1) | 0.4 ( 7) | 254 (196) | 2 (34) |
| Secondary modern or other non-selective state school | 25 (19) | 51 (45) | 27 (33) | 17 ( 2) | 4 (20) | 93 ( 49) | 6 (42) |
| Fee-paying school | 11 (14) | 79 (49) | 2 (37) | 19 (10) | — ( 5) | 43 ( 41) | 2 (35) |
| *Manual family of origin* | | | | | | | |
| Grammar or other selective state school | 52 (50) | 72 (52) | 8 (37) | 15 ( 4) | 6 ( 6) | 233 (177) | 5 (26) |
| Secondary modern or other non-selective state school | 45 (46) | 39 (21) | 12 (55) | 36 ( 5) | 12 (18) | 232 (168) | 4 (37) |
| Fee-paying school | 3 ( 4) | * (*) | * (*) | — | — | 15 ( 14) | — (*) |

*Numbers are too small for calculation of percentages.

TABLE 6.1b  *Employment of men (and women, in brackets) who scored in the middle and lowest thirds on attainment tests at 8 years, and the home and school routes to employment (Weighted data—see Appendix 1)*

| | Percentage of total population at these schools | Percentage in each social class of those employed at 36 years | | | | Total (=100%) | Percentage not employed at 36 years |
|---|---|---|---|---|---|---|---|
| | | I and II | III non-manual | III manual | IV and V | | |
| *Non-manual family of origin* | | | | | | | |
| Grammar or other selective state school | 20 (23) | 82 (54) | 9 (38) | 8 (3) | 1 ( 5) | 88 ( 74) | 6.4 (20.4) |
| Secondary modern or other non-selective state school | 69 (59) | 37 (23) | 8 (41) | 46 (14) | 9 (22) | 303 (151) | 6.5 (37.9) |
| Fee-paying school | 11 (18) | 80 (28) | 10 (61) | 6 ( 3) | 4 ( 8) | 50 ( 36) | 2.0 (50.7) |
| *Manual family of origin* | | | | | | | |
| Grammar or other selective state school | 12 ( 8) | 59 (22) | 13 (48) | 19 (1) | 9 (29) | 227 ( 83) | 1.7 (47.1) |
| Secondary modern or other non-selective state school | 87 (91) | 21 (14) | 9 (34) | 49 ( 9) | 21 (43) | 1,488 (1,157) | 9.8 (36.7) |
| Fee-paying school | 1 ( 1) | — (*) | * (*) | * (—) | — (*) | 17 ( 28) | — (*) |

*Numbers are too small for calculation of percentages.

gain employment in that sector, as the authors of the Crowther Report (1959), and others at the time of its publication (e.g. Sampson 1962) had feared.

This evidence may, in one sense, be interpretable as showing a waste of talent, in that at a time of demand for workers with relatively high educational attainment a surprisingly small proportion of those who were high attainers at primary school went on, in fact, to the more academically inclined secondary schools (see Chapters 4 and 5) and then to professional or salaried non-manual employment. A sifting out process occurred at a number of points, so that girls, children from lower social class families, and those who went to non-selective schools had the lowest chance of professional or salaried careers, even if they had apparently high attainment potential. At least five adverse factors, sometimes acting cumulatively, influenced this process of sifting. First, low parental interest and concern for the child's education were both associated with reduced chances of good educational attainment. The second adverse factor was low parental social class, which was found in other studies to be associated with parents' worries about the risk of highly educated children moving away from the family, and worries about the cost, for example in lost income, of a child staying on at school after the minimum leaving age. Low social class was also believed, in this study, to be related to problems of overcrowding and lack of encouragement reducing the chance of completing homework, and to an increased likelihood of pressure from friends and siblings to earn rather than learn. The third adverse factor was low assessment by primary school teachers of the child's educational potential, however it related to the child's test scores, and was an influence that was hard to escape (see Chapter 4). The fourth adverse factor comprised the contemporary popular attitudes which did not favour the further and higher education of girls. The final adverse factor was that the relatively low average of 20 per cent of grammar school places available at that time restricted entry into these academically inclined schools.

For the majority of jobs, particularly manual occupations, entry qualifications are usually a matter for employers, and acquisition of appropriate skills comes mostly from on-the-job training, sometimes with the attainment of a qualification to a nationally agreed standard. Cherry (1978) found that of the men who had left school without educational qualifications and who had been in manual work when they were 18 years old only a third (32 per cent) were still in unskilled or semi-skilled work eight years later at age 26 years; the others had gone on to non-manual work (20 per cent) or to skilled manual occupations (48 per cent). In terms of educational qualifications a third (33 per cent) of men who left school with none had acquired some recognized qualification by the time they were 26 years old, 17 per cent of them at the standard of Advanced level (the 18-year-old school-leaving examination), Higher National Certificate, or a university degree (Cherry 1978).

This continuing increase in qualifications and attainment is in accordance with the findings of change in scores on tests of reading ability in this study, which rose from 23 per cent of the study population scoring higher than the average at 15 years, to 59 per cent at age 26 years, contrary to what had been the generally accepted view that such ability stopped developing with the cessation of formal education (Rodgers 1984, 1986).

There was clearly considerable attainment in this group of young men who had originally left school without educational qualifications. It was therefore important to see whether this degree of educational achievement was also reflected in the nature of the men's occupations, and whether those who were working at a relatively high skill level were also those who had high levels of attainment on tests taken during their primary school years.

Since conventional job titles reveal little, if anything, about the nature of the individual's day to day work, Cherry (1978) devised skill scores in order to examine associations of men's occupations at age 26 years with assessments of 'talent' made during the school years. These scores were allocated according to the adjudged level of skill that the job required in dealing with data (reading, writing, and calculating), people (supervision, teaching, dealing with public or business associates) and equipment (work with machines ranging from minding to setting-up, fast precision and diagnostic work, and driving). Using these scales Cherry (1978) found that men who were without educational qualifications at the time of leaving school, but who had relatively high attainment scores on the verbal and non-verbal tests taken at school at age 15 years (see Appendix 2), were indeed in jobs requiring high skill levels by the age of 26 years. These high skill level occupations tended to be in smaller firms or were self-employment, and 17 per cent of intermediate non-manual jobs men held at 26 years (mainly managerial positions) were occupied by those who had no formal educational qualifications. The factors which best predicted such achievement were, at age 14 years, a high level of ambition for a middle class job (Cherry 1974*a*), and the extent to which scores on the 15-year tests were higher than expected from scores taken at earlier ages. However, a high level of ambition did not compensate for low ability scores (Cherry 1978). Neither the type of secondary school last attended nor the social class of the family from which the men came was associated with this kind of achievement in these early adult years.

Considered over a longer time scale the suggestion that a very serious waste of talent had occurred amongst men was not wholly borne out. The most able and the most ambitious who had left school without educational qualifications were, by 26 years, in jobs which required high levels of skills, although they had not achieved the skill levels and the prestige of occupations which were open to men who had gone on to achievement in further or higher education. Even amongst men who at 26 years lived in areas where employment prospects were poor, personal ambition and high measured ability on the tests taken at school were the best predictors of a high skill level in their jobs (Cherry 1978).

Because high proportions of women were not in paid employment at 36 years (see tables 6.1*a* and 6.1*b*) detailed analyses of their occupations has not yet been undertaken; but women who were in professional or skilled manual jobs when they married were those most likely to be employed when their first born was aged four years, and most likely still to be in professional or skilled occupations at that time (Wadsworth 1981).

## INCOME

At age 36 years most men and women who were in paid employment felt that they had managed comfortably or fairly well on their income during the previous year, but 18 per cent of men and 15 per cent of women said that they had found it quite hard to manage. However, among couples where neither was employed, and among single people who were not employed 67 per cent of men and 24 per cent of women said that they found it hard to manage. Those who said this significantly more often than others had higher levels of educational attainment, whether they were in employment or not.

So far only men's incomes have been studied, and their achieved level of income reflected the continuing and powerful influence of the social and economic status of the family of origin, of educational attainment, and of the route taken through the school system. Those who had scored in the top third on the tests of educational attainment taken at 8 years had the highest average earnings at 36 years. Those who were from upper non-manual social group families were also those most assured of earning above the average (median) for this study population by 36 years (79 per cent), compared with the 36 per cent of men who originated from lower manual social group families who were earning above average salaries by this age. Similarly, those who had been at selective schools and those who had attained qualifications, or equivalents, at GCE Advanced level or above were at least twice as likely to be high earners. In real life, of course, all these influences were combined, and the net effect is summarized in table 6.2. For men from a manual social group family of origin, educational attainment at a high level went a long way, but not all the way, to making up the gap in income between them and men who came from a non-manual family of origin. However, the chances of higher educational attainment were very much reduced for men from the lower social group families of origin, for the reasons discussed in previous chapters.

Perhaps now that increasing numbers of people have educational qualifications at all levels (see Chapter 7), and the system of secondary education has changed, such large differ-

TABLE 6.2 *Family origins and educational attainment of high earning (top third) men at age 36 years[a]*

| Highest level of education by 36 years | Manual families of origin | | Non-manual families of origin | |
|---|---|---|---|---|
| | Bottom two-thirds of attainment scores at 8 years | Top third of attainment scores at 8 years | Bottom two-thirds of attainment scores at 8 years | Top third of attainment scores at 8 years |
| Below O level | 13 | 17 | 23 | 32 |
| O level (earliest school leaving exams) and equivalents | 26 | 25 | 36 | 49 |
| A level (latest school leaving exams) and equivalents | 29[b] | 39[b] | (45) | (48) |
| University level and equivalents | | | (65) | (68) |

(Manual A level & university combined = 29[b] bottom two-thirds, 39[b] top third; Non-manual A level & university combined = 49 bottom two-thirds, 58 top third)

[a] Each percentage shows the proportion of high earning men from the stated origins.
[b] These education levels have been combined because of small numbers.

ences in opportunities in income and occupation associated with the social class of family of origin will be reduced.

## STRAIN AT WORK

Very similar proportions of men and women in full-time occupations at 26 and 32 years reported nervous strain at work (Cherry 1978, 1984a, 1984b). In both sexes strain was more often reported by those in non-manual occupations, particularly those in intermediate level jobs such as industrial managers and those who supervised others. Night time and shift workers also significantly more often than others reported nervous strain at work, and those in part-time jobs reported significantly less strain. There was a very strong likelihood that a man who reported nervous strain at work at 26 would do so again six years later; even those who changed to what appeared to be less stressful jobs were still significantly inclined to report strain at 32 years.

Three sets of information (reports of nervous strain at home at 26 years, consulting a doctor for nervous troubles whilst 16–32 years, and high neuroticism score on the Maudsley Personality Inventory at 16 years) were used to see whether nervous strain at work at 32 years was associated with susceptibility to nervous problems in earlier life. Women had much higher rates than men on each of these indicators of susceptibility, and both sexes had higher rates of nervous strain at home at age 32 than at 26 years. Analysis of all these factors together showed that they were each (except nervous strain at home in men aged 26 years) associated with nervous strain at work at 32 years, and the most powerful predictor was concurrent nervous strain at home.

Nervous strain at work at 32 years was for many men and women associated with reports of sleep problems, frequent headaches, pain in the pit of the stomach, and back trouble, and at 26 years four out of five men under strain also felt unduly irritable, depressed, or tired. Cherry (1984b) noted that such complaints 'may considerably reduce the quality of life both for the man and his family'.

From these studies it was concluded

that although a reduction in the stressful features of work may well reduce the level of reported strain, it is unlikely to reduce the incidence of these symptoms.

This finding does not imply that stress at work is harmless. The range of factors considered . . . is small, and even amongst these there is some indication that men on irregular night work have more sleep problems and stomach pains than others. There also remains the possibility that men in the more highly demanding jobs will have more health problems in the longterm, but there is no indication of this at the age of 32 years. (Cherry 1984*b*)

Findings from the studies of women came to essentially the same conclusion (Cherry 1984*a*).

Amongst the population in paid work at age 36 years a significantly greater proportion of men and women with highest level educational qualifications (university degree level and equivalents) felt that their skills and talents were not being fully employed, compared with those with lower level qualifications. Men more often than women expressed a view on this question, and amongst those with highest level qualifications 52 per cent of men and 35 per cent of women felt that their skills were not fully employed.

## LEISURE TIME

Table 6.3 shows how often men and women at age 36 years took part in nine leisure time activities, selected because they involved contact with others. Few people (9 per cent of men and 6 per cent of women) did none of these things. The most common of the activities for men was going to a pub or club once a week or more often, and for women the most usual activity was having friends to visit at home in the evening or at the weekend. Differences in the proportions of men and women who took part in these activities were small, in terms of their social class of origin, but were much greater according to their education. Participation was greater amongst those with relatively high educational attainment, whatever their class of origin, not only as anticipated in such activities as playing musical instruments, but also in some other leisure activities of greater significance to the life of the community. For example, proportionately more men and women with high attainment

TABLE 6.3   *Leisure time activities of men and women at 36 years, according to their class of origin and their education*[a]

| | Non-manual families of origin | | Manual families of origin | |
|---|---|---|---|---|
| | High educational attainment[b] | Low educational attainment | High educational attainment[b] | Low educational attainment |
| **Chess** | | | | |
| *Men* | 25.6 | 32.4 | 23.4 | 24.9 |
| *Women* | 24.0[c] | 18.3[c] | 19.6 | 14.3 |
| **Church and religious activities** | | | | |
| *Men* | 29.3[c] | 15.8[c] | 21.0[c] | 10.9[c] |
| *Women* | 43.4[c] | 32.6[c] | 43.9[c] | 22.4[c] |
| **Going to the theatre, cinema, or concerts** | | | | |
| *Men* | 67.4[c] | 50.0[c] | 61.7[c] | 36.8[c] |
| *Women* | 70.8[c] | 55.9[c] | 74.8[c] | 41.4[c] |
| **Help to run a club or play-group** | | | | |
| *Men* | 20.6 | 19.1 | 23.5[c] | 15.0[c] |

| | | | | |
|---|---|---|---|---|
| **Play a musical instrument** | | | | |
| *Men* | 8.8[c] | 3.2[c] | 5.6[c] | 2.6[c] |
| *Women* | 9.8[c] | 1.8[c] | 4.6[c] | 1.2[c] |
| **Undertake voluntary social work** | | | | |
| *Men* | 12.3[c] | 6.1[c] | 8.1[c] | 4.6[c] |
| *Women* | 16.6 | 12.1 | 8.3 | 7.2 |
| **Take part in local government or trade union activities** | | | | |
| *Men* | 8.5 | 5.0 | 9.5[c] | 5.0[c] |
| *Women* | 5.6[c] | 1.3[c] | 7.0[c] | 0.6[c] |
| **Go to evening classes** | | | | |
| *Men* | 9.8 | 7.2 | 8.9[c] | 4.3[c] |
| *Women* | 30.2[c] | 15.2[c] | 15.9 | 14.0 |
| **Take part in vigorous sports** | | | | |
| *Men* | 52.6 | 46.0 | 52.3[c] | 37.3[c] |
| *Women* | 54.9[c] | 40.9[c] | 47.9[c] | 35.5 |

[a] Each cell shows the percentage of people in that cell who take part in the specified activity.

[b] Senior school leaving examinations (A levels) and equivalents and all higher and professional qualifications.

[c] Statistically significant comparison of proportions between educational attainment categories in the same social class band.

undertook voluntary social work or took part in local government or trade union activities or vigorous sports, or helped to
run a club or play-group. Variations in leisure time activities
seemed largely the result of the experience of further and
higher education, rather than intelleciual capability, since
amongst the men and women with no educational qualifications those with high (top-third) educational test scores
differed from others in their leisure pursuits only in going
significantly more often to a theatre or cinema, and men were
also more likely to do voluntary social or welfare work.

Vigorous sporting activity during the four-week period
before interview at age 36 years was slightly more often
reported by men (39 per cent) than by women (36 per cent),
and very similar proportions of men (6 per cent) and women (5
per cent) had taken such exercise as frequently as three or more
times during this period. Participation in vigorous sports,
however often, increased significantly in both sexes with
increasing educational level, rising from below half the
population with no educational qualifications (36 per cent of
men with no qualifications and 34 per cent of women) to
significantly higher proportions of those with university
degrees and equivalents (55 per cent of men and 51 per cent of
women).

## MARRIAGE AND CHILDREN

### (a) Marriage

By age 36 years all but 10 per cent of men and 6 per cent of
women had married at least once. More than half of first
marriages took place whilst study members were aged 19–24
years, and although men and women with qualifications in
further or higher education married later than others, even
within the late marrying group there was conformity to the
overall pattern that those from manual social families of origin
were first married at earlier ages than those from non-manual
families.

By 36 years of age 14 per cent of men and 17 per cent of
women had separated or divorced. This was most common of

all in women from manual families of origin (19 per cent of
them) who had tended to be the first to marry. Divorce was
much more frequent amongst those with lowest or with no
educational qualifications, and they too had been inclined to
marry early. It is therefore not likely that the true picture of the
risk of separation and divorce can be seen until a sufficiently
high average number of years of marriage has been achieved by
those who first married at later ages. But so far by this age men
and women who divorced were themselves significantly more
prone than others to have had parents who divorced (Wadsworth 1984). It cannot be known from information available in
this study how far the increased risk of divorce amongst those
whose parents had divorced may be the result of a precipitous
marriage, perhaps brought about by emotional vulnerability,
perhaps because of problems of income among offspring in
divorced families, or because divorce was seen as a possible
way of managing emotional problems, which themselves
might well be more frequent in this group of people who
already seem to be more emotionally vulnerable.

Although it is sometimes said that education tends to
separate offspring from their families of origin, there was a
significant tendency for men and women to marry others from
similar social class backgrounds, whatever their educational
attainment. Choice of husband was also associated with
women's height, in that of the women who married, the taller
were more likely than others to marry men in higher social
classes than themselves (Wadsworth 1986a). This is not a
finding peculiar to this study (Illsley and Kincaid 1963). Tallest
women tended also to be those with highest educational
qualifications (Wadsworth 1986a).

### (b) Children

By the age of 35 years 89 per cent of women and 82 per cent of
men had become a parent of one or more children. The highest
average (mean) numbers of children by this age were 2.04 born
to women from manual class families of origin, as compared
with an average of 1.86 children born to women from non-
manual families. The birth of the first child happened earlier in
life to men and women with the lowest educational qualifications,

and took place at increasingly later average ages as the
level of qualifications increased; even so, whatever the level of
qualifications achieved those from manual class families of
origin were inclined to be parents at a younger average age
than others. Men who were ambitious ubout work tended to
become fathers later than those who were less ambitious
(Kiernan and Diamond 1983).

Women who gave birth to their first child before age 25 years
were the most inclined to have parents who had married at a
relatively early age, who had the minimum of education, to
come from a relatively large family of origin, of low social class,
and they were themselves significantly inclined to have
achieved no educational qualifications (Kiernan and Diamond
1983). The younger the woman at the age of her first birth the
more exaggerated were these characteristics. Conversely,
women without children were significantly more likely to
come from small non-manual social class families with at least
one well-educated parent, to have achieved a further or higher
educational qualification themselves, and to have occupational
ambition (Kiernan and Diamond 1983). Among the women
who first gave birth during their teenage years the majority (57
per cent) conceived after marriage, a quarter (26 per cent)
conceived before marriage but gave birth afterwards, and 17
per cent gave birth outside marriage. For a number of reasons,
including under-reporting of pre-marital births, the exclusion
of the illegitimate from this study's follow-up, and more recent
changes in sexual behaviour of young people, these figures
may be an underestimate of what is happening today. But
amongst the women who gave birth before marriage and
during their teenage years, only 13 of the 40 women followed
up had had their child adopted, and by age 26 years only one
woman was bringing up her child alone. Kiernan (1980)
pointed out that 'Pregnant teenagers in this birth cohort did not
have the option of legal termination of their pregnancies.'
Teenage mothers who conceived their first birth after marriage
were most often girls from manual social class families who
married men from very similar home and educational backgrounds. By contrast those teenagers who conceived their first
birth before marriage were far more varied in their background
and their choice of spouse (Kiernan 1980).

## HOUSING

At age 36 years all but 10 per cent of the study population lived in a house or bungalow; most of those who lived in flats had unfurnished accommodation (7 per cent), and 1 per cent lived in lodging houses or institutions. Three-quarters (75 per cent) of study members owned or were buying their accommodation. The most usual form of renting at that time (1982) was from a local authority (14 per cent) rather than a private landlord (3 per cent). Only a very small proportion of people (1 per cent) shared their kitchen, lavatory, or bathroom facilities with another household, and practically everyone (98 per cent) had hot water on tap. However, 5 per cent felt unhappy with the district in which they lived, and 4 per cent were unhappy with their accommodation; those who felt discontented were significantly more often those from lower social classes and with little or no educational attainment.

Contrasts of housing circumstances of study members with that of their parents are given in Chapter 7.

## LIFE REVIEW

At 36 years most men (95 per cent) and women (94 per cent) felt that so far 'life had been good' to them, and this feeling was significantly more often expressed by those with good educational qualifications than by others. But these best-educated men and women were also more inclined to wish that, on looking back, things had been different in their family life. For the 36 per cent of women who wished things had been different the most common concern was about the ill health or death of a parent, then, in order of frequency, a wish that their own childhood had been more harmonious, that their upbringing had been less strict, that their parents had not separated or divorced, that they had not married their first husband, and that they had not been an only child. The 29 per cent of men who wished things had been different also most often wished that a parent or parents had not died or did not now suffer ill health; next came the wish that they had not married their first wife, that their parents had been more concerned for them, that they had not separated or divorced, that their childhood had been more harmonious, and that they had not been only children.

Similar proportions of men (38 per cent) and women (32 per cent) wished that things had been different in their working life, but much higher percentages (54 per cent of women and 47 per cent of men) wished that things had been different in their education. Mostly people wished that they had had more career advice (19 per cent of men and 16 per cent of women), as well as regretting that they had not stayed on longer at school and gained more qualifications, or gone to university.

In looking forward, however, differences between views of men and women were much greater. Those who were in paid employment were asked about promotion. Far more men (56 per cent) than women (23 per cent) said that they wanted promotion, and this degree of difference between the sexes was found whatever the level of education achieved. There were also proportionately many more men (55 per cent) than women (27 per cent) who felt that chances of promotion in their present occupation were reasonably or very good. This was hardly surprising in view of the evidently low level of enthusiasm which parents and teachers had shown towards daughters going on to further or higher education.

## CONCLUSIONS

Discussions about the importance of education which had taken place during preparations for the 1944 Education Act divided the benefits into those to be gained by the individual and those which would ensure a continuing supply of appropriately skilled labour (see Chapter 1). This study's findings showed benefits gained in both of these respects.

For individuals educational qualifications not only increased the chance of a relatively high income and a salaried occupation, but were also associated with greater receptivity to new ideas in health education, a wider range of leisure time interests, and a greater likelihood of active participation in sports and in activities in the local community.

Benefits in terms of a skilled labour force were difficult to evaluate. Average number of years spent in full-time education have increased in comparison with earlier times. The proportion of those with educational qualifications has risen at every level of qualification, and this is an indicator of how effectively the labour force has been transformed from the pre-war predominantly skilled manual basis to the post-war basis of professional, salaried, technical, sales and administrative occupations (Goldthorpe *et al.* 1980, Price and Bain 1988). In this study population born in 1946 39 per cent of men and 26 per cent of women attained qualifications at A level or equivalent and above; in the follow-up study of those born in 1958 the corresponding proportion was 42 per cent of men and 29 per cent of women (Fogelman 1985). An estimate of the proportions of occupations requiring this level of qualification can be gained from the national representative sample of the 1987 British election survey which showed that 32 per cent of men and 23 per cent of women were employed in higher and lower service class occupations (on the short Goldthorpe scale: Heath, personal communication). By this criterion a sufficient proportion of the men and women in the 1946 and the 1958 birth study were qualified for such occupations.

In addition to benefits for the individual and for the community the increase in the number of years of education experienced by many more people than in earlier times is likely to increase the population receptive to new ideas, as the findings on acceptance of new ideas in health show, and gradually to increase the proportion of those with a concern for education and an appreciation of 'book learning'; further evidence for this is given in Chapter 7.

Those who had no educational qualifications, or only the minimum, but who also had relatively high test scores and were ambitious, tended to achieve responsible positions in their work, although not all occupations were open to them because of their lack of qualifications. In this respect the talent they had shown in childhood was not wasted, but some individual and community benefits which might have followed the experience of higher and further education were probably lost.

During these early adult years some important aspects of health showed both a considerable social class difference and links with earlier life. Risks of death and serious illness were greatest for those who had been brought up in the lowest social classes, and so were chances of relatively high blood pressure, poor respiratory health, obesity, being overweight, and shortness of stature.

Adverse health habits in smoking, eating, and alcohol consumption were also more common among those in the lower social classes and in those who had been in lower social class families in childhood. Although in general the experience of a rise in social class between childhood and own adult life, and gaining educational qualifications were associated with improvement in these health habits, this was not invariably so. Sex differences in health habits were also striking, and proportionately more women than men took less than the recommended intakes of fibre, iron, calcium, and vitamin C. These differences have important implications not only for present day health in middle life but, looking forward, they may well also be part of the process of perpetuation of sex and social class differences in the longer term. In this study population it is notable that the smoking and eating habits of those who had been in lower social classes all their lives were most similar to the habits of their parent's generation, who were young adults at the time when smoking was not seen as carrying a health risk, and when dietary habits were different in many respects.

The suggestion was made in the early years of the National Health Service that the maternity and child welfare services in the community should be reduced (see conclusions to Chapter 3), but on the basis of findings from this study Douglas and Blomfield (1958) suggested instead that these aspects of the service should be developed. Now the findings from this and other studies on the importance of child health to health in adult life all show the value of investment in child health. Mothers and young children must also have the benefits of good housing and nutrition if health in childhood is to be properly cared for, and the trend of increasing poverty and homelessness since the 1960s (see the introduction to this and the previous chapter) is a serious obstacle to achieving this aim.

In adult health signs of anxiety and depression in early middle life were, like problems with physical health, linked with recent and current experience and with childhood. They were more than twice as common in women as in men, and of greater prevalence than high blood pressure at age 36. Links with childhood were found through relatively high neuroticism and anti-social behaviour in adolescence, and in the childhood experience of what were disturbing events for some members of the study population, for instance parental divorce. Possibly these long-term links with parental divorce were the results of differences in behaviour used in coping with emotional stress, which may have been brought about by such a stressful experience, or perhaps they were associated with consequent changes in self-image, in the family's financial and housing circumstances, and in their own reduced chances of good educational attainment.

Links between childhood and adult life do not necessarily imply a fixed, irrevocable, or unchanging effect. It is possible to recover from some kinds of problems that have put an individual on the wrong track, for example by taking educational courses or in changing dietary and exercise habits or professional help, even though it may take a great deal of personal effort to reverse a trend or to solve a problem originating in earlier life. The influence of an earlier experience may also be changed through later experience as well as through intervention, as studies of emotional risk have shown.

There were many differences between the generations of the study members and their parents in the material circumstances of life and in the nature and availability of work and leisure time activities, in attitudes to sexual and marital behaviour and to the gainful employment of women, and in chances of good health and long life. But there were also, for the individual, strong links between the generations in the sense that the imprint of childhood was found in adult life in occupation, income, marriage, leisure time activities, health, health related habits in adult life, and in the nature of the relationship between study members and their parents.

# 7
## Generation Differences

### INTRODUCTION

By the late 1980s the changes in many aspects of life in Britain since the end of the Second World War amounted to a considerable difference between the generation of those who were children in 1946 and their offspring. There were also striking differences in the circumstances, attitudes, and expectations of those who were parents in 1946 and their parents before them, especially in ideas about bringing up children, as illustrated at the beginning of Chapter 3.

Now it seems almost natural that there should be differences between generations. Gellner (1964) summarized the expectation of change: 'Life has come to be lived on an upward slope. Improvement is both anticipated and required. This is sometimes an explicit doctrine, but generally a tacit assumption, the recognition of a manifest truth.' (p. 4)

It seems now also to be almost a natural assumption that life should comprise a series of upward steps, in education, in occupation, and in the accumulation of possessions and wealth, a series of progressions that individuals and society are both expected to make. This is perhaps associated with our Western, linear concept of time passing in life and in history, contrasted by Butler (1989) with the older view of time passing in a cyclical fashion, marked for example by the liturgical calendar or the annual round of the agricultural year. Connerton (1989) described the denial of recurrence in life as a principle of modernity.

Such expectations of change and the differences between generations matter, not least because they must to some degree be anticipated in future policy planning.

There have been confusions among policy makers in medicine, for example about the necessary numbers of medical students (see the introduction to Chapter 5), and about the extent to which medical services should be hospital based (see discussion in Chapter 3). In education there were comparable problems about the methods appropriate to make available equitable opportunities for attainment, as well as the desirability of achieving equality of opportunity (see introductions to Chapters 4 and 5).

Some degree of anticipation of generation difference is possible using readily available information. For example, in spite of an increasing expectation of length of life and a falling death rate, the birth rate has remained at or very close to the replacement level, and it is evident that the proportion of the elderly in the national population will in future rise. The fall in the proportions who worked in manual occupations in 1951 (72 per cent of men and 64 per cent of women) compared with 1981 (58 per cent of men and 44 per cent of women) (Halsey 1987), forecasts an increase in health problems associated with sedentary occupations. But the link between such structural changes and people's attitudes and demands in everyday life is hard to understand and even harder to predict.

In this chapter examples are given of differences and associations between the generations of people in this study. Information is taken from questions asked of study members' parents about themselves and the families from which they came, and about study members when they were children, as well as from questions asked of members themselves. Study members also gave information about how they were bringing up their first born when the child was 4 years old, and again at 8 years. All these sources of information are used in this chapter.

## HEALTH

As poverty and atmospheric pollution were reduced and improvements made in housing, purchasing power, and the National Health Service made medical care freely available, it was widely expected that the levels of both ill health and demand for medical care would fall. Beveridge put this forward as something to be expected in due course, following the establishment of the National Health Service. However, the great increase in what medicine could do was not foreseen, and the range of advances in pharmacology, surgery, diagnostic techniques, physical medicine, and public health briefly described in earlier chapters, helped to reduce infection and chances of premature death. Improvements in nutrition and housing contributed also to this change. However, increases in the length of life, and the consequent rise in prevalence of chronic diseases and the disorders of later life showed the need to examine the natural history of such conditions, and the possibility of a long developmental phase in many of the serious illnesses of later life. Thus early detection and treatment in a wide range of conditions were increasingly accepted as proper concerns for medical care. The growing proportion of the elderly in the national population described in the introduction to Chapter 6, emphasizes the importance of these changes and increases in requirement for care.

The scale of improvements in health may be seen in the gains in life expectancy at birth shown in table 7.1. Expectations of years of life at the time of birth improved greatly over the three generations in the study, and particularly in the time between the birth of study members' parents and the birth of study members themselves. The effect of improvements in health can also be seen in the gains of life expectation among survivors to age 40 years in the parents' generation.

Comparisons of health in childhood between generations in this study show the complexity of the changes which have taken place. The establishment of specialist medical and nursing staff for child care, and improvements in ideas about how to treat children in hospital, have ended the practices, common in the 1940s, of keeping children in adult wards and of severely restricted visiting hours. In 1959 the Platt Committee was concerned with care of children in hospital, with their continuing education, and with provision for mothers to stay in hospital with young and very sick children; the National Association for the Welfare of Children in Hospital was founded in 1961. But 'As late as 1970 some children's wards had notices proclaiming "Parents may visit on Saturdays and Sundays between 4 and 5 p.m."' (Meadow 1988). These improvements were necessary not only because earlier care had not in these respects been good, but also because increasing numbers of children received hospital treatment. Between

TABLE 7.1 *Expectations of life at birth and at 40 years, and gains in expectations, for males and females in three generations of the United Kingdom population*

| | Study members' parents' generation | | Study members' own generation | Study members' children's generation | |
|---|---|---|---|---|---|
| | 1901 | 1931 | 1951[a] | 1971 | 1981 |
| *Expectation of years of life at birth in each year* | | | | | |
| Males | 48 | 58 | 66 | 67 | 70 |
| Females | 52 | 62 | 72 | 75 | 76 |
| *Expectation of age at death among those born in the given year and surviving to age 40 years* | | | | | |
| Males | 67 | 69 | 71 | 72 | 72 |
| Females | 69 | 72 | 75 | 77 | 78 |
| *Gains in expectation of years more life after age 40 years compared with expectation at birth* | | | | | |
| Males | 19 | 11 | 5 | 5 | 2 |
| Females | 17 | 10 | 3 | 2 | 2 |

[a] Year nearest to 1946 for which national data are available.

*Source: Social Trends* (1987).

birth and age 4 years, that is between 1946 and 1950, 139 per thousand first born study children were admitted to hospital (Douglas 1975): the comparable rate of admission of their first born offspring during the 1970s and early 1980s was 200 per thousand (Wadsworth 1985). Even though the average number of days spent in hospital during any one admission fell from 24 in the late 1940s to 8 in the following generation, almost a quarter (23 per cent) of hospital admissions in the second generation were for eight days or more. Greatest increases were found in admissions for injury, genito-urinary conditions, diseases of early infancy, and ill-defined conditions; rates of hospital admission fell for infectious diseases (Wadsworth 1985). Reasons for the rise in hospital admissions include the growing ability to correct such problems as squints, and to head off the development of later illness, as well as the changes in medical practice, seen for instance in the intergenerational fall in tonsillectomy and adenoidectomy rates from 20 per thousand in members of this study in childhood to 7 per thousand in children born in 1958 (Calnan *et al.* 1978). It is also said that there has been a growth in willingness to admit children, and sometimes to keep them in hospital longer than is strictly necessary for medical reasons, in order to ease family circumstances, or to provide better care than can sometimes be given at home, or to guard against the development of complications.

Some conditions have a strikingly changed prevalence in the offspring of study members; for example medically treated eczema rose from 2 to 12 per thousand children, and asthma from 6 to 19 per thousand. Prevalence of lower respiratory illness before the age of 2 years, however, fell from 250 per thousand of the study members to 130 per thousand among their first born children (Mann *et al.* forthcoming). Comparisons between the national birth cohort studies showed juvenile diabetes up to age 11 years to have risen from 0.2 to 1.3 per thousand children (Stewart-Brown *et al.* 1983). Comparing the generations in this study at age 7 years obesity had increased from 20 to 40 per thousand boys, and from 38 to 63 per thousand girls. Interpretation of such information must be cautious; definitions of illnesses may have changed between generations both in parents' and in professionals' ideas, for example, about the degree of ezcema which needs to be treated; caution in interpretation is also necessary because actual numbers of cases of some serious conditions, for instance diabetes, are relatively small. Nevertheless, these findings illustrate the scale of change in supply and requirement for care during the years since the National Health Service began.

As well as these kinds of changes in rates of particular illnesses it is important to emphasize the increased benefits to child health of the improvements in environment and medical care. Just as improvements in health and nutrition are believed to have increased the average height of the study population of men and women when compared with their parents (Kuh and Wadsworth 1989), it is clear that the average height of children born twelve years after this study's population, in 1958, is again greater still, although significant differences between social classes persist (Kuh *et al*. forthcoming, Rona *et al*. 1978). Height is generally taken to be an indicator of health, and probably reflects the state of physical development in body systems and organs. Intergenerational increases in average height reflect, therefore, the great general improvement in health. Improvements in home circumstances, in medical care, in preventive medicine, and in nutrition have also meant a childhood with less risk of death, less infectious illness, less long-term debilitating illness, and therefore fewer long-term effects of such conditions (the Court Report 1976, Court and Alberman 1988, Forfar 1988). Advances in diagnosis and in surgery have also reduced the potentially disabling effects of conditions such as congenital deformation of the hips and phenylketonuria (Forfar 1988) and the stigmatizing aspects of such problems as squints, injuries, and harelips.

Improvements in care have, however, not only increased the current work of health services, but have had the effect of increasing the future workload as well, at least simply in numerical terms, as improved health and reduced risk of death enable more people to live a full lifespan. The extent to which improvements in care and environment have had this effect on child health has not yet been accurately determined. However, now that the risk of death in the first year of life has dropped so much, falling in England and Wales from 36 deaths per thousand live births in 1946–50 to 9 in 1988, and now that very low birth weight babies are much more likely to survive (neonatal death rates in babies of birth weights of 2,500 g. or less in 1953 in England and Wales were 154.4 per thousand live births compared with 57.9 in 1981: Macfarlane and Mugford 1984), the question of their health in later life becomes important. Research is currently investigating the infant growth and development and the learning abilities during the early school years of very low birth weight babies in comparison with others.

However, as in housing the improvements in child health have not been uniformly distributed across the national population, and it is evident that there are still wide social class differences in growth, as described above, in nutrition (Nelson and Naismith 1979), in chances of survival (Blaxter 1981, Townsend and Davidson 1982, Macfarlane and Mugford 1984) and in risks of ill health (Blaxter 1987, Whitehead 1987, Mann *et al.* forthcoming).

Some aspects of these improvements, persisting social differences, and changes in child health and survival will move on in the population as it ages, and be seen in health in the early adult years, in mid-life, and eventually in old age. This aspect of intergenerational change in health is discussed in the following chapter.


## HOUSING

Government and other statistics make clear the huge national improvements in housing conditions which have taken place since the end of the Second World War. This has been a remarkable achievement since not only has the British population grown by about six million since that time but the number of private households has grown even faster as couples are no longer prepared to share housing either with their parents in their early years of marriage or partnership, or with their elderly parents in later life. The rising trend in divorce and separation has also created new smaller households and so too has the trend for teenagers to want earlier independence from their families, and both of these changes put pressure on the housing stock. In the early post-war years plans for housing were, like those for education and the care of the nation's health, of visionary quality. In the years since then the stock of housing has greatly increased, and planned and expected standards of interior space, plumbing, heating, and light have all risen (Burnett 1978). Between 1946 and the early 1970s twenty-two new towns were approved in England and Wales, and the proportion of dwellings owner-occupied rose from 26 per cent in 1945 to 63 per cent in 1986. Increasing expectations were, however, associated also with dissatisfaction with some aspects of new housing provision, particularly tower blocks, and there remains still a national housing shortage, especially for those with lowest incomes and with poor prospects in occupation. The findings of this study show that the general trends of improvement in housing circumstances and in chances of home ownership have not been evenly distributed throughout the population.

When study members were two years old, in 1948, almost half (44 per cent) lived in homes without running hot water, where water was heated in coppers or kettles. Some instances of the poverty of home circumstances in these immediate post-war years have been given in Chapter 3, but another example will act as a reminder of how bad things could be. Having interviewed a mother in 1950 a health visitor wrote on the bottom of the form

The above premises are condemned by the local sanitary authority, being a stable and a barn made into a home. It has an old-fashioned fireplace fitted and a tap but otherwise no conveniences. It has a leaking roof, damp walls, insufficient window space and the interior walls are unplastered. There is no washbasin, bath, copper or running hot water and all slops have to be emptied outside. The family, which is crowded at 2+ persons per room, consists of two pre-school children and two school children. The father, a building labourer, is unemployed. (Douglas and Blomfield 1958: 42)

By the time study children were 11 years old (in 1957) the proportion of families who lived without running hot water had fallen to 21 per cent, falling again to 15 per cent in 1961, to 3 per cent in 1972, and then to 2 per cent in 1982. Similarly the proportion of families who shared a bathroom fell from 39 per cent in 1948 to 2 per cent in 1982.

There were great increases in proportions of people who owned or were buying their houses. Whilst the study members were children those proportions rose from 24 per cent in 1948 to 40 per cent in 1961. However, social group differences in home ownership were very uneven. Whereas 27 per cent of non-manual families first became owner-occupiers during these years the comparable figure for manual families was 15 per cent, and the total proportion of manual families who lived in owner-occupied homes in 1961 was still little more than a half that already achieved by non-manual families thirteen years before. This is not to say that home circumstances had not improved for manual social group families, particularly in terms of the facilities described in the previous paragraph, and almost half of manual group families (48 per cent) had moved into council houses from tenancy with private landlords, as compared with only a quarter (25 per cent) in council housing in 1948.

By 1982, when the study members were 36 years old, a comparison of the housing tenure of those who had children with the tenure of their parents in 1948, and then later in 1961, showed the scale of the increase in owner-occupied accommodation. It had nearly doubled between 1948 and 1961, and then increased from 40 per cent in 1961 to 76 per cent in 1982. However, the gap betwen the social classes in home ownership during the years 1948 to 1961 continued into the following generation. In 1982 87 per cent of non-manual social class families with children owned or were buying their accommodation compared with 71 per cent of manual families. Chances of being in owner-occupied accommodation at age 36 years were much greater for those in the non-manual social groups. Within social groups the higher the level of educational attainment by the study member, the greater the chances of home ownership at age 36 years. Whatever the social group of family of origin higher educational attainment gave an added likelihood of home ownership.

This picture of the differential influence of education in this generation and social group in the previous generation is similar to that found in the study of income described in Chapter 6. Low educational attainment was associated in both social groups with a risk of intergenerational loss of home ownership.

The signs of poverty, evident in information about housing

when the men and women in the study were born in 1946, were greatly reduced by the time of their children's birth. In income this may be seen in family studies of poverty in York in 1950, and in their children in the mid-1970s. Defining poverty as the percentage income above or below the National Assistance Scale in 1950 and the Supplementary Benefit Scale in 1975–8, it was found that although half (48 per cent) of those in low income families in 1950 were still poor in 1975–8, a third had achieved an intermediate income and 18 per cent could be described as 'comfortably off' (Atkinson *et al.* 1983). Although chances of remaining in the lowest income groups in these York families were greatest for those with the least income in 1950, nevertheless half of those who began in poverty (52 per cent) had achieved higher levels of income a generation later. In these families Rowntree and Lavers (1951) did not find unemployment to be a cause of poverty in 1950, but a generation later 29 per cent of poverty was found to have been caused by unemployment (Atkinson *et al.* 1983).

## CHANGING BELIEFS AND ATTITUDES

The great majority (87 per cent) of the study population recalled in early adulthood, at age 26 years, that they had been brought up in some kind of faith or religious denomination. This was much more common amongst those from non-manual families with well-educated parents (93 per cent) than amongst manual families in which parents had the minimum of education (47 per cent). By 26 years religious affiliation was reported by 67 per cent of the study population, and those most inclined to have lost or changed the beliefs in which they had been brought up were the men and women who had been best educated (Wadsworth and Freeman 1983). This has been found in other studies, and is what Stark and Glock (1968) in their study of American populations described as the 'up and out' phenomenon. It may reflect how much easier it is for those who take higher education courses to leave home, and therefore to change their pattern of life from that of their parents, as well as the tendency for higher education to encourage independent thought and to be a source of pressure to conform to the institution's student norm. Confident expectation of future change of social class was also seen much more in those educated at universities than in others (Wadsworth and Freeman 1983).

The differences in movement away from the family of upbringing were seen also in voting. At levels of educational achievement below that of university, 72 per cent of men and women said that at age 26 years they had voted in a recent national election in the same way as their father; but only 57 per cent of those who had been to university or equivalent institution had voted as their fathers did (Wadsworth and Freeman 1983).

There were therefore at the age of 26 years signs of a drift away from beliefs and attitudes of the family of origin apparently accelerated by the experience of higher education. If this was an age effect, in the sense that the observed changes were an assertion of independence and an exploration appropriate to early adult life then correspondingly, later in life, there may be some degree of return to religious beliefs among those who had in early adulthood moved away from the beliefs of their families of origin.

In fact, by age 36 years there had been some overall reduction in proportions of believers, and by this age 54 per cent of men (as compared with 60 per cent of men at age 26 years) and 69 per cent of women (compared with 75 per cent ten years earlier) said that they had a religious belief or faith, whether or not they went to church. Percentages of those who had given up religious belief during the ten years whilst they were aged 26 to 36 years were greatest in those with no educational qualifications (29 per cent of such men and 24 per cent of women) and least in those with university degrees and equivalents (13 per cent in men and 7 per cent in women). During the same period the proportions of those who had acquired a religious belief were greatest among those with degrees and equivalents (18 per cent in men and 12 per cent among women) and least in those with no educational qualifications (11 per cent in men and 8 per cent of women).

Thus, although those who went to university or took equivalent level courses had been the most inclined to give up belief in early adult life, by their mid-30s they had become the group who reported the most rapid return to belief. Those who by age 36 years had gained belief, having been non-believers at 26 years, had a significant tendency to have been brought up, as children, in a religious belief or faith.

## EDUCATION

The wartime and post-war debate about whether education was to be seen as primarily for the development of the individual, or for the supply of skilled workers (Barnett 1986, and see the introduction to Chapter 1), has of course continued, but for parents the choice of education for their children is based on other, more immediate concerns. This difference between the public debate and parental wishes is revealed in the public discussion about the provision of pre-school education, and in the study members' views on the value of nursery and play-group experience for their first born child.

Educational philosophers and theorists have played an important part in the origins of the differences in this debate. Froebel wrote that 'every human being, even as a child, must be recognized, acknowledged, and fostered as a necessary and essential member of humanity' (Blackstone 1971: 13), and Bertrand Russell (1926) asserted that

the nursery school, if it became universal, could, in one generation, remove the profound differences in education which at present divide the classes, could produce a population all enjoying the mental and physical development which is now confined to the most fortunate and could remove the terrible deadweight of disease and stupidity and malevolence which now makes progress so difficult. (p. 181)

In her history of pre-school education Blackstone (1971) describes how psychological work on the development of speech and language and the foundations of intelligence strengthened arguments for pre-school education for all children, which at the beginning of the century had been seen as only for the 'physical and medical nurture of the debilitated child' (Blackstone 1971: 53). Van der Eyken (1974) went so far as to extend the idea of the value of pre-school education by arguing that

However enlightened, financially secure and socially aware the parents, however affluent the neighbourhood, the home environment provided for the pre-school child is inadequate if measured in absolute terms against the child's potential and intellectual development during this period. (Van der Eyken 1974: 35)

Studies of teachers' views also find a change in attitudes over time, described by Taylor *et al.* (1972) as a generation gap. Their sample of local authority nursery school teachers saw as their purpose 'the social education of the young, particularly that form of social education through which personality and character begin to develop' (p. 60). Taylor *et al* (1972) say that older teachers in their study 'may not yet see clearly the relevance of educational sociology to the professional education of the nursery teacher' (p. 60), whereas younger teachers apparently thought this of the greatest importance.

The views of parents are harder to come by. In a study of children born in Nottingham John and Elizabeth Newson (1968) found social class differences in mothers' ideas about the form care should take during the pre-school years.

These mothers [non-manual], mainly in the professional class, are the ones who organise play-groups and tea-parties, pay for private nursery school education (but not for day nurseries), keep a close watch on their children's play, and in general expect to *provide* suitable company, just as they provide food, clothing and education: the child is not expected to find his own friends or else do without. For these mothers, the principles which they are trying to lay down at this age are not those of survival through aggressive competition [as previously illustrated with reports from manual workers' wives], but of peaceful co-existence, with the accent on peace. (p. 109).

At much the same time the Plowden Report (1967) noted that 'nursery school education on a large scale remains an unfulfilled promise' (para. 291), but in the years since then parental demand, in particular, has brought a great increase in provisions for pre-school education, especially in playgroups begun by parents (Osborn 1981). In this study of men and women born in 1946 82 per cent of their first born offspring had been to some kind of nursery or playschool by the time they were 4 years old, compared with 14 per cent of the study members themselves. Many mothers of the study population's first born offspring said that they wanted their children to go to nursery or playschool to increase their experience of playing with other children (41 per cent), and as a preparation for infant school (30 per cent); these proportions did not differ significantly between the social classes. There was no social class difference in the proportions of children going to local authority nurseries (25 per cent of children), but the chances of a child from a non-manual family going to a privately run pre-school group were greater (65 per cent of these children) than those for a child from a manual family (41 per cent) (Wadsworth 1981).

Pre-school facilities were of some importance and help to this sample of 1,676 first born offspring of study members. Mothers who saw their own parents or in-laws less often than once a month were the greatest users (89 per cent of the children of these mothers went to some kind of pre-school), compared with those who saw one or more of the child's grandparents at least once a week (76 per cent of these children went to pre-school).

Study members who chose to send their first born to any kind of pre-school had themselves generally been more successful at school than those who kept their children at home during their first four years. Study member parents whose children went to nursery or playschool had themselves been significantly more often assessed as hard workers by their primary school teachers, had achieved significantly higher average scores on the tests taken at 15 years, and were significantly better qualified. Looking back it was clear that the greater the amount of educational attainment in the two previous generations the greater was the likelihood of the study member's first born child going to a nursery or play-school, (Wadsworth 1981). This was foreseen before study members became parents when, in writing about educational attainment at secondary school, Douglas *et al.* (1968) suggested that

education widens the horizon for each generation and this in turn affects the level of attainment of the children, shaping their ambitions for the future. Parents who have themselves enjoyed a high standard of education see the necessity of education for the future employment of their children while others, who have failed to get the education they aimed at for themselves, try to ensure that the chances they have missed will be taken up by their children. (p. 90)

Study members who were optimistic about their own and

other's opportunities of changing social class were also significantly more inclined, whatever their current class, to send their first born to some kind of pre-school (Wadsworth 1981).

Mothers whose children went to nursery or playschool differed from others in reports of their play and communications with their first born; they were significantly more inclined than other mothers to say, when the child was 4 years old, that they generally reacted without anger to bed-wetting, that they relatively less often used punishment, particularly threats not to love the child any more or to send the child away from home, and they less often reported threatening to spank or actually having spanked the child. They also reported significantly more story-telling than other mothers, more joining in with games, and more expressions of affection between themselves and the child, and they less often felt that their child was highly strung or particularly excitable (Wadsworth 1986*b*).

By contrast, children of mothers who seemed to be less communicative with their first born, who had no educational qualifications and the minimum of years at school, were the most likely to be from a relatively poor family and to be in need of the extra attention and encouragement that pre-school would have provided; they were also those least likely to have gone to nursery or playschool of any kind.

When asked about generation differences in childhood study member parents reported more than anything else that they had tried to achieve better communication with their children than their parents had managed with them. Whilst this may have had the effect of bringing parents and children closer in some ways, it may also have added to the impression that childhood passes more quickly now than in previous generations. Such closer communication, the enormous increase in exposure to television and radio, and the commercial value of children in the market for clothes and other goods which change with fashion, have all helped to draw children nowadays faster towards apparent independence than the children of previous generations. In his historical review of children's literature Carpenter (1985) described the work of the English 'Golden Age' authors from Kingsley and Lewis Carroll to J. M. Barrie, Beatrix Potter, A. A. Milne, and Kenneth

Grahame, and finally in the years after the Second World War through to Tolkein and C. S. Lewis, 'who believed in childhood as a self-contained state which is ultimately preferable to maturity' (p. 215). Carpenter compared their work with the particular concern of modern children's fiction for their readers to come to grips with the world: 'the modern British children's author is actually encouraging children to grow up' (p. 216); he concludes that, in these terms, 'the child is no longer occupying a separate world' (p. 218).

The speed of intergenerational change was also revealed in this study's preparatory work for comparisons of verbal test scores attained by the study population when they were 8 years old and by their first born child at the same age; the tests are described in Appendix 2. When the study of first born offspring began in 1974 two words ('muslin' and 'guineas') in the 1954 vocabulary test had become too obscure for this purpose, and two of the words considered to be quite difficult in 1954 ('antique' and 'secretary') were found to be much more readily understood in 1974; the ranking of words in order of difficulty of reading and comprehension was also changed to accord with current speech.

Comparison of verbal attainment by the age of 8 years in the two generations showed the significantly higher average scores attained by offspring who took the tests in the 1970s and early 1980s, as compared with the average scores their parents achieved in 1954. Figure 7.1 shows that the rise in test scores between the generations was accounted for more by improvements in average scores of boys and girls from manual social class families than by improvements in scores of those from non-manual families. All the differences in averages between the generations, within sex and social class groups, were statistically significant, with the exception of the rises in non-manual boys' and girls' sentence completion scores. In the study members' generation girls' average scores in reading and in sentence completion were significantly higher than those of boys, but by the next generation there were no significant sex differences in the scores within social classes. Figure 7.1 also shows that, despite the intergenerational increase in average verbal attainment scores and the shrinking proportion of the population in the manual social classes, the average scores of

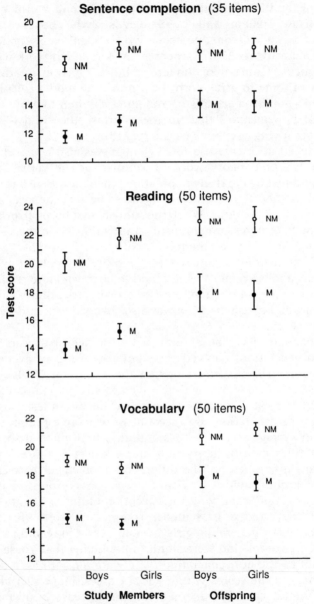

FIG. 7.1 Average scores (and confidence intervals) on tests taken at 8 years

offspring from manual social class families all remained significantly lower than those of offspring whose fathers or mothers were in non-manual occupations. Thus, although improvements in verbal attainment have been striking and the difference between the sexes has disappeared, nevertheless, like the great improvements in infant survival rates since the 1940s, these improvements have not been matched by an equivalent narrowing of differences between the social classes. It is important to improve the average scores of these children who have a poor start in life in this and in many other ways.

These average score increases were undoubtedly associated with improvements in parents' education and in education in primary schools, as well as with the much higher proportion of study population offspring who went to pre-school of some kind (82 per cent), compared with 14 per cent in the previous generation. Elimination of sex differences may show that parents', teachers' and pupils' expectations of girls' educational attainment are now as great as those for boys. Significantly higher average scores were achieved by children whose study member parent had attained relatively high scores on attainment tests and in examinations, by children who had been to pre-school of any kind, and by those whose mothers had been relatively stimulating and involved with them at age 4 years. But by far the most powerful effect on the child's verbal attainment score was the mother's achieved educational level. Once this had been taken into account the effects of going to nursery or playschool and of having a stimulating and involved mother played a small part in increasing verbal attainment. Nevertheless, pre-school attendance significantly raised the verbal attainment at 8 years of children whose mothers had seemed relatively under-stimulating four years before (Wadsworth 1986*b*).

Like improvements in health over the same period, it is evident that not all of this improvement in verbal attainment could be ascribed to the work of the services. Improvements in health and education have been influenced by increased parental concern and awareness of their child's development, which was itself a product of improvements in previous generations. Better communications of all kinds will also have helped to raise verbal attainment; for example the vocabulary used on television, as well as at pre-school, will be wider than that generally used at home for many children. The rising sales of books and printed material of all kinds also show the increased interest in literacy. Now we need to know whether this flood of communication and the apparent foreshortening of childhood threaten children's imagination and curiosity.

## FAMILY LIFE

At age 36 years a little over half (56 per cent) of men and women had both parents alive, 37 per cent had only one living parent, and 7 per cent had lost both parents through death. Non-manual class men and women were the most likely to have both parents alive, because of the social class differences in death rates.

At 36 years only 5 per cent of men and 2 per cent of women lived with their parent(s), and almost all of the study members who did so were single.

Among those with one or more surviving parent 10 per cent of study members of each sex rarely or never had contact with them. This was much more common in the best-educated group, that is those with qualifications at further or higher education levels. At its maximum, amongst these best-educated study members, 24 per cent of women had little or no contact with their parents compared with 15 per cent of men. Among those with no educational qualifications, by contrast, 7 per cent of men and 9 per cent of women rarely or never saw their parents. However, the majority (79 per cent of men and 77 per cent of women) saw their parents at least once every two weeks. Rates of contact with parents were not altered by the presence of children in the households of study members.

Pressures on children to grow up quickly and to escape from childhood and dependency, and the growing counter-pressures to continue in education with a consequently low income during the student years, have become more of a problem for those in the study members' generation who are parents than it was for parents at earlier times. Parents of study members had had to contend with the changes in ideas about bringing up children as they altered from the pre-war system of relatively clear aims and methods to be followed, to the less didactic post-war approach of advice to parents to help them decide for themselves what best to do (see Chapter 3). Now study members who are parents

have lived through a dramatic shift in the standards expected of them . . . Parents must also answer for the mental and moral character of their sons and daughters, despite influences from the street, the so-called peer group, the mass media and youth culture which children cannot escape, and with which parents cannot contend . . . Hoggart's working class family is romantically remote in the 1980s. (Halsey 1987: 112–14)

Hoggart (1957) had described his childhood in Leeds in the 1920s, but the circumstances of the study members' childhood in the late 1940s and 1950s now seem almost as remote. Material circumstances are much better, and holidays and travel are far more common because of the technological improvements in transport, the better terms and conditions of work, and the increase in purchasing power for the great majority. But parents and children are likely to live much further now from grandparents and other relations than they did in the 1950s, because of the demands of work, and are therefore less able to benefit from such contacts, and more subject to the strains of living in small close knit groups (Young and Willmott 1973). These family changes and the reasons for them have brought community change. What were once towns and villages in which many families had lived for two or more generations are now very different as children go away to further and higher education and to work, as adults' work may well involve commuting, and as older people move into or away from the town to retire. Comparison of the two studies of Banbury (Stacey 1960, Stacey *et al.* 1975) illustrates these changes, and weakening of the perceptions of social class barriers, a process which owes much to increases in standards of education as well as to improvements in mass communication.

Continuing high divorce and separation rates (see figure 3.1) are likely, according to the findings in this study of men and women born in 1946, to increase the risk of emotional problems among the children who experience such family change, and to increase the risk of long-term emotional difficulties and reduced chances in education and subsequent career choice, and even income (see Chapter 6). Compared with previous generations, however, children's experience of the emotional disruption brought by death of a parent or brother or sister is now much less as a result of the fall in death rates, but may be more difficult to cope with than at earlier times because of the tendency for grandparents and other family members to live too far for frequent contact.

Although information has been collected on satisfaction with past and current home and family life, with work and education, and self-assessments have been made of future prospects, nevertheless measures of other aspects of happiness have not so far proved possible; nor has an assessment of the role and power of conscience in middle life, which may be a link between childhood and adolescent family life and some kinds of decision taking in adult life.

## LABOUR MARKET CHANGE AND THE INDIVIDUAL

Just as comparisons of study members' educational attainment with that of their parents showed very large differences, so too did comparisons of employment in the two generations. During the years since the Second World War great changes in the country's methods of production, wealth generation, and marketing have required changes in the skills of the work-force in what must have been the greatest increase in the proportions of salaried and clerical workers since the Industrial Revolution required a corresponding revolution in literacy and in clerical ability. The scale of the change for men and women in this study is illustrated in table 7.2 by comparison of employment in the parents' generation in 1950 with that of the study members themselves in 1982, when they were 36 years old. As well as the large rise in unemployment in men and the large rise in the proportion of women employed, there has been a decrease in the proportion employed in manual work. Whereas 75 per cent of fathers had been in manual work in 1950 only 46 per cent of their sons were in 1982 and, reassuringly, the smallest proportional fall was amongst skilled workers. Among women there was a striking rise in the proportion employed, up from 26 per cent of mothers to 65 per cent of daughters, and although the proportions of manual workers

Table 7.2 *Employment and unemployment amongst study members and their parents[a]*

| Social class and employment status | 1950: Parents of study members | | 1982: Study members | |
|---|---|---|---|---|
| | Fathers (%) | Mothers (%) | Men (%) | Women (%) |
| Professional I | 2.7 | 1.2 | 8.2 | 0.8 |
| Salaried II | 11.6 | } 5.0 | 29.4 | 15.3 |
| Clerical IIINM non-manual[b] | 9.9 | | 9.3 | 24.0 |
| Skilled manual IIIM | 45.0 | | 33.0 | 4.5 |
| Semi-skilled IV | 19.8 | 19.4 | 10.7 | 13.5 |
| Unskilled V | 9.4 | | 1.4 | 4.5 |
| Not working but seeking work | } 1.5 | } 74.3 | 5.6 | 3.5 |
| Not working and not seeking work | | | 2.3 | 33.9 |
| Total (=100%) | 10,750 | 10,939 | 3,801 | 3,781 |

[a] Figures weighted to compensate for original sampling. Parents' jobs in this analysis were classified according to the Registrar-General's 1970 classification of occupations, and study members' jobs according to the 1980 classification.

[b] All the titles of social classes have been much abbreviated and this one, for example, also includes hairdressers, sales representatives, and many shop and restaurant workers, as well as clerks, cashiers, office machine operators, and secretaries.

changed very little, the proportion of women in salaried and clerical work rose from 5 per cent to 39 per cent across the generations. The proportion of women study members employed in professional occupations will probably increase a little more in future years, since this highest qualified group were the last to begin having children, and at 36 years 2 per cent of women who were not in paid work had educational qualifications at a level which would permit them to take up professional (social class I) occupations. But even if all these women worked in social class I occupations the percentage of all employed women in that category would still rise only to a maximum of 3 per cent compared with 8 per cent of men.

Such differences in the population's patterns of work was also a powerful source of generation difference within families. As office based employment and demands from the service industries increased, workers had to be recruited not only in the traditional way from that section of the population whose fathers had been in similar employment, but also from those who had grown up in working class families. More than half the men and women who were in professional, salaried, or clerical jobs (social classes I, II, III non-manual) at 36 years had been brought up in families where the father was a manual worker, as tables 7.3*a* and 7.3*b* show. Those who changed social class in this way, by moving from a manual class family of origin to non-manual occupation in their own working life at 36 years, amounted to a third (32 per cent) of employed men and almost half of employed women (45 per cent).

Generation differences in the nature of parents' and study members' employment represent a fundamental change. The fact that such changes could occur showed that there was an increased hope of release from a life of long, hard labour for those at the lowest end of the spectrum of occupations (Goldthorpe *et al* 1980), which had seemed much less likely to be a reality for many people in the parents' generation (Glass 1954).

Education has increasingly become the way in which the individual prepares for the new demand from employers for numeracy and literacy, compared with the now less prevalent on-the-job training schemes, such as apprenticeships, which were an important mechanism of social change for the individual in previous generations (Halsey *et al.* 1980, Goldthorpe *et al.* 1980). In the Goldthorpe study of men aged 20 to 64 in 1972, those who achieved better jobs and better status than their predominantly manual class fathers wrote of their good fortune in joining the labour force at a time when the demand for non-manual workers was high, and of their persistence in work and study in order to take the opportunities that these changes offered. But as this study of men and women born in 1946

TABLE 7.3a  *Women's employment and unemployment at 36 years, and the social class origins of those in each group (data weighted to adjust for sample selection described in Appendix 1)*

| Social class of family of origin (father's) when study member aged 4 years | Social class of study women's employment at age 36 years (%) | | | | | Not employed (%) | |
|---|---|---|---|---|---|---|---|
| | I and II^a | III non-manual | III manual | IV | V | seeking work | not seeking work |
| *Non-manual* | | | | | | | |
| I | 6.4 | 1.9 | 0.6 | 1.6 | — | 2.3 | 2.3 |
| II | 15.6 | 10.9 | 10.1 | 9.8 | 0.6 | 10.5 | 14.3 |
| III | 14.2 | 10.5 | 5.9 | 4.1 | 3.5 | 12.8 | 9.0 |
| *Manual* | | | | | | | |
| III | 36.9 | 47.9 | 33.1 | 48.3 | 42.4 | 39.8 | 38.7 |
| IV | 13.5 | 15.9 | 24.9 | 17.5 | 33.1 | 20.3 | 19.3 |
| V | 5.8 | 6.7 | 14.2 | 10.0 | 14.5 | 9.8 | 9.5 |
| Unknown | 7.6 | 6.3 | 11.2 | 8.6 | 5.8 | 4.5 | 6.8 |
| TOTAL(= 100%) | 607 | 907 | 169 | 509 | 172 | 133 | 1,284 |

^a Combined since only 29 women were in social class I occupations.

TABLE 7.3b  *Men's employment and unemployment at 36 years, and the social class origins of these in each group (data weighted to adjust for sample selection described in Appendix 1)*

| Social class of family of origin (father's) when study member aged 4 years | Social class of study men's employment at age 36 years (%) | | | | | | | Not employed (%) | |
|---|---|---|---|---|---|---|---|---|---|
| | I | II | I and II | III non-manual | III manual | IV | V | seeking work | not seeking work |
| *Non-manual* | | | | | | | | | |
| I | 11.3 | 3.0 | 4.8 | 2.3 | 1.0 | 0.5 | — | 0.9 | 1.1 |
| II | 17.7 | 20.7 | 20.1 | 9.3 | 5.9 | 4.9 | — | 5.2 | 19.3 |
| III | 16.7 | 13.0 | 13.8 | 13.3 | 6.6 | 2.7 | 1.8 | 4.2 | 13.6 |
| *Manual* | | | | | | | | | |
| III | 34.1 | 35.0 | 34.8 | 43.5 | 48.0 | 43.6 | 52.7 | 52.6 | 25.0 |
| IV | 10.3 | 15.9 | 14.7 | 23.7 | 20.8 | 25.4 | 14.5 | 16.4 | 14.8 |
| V | 4.5 | 5.5 | 5.3 | 3.7 | 8.8 | 13.3 | 16.4 | 15.0 | 23.9 |
| Unknown | 5.5 | 6.8 | 6.4 | 4.2 | 8.8 | 9.6 | 14.5 | 5.6 | 2.3 |
| TOTAL(= 100%) | 311 | 1,119 | 1,430 | 354 | 1,255 | 406 | 55 | 213 | 88 |

showed, persistence and success in education were associated with parents' concern for their children's education, which was in turn related to parents' own educational attainments, and was not equally distributed across all social groups. The family elements behind the educational attainment necessary for achievement of occupations in the non-manual classes helped to increase the proportion of those in non-manual jobs who came from manual social class families of origin, but the uneven class distribution of educational attainment and of concern for and interest in their children's education in parents of study members did not give such good chances of moving into social class occupations higher than those held by their fathers to those from the lowest social classes of origin as to those from highest classes, as Glass (1954) and Halsey *et al.* (1980) also found. For women in the study members' generation chances of such change were slimmer still, since their likelihood of further or higher educational attainment was generally much lower than that for men, in all social classes.

As in this study, Goldthorpe *et al.* (1980) found greater social participation and club membership among those in the service classes, that is among all those in non-manual occupations higher than the routinely clerical and administrative, and evidence that those who rose into the service classes tended to 'extend and diversify' their patterns of social involvement. In the Goldthorpe study no evidence was found, as others had expected, of social isolation in those who had risen in job status between the generations, and no evidence of problems of relationships with others in the class they joined. Looking further back in this study, to childhood, there is evidence of something like the process Goldthorpe *et al.* (1980) called 'anticipatory' change, in the increase in average test scores and in height among those whose fathers were then rising in social class (Douglas 1964, Kuh and Wadsworth 1989). Perhaps such changes were associated with an increasing optimism in the family, with increasing income, better nutrition, and a growing parental concern for educational attainment and similar success in their children.

## CONCLUSIONS

The rapid advances in medicine, technology, and industry, and in the average level of education attained in the years since the end of the Second World War brought very great differences between generations. These differences can be seen in improvements in housing, transport, and diet, as well as in increases in the purchasing power of many families, in changes in the nature of work and the work-force, in such socially important aspects of behaviour as marriage and divorce, in mass communications, and in the spread and acceleration of change in fashions in taste and entertainment.

Less visible are the differences in attitudes. Particularly striking has been the difference in perception of distance between the classes, and the reduction of fear of disapproval of authority seems to have lessened as Titmuss (1958) anticipated.

This study showed that intergenerational improvements in housing, health, and pre-school education benefited most those who had gained some educational qualifications, and those whose fathers had been in non-manual employment. Study members' parents with education beyond the minimum and with qualifications above those of basic school-leaving examinations had a particular concern for their children's education, and this was strongly associated ultimately with good educational attainment. Study members with this advantage went on, in their own lives, to become concerned about education, and their offspring had higher average test scores than others at the age of 8. An increased level of education in the study member was associated also with an increase in response to new ideas about own care of health, for example in diet and in smoking habits. Thus, like the study of poverty in York, it seems that the general rising levels of health, housing, and education during the period of the study were interlinked. Those who benefited most from the rise were those who began with some advantage, of which the most powerful was education. Those who benefited least had not attained educational qualifications, and had remained in low social class circumstances.

Generations in this study were both linked and separated by the changes in medicine, education, and occupations. They were linked in the sense that individuals' chances of good health, growth, and educational attainment were strongly associated with those of their parents. Children of parents with highest educational attainment were significantly more likely than others to continue on into further and higher education, and children of tall, healthy parents were themselves the most likely to be tall and relatively healthy. Children of parents who did not have these advantages had commensurately reduced chances in health and education.

The generations were separated by the improved general level of health and education in offspring compared with the parents, by changes in family closeness and generation differences in relationships between sexes, by the apparent earlier desire for independence, by the changing demands of the labour market, and by great increases in average purchasing power and availability of credit for the individual and the family. Important aspects of this distance between generations are likely to continue, so that when the study population's offspring themselves reach early adulthood they will be on average fitter, less inclined to premature death, and better educated than their parents had been at this stage in life. The generations were separated too by differences conferred by the advances in medicine, in public health, and in improvements in care of their own health, and in the changes in education. Medical advances, for instance, brought control of conception and reduced risk of infections, which helped to release women from many unwanted pregnancies and to free mothers from much of the heavy burden of their own and their children's illnesses, and thus changed women's employment prospects. Medical advances in care, in diagnosis, and in public health also helped to extend the expectation of life, and the period of good health most people can now enjoy in their middle years, which in turn brings fitness for continuing employment, and a prospect in middle age of another twenty or more years of vigorous life. Just as this immediate post-war generation was the first in the new wave of youth culture in the 1960s, so they are now in the vanguard of the newly vigorous and relatively well off middle-aged. Changes in education have brought more years of opportunity to learn, wider curricula, and improved chances of gaining qualifications, at all levels. Changes in the job market have brought a greater likelihood of non-manual work and these, like the changes in education, brought differences between generations in interests and tastes.

Education played a notable part in the processes leading to generation links and differences. Educational attainment was associated not only with high chances of acquiring professional and other salaried occupations, but also with greater receptivity to new ideas in health, politics, and religious beliefs, and with greater participation in community activities and the arts, but with comparatively less contact with the parents' generation. Significant educational attainment by study members' parents, and their belief in the importance of education for their children, had originally provided the impetus for study members' own attainment in further or higher education. Parents' help and encouragement for their study member children to persist in their efforts, and the widening opportunities opened by increased numbers of secondary school, technical college, polytechnic, and university places reduced the base of those without qualifications in the generation now in middle age, but with little narrowing of the gap between the sexes; this only began to reduce ten or fifteen years after members of this study population had completed their education. The broader base of study members with higher education and qualifications, made possible by their experience of the grammar school system, is likely now to have increased the proportion of those who were concerned for their sons and daughters to stay on after school-leaving age and to go into further and higher education. This will also have increased because education is more than ever seen as the basis for occupation. However, since most parents will be in non-manual employment, and since the proportion of manual worker force is shrinking, this will do little to narrow the social class differences in those going to further or higher education. But, if the system will allow, it will increase the numbers of those prepared to continue their education after leaving school.

By early middle life, however, there were signs that those with experience of higher education who had diverged in their mid-20s from the beliefs of their families during childhood were tending to return to them, or to something like them, whereas those who had not diverged earlier from their family's beliefs began to show signs of doing so. The implications of this are discussed in the following chapter.

It would undoubtedly be wrong to expect that these changes and intergenerational differences during the life of the study men and women and their parents are the last that will take place; had that been assumed when members of the study population were in their 20s it would evidently have been wrong. Studies of intergenerational differences which take only university students as their populations, or collect information only once on this topic, are not likely to give a reliable picture of such differences (Greenberg and Nay 1983). It would also be unwise to assume that the differences between future generations on such topics as religion and family relationships will continue to be as they have been found in this study. No doubt changes, at least in the general level of education and in the nature of employment, will bring about other differences between future generations of parents and children (Troll *et al.* 1979, Leigh 1982, Riley 1987).

Changes with increasing age during the lifetime of a generation show that big differences between generations can be tempered by the changes in perspective which tend to occur in middle life. Adolescence and early adult life are characterized by energy, exuberance, and the desire 'to take on the world' and to make changes. By middle life expectations of change are likely to be less and time, which may have seemed endless and stretching infinitely forwards in adolescence and early adult life, will begin to seem circumscribed. The view from the changed perspective of middle life will tend to exaggerate perceptions of generation differences, whereas in fact generations are strongly linked through education and health in the ways described above, and through shared customs within social class, religion, family, work, and other groups (Halbwachs 1980), sustained by such rituals and commemorations as Christmas and birthdays (Connerton 1989), and through shared recollections (Yarrow *et al.* 1970, and see Appendix 1).

In the study of generation difference and change and the things that link generations it is therefore necessary to differentiate the influence of current social, family, and work circumstances, attitudes, and concerns from those of age, and from those of childhood and adolescent experiences of health, education, and family life. Understanding generation differences and links, as well as the processes of individuals' change with age, are important in the practical matters of policy design and the evaluation of its effects in education and health.

# 8
## *Conclusions*

Attempts to anticipate generation differences cannot rely on consistent change, even when good information on some population characteristics and structure is available. Few technological changes or epidemics and their effects can be predicted far ahead in time, any more than it is possible to anticipate change in such fundamental things as religious belief, political concern, and attitudes to family life. A degree of anticipation is possible within lifetimes, however, through those things which make an imprint on life at one point, and which are carried on into later life, or the following generation. These may have their effect because they occur at a critical stage in life, either in terms of biological or social development, and the nature of that effect is likely to be influenced by the cultural or historical time during which the critical stage occurs.

### INFLUENCES ON CHILD DEVELOPMENT

It is popularly believed that infancy and childhood are particularly impressionable times, likely to affect the whole of later life, and in terms of growth and development this is certainly so. Critical periods of development can be shown in human biology, critical in the sense that particular kinds of growth have to occur at specific periods of development or not at all. Their failure can mean that a unique opportunity is missed, with consequent risk of permanent impairment to the child. Faced with a challenge during such critical periods before birth the developing foetus must use what resources are available to resist or adapt, or else risk possible permanent damage or death (Stein *et al.* 1975, Barker *et al.* 1990, Bock and Whelan 1991). Risk in early life may come from poor diet and environment, and both retrospective and prospective studies show that those brought up in poor circumstances are at greater risk, for example, of respiratory or cardiovascular illness, and of premature death in adult life (Barker and Osmond 1986*a*,

Marmot 1986, Mann *et al.* forthcoming). Poor diet in early life may be a source of risk to childhood health, for example by raising vulnerability to infection, and to health in later life through failure to stimulate appropriate growth, or organ or biochemical development, thus in effect failing to programme correctly during the unique time in life when it must occur (Lucas 1991). Damage may also occur to the developing child through infection which may have long-term consequences (Martyn *et al.* 1988), and as a result of exposure to such harmful agents as cigarette smoke and atmospheric pollution (Mann *et al* forthcoming). Many questions remain to be answered, particularly those concerning the extent of risk of genetic origin. When it has been identified it will be possible to see how far preventive health care can work against this source of risk.

Whereas in human biology questions about the childhood origin of risk have tended to concentrate on the demonstration of critical periods and long-term effect, and the adaptability of organs and senses when impaired (Bock and Whelan 1991), in mental health the subject cannot be approached in the same way, because neither the concept of function nor that of damage is so clear. Function in human biology can be assessed in terms of organ performance, but in mental health function is a far more difficult concept to measure. Damage from a particular circumstance is assessed by concurrent distress and by apparent long-term problems. In this study, for instance, impact of parental separation on infant or school-age offspring was assessed through the study of children's bed-wetting and nightmares soon after the event (Douglas 1973*a*), and by the comparison of the adult mental health of those who experienced parental separation with that of others (Rodgers 1990*b*, 1990*c*). In mental health studies the question has been how such apparent long-term effects could be sustained. Studies have therefore been concerned with how far long-term effects may be the results of continued adversity, of problems in the development of styles of response, of vulnerability through such extrinsic factors as poor life circumstances or intrinsic factors such as temperament (Rodgers 1990*b*). Investigation has also been undertaken into the question of how far effects of the original risk may be mitigated by improving circumstances, for instance through a 'good' marriage (Brown and Harris 1978, Quinton and Rutter 1988) or through alterations in the subject's own concept of the original source of adversity (Hetherington 1988). The biological notions of critical period and of programming in early life are also less certain in mental health. It used to be thought that childhood experience was the determinant of the risk of adult emotional vulnerability, but this is no longer seen as inevitable (Rutter 1972, Clarke and Clarke 1976, Skolnick 1986, Magnusson *et al.* 1986). In raising the questions of adaptability and later mitigating effects, more recent work shows that the inevitability of adverse outcome is not an appropriate criterion for assessing the critical nature or otherwise of a particular early life adversity, since some of those 'damaged' may not have an adverse outcome because they have been able to cope (Rutter 1988, Robins and Rutter 1990).

Childhood is also a formative time in terms of education. Although it is not a unique time in life when learning of this kind is possible, in our society it provides the basis from which employment opportunities and earning capacity are usually developed, and these form part of the development of identity separate from that of the family of origin. In this study further and higher educational attainment was associated with greater than average occupational and income attainment, with greater involvement in the arts and community activities, and with receptivity to new ideas in health education which affected choice of diet and habits of smoking, alcohol consumption, and exercise. There was an evident long-term and far reaching effect of education as Russell (1926) and others anticipated (see Chapter 7). The particular value of a well-designed beginning to the process of education has also been shown in two longitudinal follow-up studies of American children (Lazar and Darlington 1982, Berrueta-Clement *et al.* 1984).

None of this is to deny that powerful influences on mental and physical health, occupational achievement, health related habits or taste, or on any other aspect of adult life occur after adolescence. It emphasizes that such later life influences can only build on what has already been established in earlier life, and the reaction to new influences and the capacity to handle them will also be related to earlier life experience.

Mental health studies have introduced the notion of chains of effects which link an aspect of childhood with a particular adult outcome. For example in their study of girls brought up in institutions Quinton and Rutter (1988) found that the protective effect of a supportive marriage was more likely to be experienced by girls who considered the future when making decisions about occupation and choice of partner and, in turn, those who did so had been more likely than others to do well at school. In this study of men and women born in 1946 chains of influences on physical and mental health and in education and occupation were traced back into childhood and into the previous generation. Such chains usually involved home and family circumstances, parents' health, attitudes and education, the availability of services in education and health, as well as current public attitudes towards, for example, divorce, disability, or the role and value of education. These chains were rarely a matter of a straightforward progression to a predictable outcome. As this study's work on the question of wasted talent showed many of those of high measured attainment at 8 years who did not get into grammar school or further education eventually achieved good occupational positions.

Many of the things which will in the long run affect the life of the child or adolescent do not have an immediately apparent impact, either because they are only the first link in a long-term chain or because the vulnerability they bring will be added to gradually as age increases, and they will not in this respect be vulnerable to challenges until an accumulation of problems has developed. Influences on the development of chains of effects and on the accumulation of problems are, like the factors which influence children's and adolescents' development, subject to contemporary and family circumstances. The influence, for example, of parental smoking on children's health is now more likely in lower social class families but less than it was in the immediate post-war period. Similarly parental concern for children's education, educational opportunities, dietary and exercise habits, and atmospheric pollution all vary in their influence with historical time and with current social circumstances. In looking back to earlier times it must be remembered that individuals were not isolated and 'acting in a vacuum: they acted in the context, and under the impulse, of a past society' (Carr 1964: 35).

## EFFECTS OF HISTORICAL OR SOCIAL TIME

Cultural or historical time makes an imprint on childhood both socially or historically, as well as biologically.

Elder and his colleagues (Elder 1974, Elder *et al.* 1984) used a follow-up study of children into adulthood to show how the American depression acted on parents, obliging them to contend with the problems of large-scale unemployment. Mothers' and fathers' reactions and methods of coping were associated with the state of their own marital relationships and with their ways of bringing up their children, and these were in the long run associated with aspects of their children's behaviour in their own marriages and employment. Hareven (1978) and Hareven and Adams (1982) used historical information to show how a community's changing conditions of work affected home and family life. In epidemiological studies of historical data Barker and Osmond (1986*a*, 1986*b*) found variation in adult death rates from stroke and chronic bronchitis according to the social conditions prevailing at the time of birth. It was concluded that improvements in housing and living standards were associated with reduced risk of childhood bronchitis, which was itself a risk for death from bronchitis in adult life (Barker and Osmond 1986*a*). These environmental improvements were also argued to have improved maternal physique, and thus the intra-uterine environment, which was associated with later life blood pressure and pulse rate (Barker *et al.* 1990). The trend in Britain of increase in achieved adult height since the turn of the century is thought to be related to improvements in social circumstances, nutrition, and child welfare (Kuh *et al.* forthcoming).

Thus children brought up at earlier times will have a different start in life, with different consequences for adult life, compared with those born recently. Children born in the 1940s had very different experiences of childhood illness, of nutrition and its consequences, of school, of further and higher education, of parents' employment and parents' health, of smoking and other health related habits, as well as different chances of survival and of parental death and divorce, compared with children born twenty or more years later.

Compared with children born before the 1940s men and women in this study had better chances of survival in infancy

and of good health in childhood, with a much greater
likelihood of medical and infant welfare care because of the
newly introduced National Health Service, and a reduced
chance of getting some kinds of infections and viral illnesses
because of improvements in vaccines and in the programmes of
immunization and vaccination. They had also a better chance of
a good and balanced diet in childhood, because of increases in
spending power and partly because of wartime food rationing,
and they grew taller than children born at earlier times. Their
mothers and fathers were more likely to be in employment
than parents of children born in the pre-war years, and to have
experienced more years of education or training for some kind
of academic or work related qualification. The study children
had on average more years of education than those born at
earlier times, and they had improved chances of gaining
qualifications, particularly if their parents had already done so
and, proportionately, this gain was probably greater among
girls than boys.

Compared with children born since 1946 members of this
study have in some respects not had such a good start in life.
Health and survival in childhood have since improved im-
mensely, and children have on average again grown taller,
although these advantages have been much less for children from
lower social class families than for others. It is difficult to know
whether diet has improved, but it is certainly much more
varied. Smoking, alcohol drinking, and sexual experience now
begin at earlier ages. Parents have in general a higher level of
education than those of earlier times, and although for men
chances of employment have been reduced in the last decade,
for women they have greatly increased. The study of the
offspring of study men and women showed that high interest
in their children's education was greatest among parents with
most education (see Chapter 7), and so nowadays, as population
levels of educational attainment rise, this may help to provide a
gradual, beneficial change. Parents are also now more confident
about discussing their children's prospects and in expressing
their concerns. Working class parents are probably now less
concerned that the further or higher education of their children
risks alienation of the generations, as was feared among their
parents.

When the generation of the study's population become the elderly of the 2020s they are likely to be a fitter elderly population than that of the 1990s, because of differences in the imprint of time in childhood and in adult life. But the differences which may be brought about by their experience of weaker ties of tradition and family are impossible to anticipate.

In a society which has experienced great change and upheaval during this century there now exist many layers of varied imprints. The scars and long-term effects of the childhood illnesses which were common during the last war and the years before can be seen now in the population born before 1950. The long-term effects of childhood tuberculosis, rheumatic heart disease, rickets, relatively poor nutrition, and far worse working conditions for instance, will be greater in those now aged 50 years or more compared with future 50-year-olds and will be of greatest prevalence among those now in the oldest age group. Similarly, adverse long-term effects of the poorer growth rates experienced at earlier times, and the worse smoking and exercise habits will become less as the population ages. Long-term effects of the differences between generations in such things as religious beliefs, in family life, and attitudes to care of the elderly have yet to become apparent.

## ATTACHMENT TO A PARTICULAR PERIOD OF TIME

People are thus in many ways attached to the historical time of their childhood and adolescence when development took place. Attachment to that time is also likely to be an important part of identity (see Chapter 1), and memories of that time are part of the process of maintaining 'the sense of continuity across the life course . . . a sense of coherence of self and consistency of the life history' (Cohler 1982).

In middle age any review of life will see the developing years in the context of later achievement and failure. By their mid-30s most men have settled into an occupation. For most women of that age the style of life with children will have begun, and occupations which may be taken up or continued later as children become independent, represent a change still to come. For many women and men middle life will provide not only a vantage point from which to look forwards and

202Conclusions

backwards in time across two or even three generations of the family, all at different stages in life, but also an increased awareness of mortality and perhaps a tendency to desire less change, less sweeping away of the things of earlier life. The study provides what may be evidence of mid-life review in the tendency for those with highest educational qualifications to return, at this stage, to the religious beliefs of their families of origin, and for others to begin for the first time to break away. Perhaps later on in life those who seemed first, in their own middle age, to break away from the conventions of their parents will return to some extent, as those with higher education have already begun to return.

The power of education to bring about differences between generations, and differences within generations was evident in occupations, in attitudes and beliefs, and in optimism about the possibilities of change. But its effect may be tempered by changes in outlook which seem to have come with the beginnings of middle age. Perhaps at this time of life the limits of acceptance of new ideas begin to be reached, and there may be a tendency to return to or to stay with the ideas and conventions of the time of youth and early adulthood. From the vantage point of early middle age, the apparent endlessness or linearity of time seen from the perspective of youth changes to an awareness of those aspects of time which may be described as circular, such as the movement of generations through life and their replacement with the following generation, and the mortality of the generation of parents (see the introduction to Chapter 7).

In a fast changing society with large generation differences in occupations and in popular taste and expression, adjustment to middle age may be just as important as it has been thought to be for old age.

Just as unemployment can threaten a sense of 'identity' and 'genera-tivity', so can changed habits and values in society threaten the individual's own interpretation of his past life in old age or more likely threaten his adjustment to present society. Living to a great age in a fast changing society as the twentieth century requires many readaptations. Adjustment to old age is not only a matter of coming to terms with eventual physical decline and loss of friends and loved ones, it also involves coming to terms with discontinuities between the past and the present. (Coleman 1986: 8)

## USEFULNESS OF THE IMPRINT OF TIME

The coexistence of imprints of time can yield a great deal of information about the development and progress of an illness or a problem, and about the impression made by the social and physical environment. Just as a core sample of glacial ice or pond mud can show layers of matter deposited at earlier times, when climate and foliage were not as they are today, so an age slice through the population reveals the differences in impacts of influences from earlier times, in the same way that layers of earlier influences accumulate and interact in the individual. These layers of influence also constitute the material for life review and for links with earlier time, and are thus important facets of identity and self-image. The population differences can be useful in a number of ways looking both backward and forward in time.

In research the layers of the imprint of time can be used to reveal the effects of an experience on individuals, particularly in rapidly changing times, just as comparisons of life in different cultures can reveal effects of cultural imprint. In studies of the effect of environment on illness, for example, improvements in housing circumstances, hygiene, and nutrition have been shown to be associated with a reduction in many kinds of disease by the comparison and prevalence of illness at different times during the years of environmental improvement (Habbakkuk 1953, McKeown 1979, Barker and Osmond 1986a, Mann *et al.* forthcoming). Mattock *et al.* (1988) studied populations who experienced epidemics of measles to seek a possible association of that disease with later risk of Parkinson's disease. Mothers who had experienced illness during certain types of influenza epidemics have been shown to have offspring with a raised risk of schizophrenia (Mednick *et al.* 1988), and epidemics of some virus disease have been studied for possible links with juvenile diabetes (Gamble 1980). It has been shown that exposure to the poliomyelitis virus in childhood may damage brain cells, with consequent raised risk of motor neurone disease in later adult life, and the current increase in motor neurone disease correlates significantly with the post-war epidemic of poliomyelitis described in Chapter 3 (Martyn *et al.* 1988). An experience such as war, which affects in the nations involved all members of a population, but not in every generation, may be used to study particular aspects of its effects on individuals. The effect of severe malnutrition in pregnancy on foetal development was investigated using data on a population of Dutch women who were at various stages of pregnancy during the time of the famine brought about by the Nazi occupation of the Netherlands during the Second World War (Stein *et al.* 1975). Similarly the long-term effects of the American economic depression of the 1930s on the development of children born during that time and on their subsequent behaviour as parents have been investigated, as described above (Elder *et al.* 1984).

These kinds of studies rely on their skill at finding people who may have been put at risk by their past experience, and on the published statistics which show trends, for example in causes of death, in years of education experienced, in qualifications attained or in housing standards. Such studies often have to cover long periods of time and to be ingenious in design. For example Barker and his colleagues found that a hospital in Preston had kept standardized records of births occurring there between 1935 and 1943. Men and women whose birth records were available were traced in order to study the relationship of adult blood pressure with birth weight and the weight of the placenta (Barker *et al.* 1990). Studies of the effects of policies and changes in policies use comparable methods, exemplified by the study of the relationship of education with later occupation among men born in the period 1913–22, compared with men born in 1923–32, 1933–42, and 1943–52 (Halsey *et al.* 1980, Goldthorpe *et al.* 1980).

In a fast changing society it is important that evaluative studies should investigate the effects of policies and the long-term effects of experiences on individuals. They will continue to depend on the existence of good information on trends, for example in illness, causes of death, growth rates, educational attainment, housing, and poverty. Evaluative studies often require better information than is usually available on such social forces as attitudes and expectations, for example to education, which have been shown in this study to be of considerable power in shaping the lives of the study members. Attitudes and expectations also affect the development of policy as well as its implementation and effectiveness, as the history of the drafting of the 1944 Education Act shows. Attitudes and expectations of lay people and professionals about health education, disability, child upbringing, parental divorce and separation, and mothers going out to work are similar examples of important social forces. Trends in a wide range of attitudes have been monitored in Britain since the early 1980s (Jowell and Airey 1984, Jowell *et al.* 1990).

To make use of the imprint of time in childhood it is necessary to have good information about the things which are thought to be risk factors for later problems, and those things which will assess progress or effectiveness in policy application.

Studies of the development of risk can make opportunistic use of past events, and use data collections that catch up in adult life on the progress of those thought to be at risk as the result of childhood experience, in ways shown in the examples described earlier in this chapter. Long-term follow-up studies, such as that described in this book, are also used and examples of these and other methods are given in Appendix 1. Published routine statistics are of relatively little help in these studies, but without good information on trends in risk factors it is difficult to make effective use of the information which single studies of risk can provide.

Investigations of policy effectiveness often begin from routine data collection but need also further information. In medical care, for example, although extensive information is available on causes of death, on some characteristics of those who have died, and on notifiable infectious diseases much less is known about the extent of sickness in the population and about other indicators of health. Assessments of health policy can therefore examine trends in sex, age, and social differences in death rates for all kinds of causes (Townsend and Davidson 1982, Whitehead 1987, Davey Smith *et al.* 1990) using published statistics, but this source provides very little of the information necessary to see whether policies to improve the health of the population are effective, particularly since some important aspects of what proved to be terminal illness may have been established many years before, in early life. The emphasis on death and infectious disease in published statistics is an example of the imprint of time; good information on population trends in these important topics reflects the requirements of earlier times when these aspects of health were predominant. Now that state of health can itself be assessed by measuring, for example, fatness, blood pressure, respiratory function, and growth in children, policy effectiveness should also be assessed in these terms, as well as providing information not yet available on trends in new cases of such disorders as diabetes or rheumatic disease. This type of information is lacking for both adults and children. Assessment of policy effectiveness in education is similarly short of information; for instance it is not possible to know whether the proportion of 'able' children who do not gain educational qualifications or go on to higher or further education is being reduced.

Without better knowledge of the population's health and education, particularly in childhood, many of the important questions of the 1940s remain the important questions of today, and answers are as difficult to find now as they were then. When *The Economist* asked in 1944 'whether the advances in social conditions have been commensurate with technical and scientific progress or the nation's productive capacity' (see Chapter 1) it had some difficulty in finding answers, and it is equally difficult today. It is still necessary to ask whether equalities of opportunity which the design of the 1944 Education Act hoped to achieve are now attained, and it is only possible to attempt to answer this question with single studies which, if funded, cannot reveal all aspects of trends. It still cannot be clearly shown whether the state of health of the population is improving, for instance in terms of prevalence of many significant illnesses, and of rates of rise of blood pressure, deterioration of respiratory function, and change of body shape with increasing age. Changes in measurement designed to provide answers to such questions would bring a longer time perspective to the assessment of policy effectiveness. They would also make use of the fact that the imprint of time is a valuable research resource, as studies of the natural history of illnesses, and of the long-term effects of education for the individual and for the community have shown. Increasingly a longer time perspective will be necessary as interest grows in the processes of ageing, in the origins of chronic disease, in the long-term effects of health education and of treatments, in the value of education, and in the effects of environmental and social change.

# Appendix 1

## Study Design and Management, and some Comments on Problems in the Use of this Research Method

### THE SAMPLE

The study began with the intention of describing maternity services received and the cost to the mother and her family of having a baby. The target population comprised those women who gave birth in England, Wales, or Scotland during the week 3–9 March 1946. Health visitors collected information eight weeks after the births from mothers and from hospital, local authority clinic, and general practice records. Of all the 458 local authorities in England, Wales, and Scotland, 424 (93 per cent) took part, and the total of births available for study was consequently reduced from 16,695 to 15,416. Information was eventually collected on a total of 13,687 births (Joint Committee (a) 1948).

For the subsequent follow-up a manageable size of sample was taken from the 12,930 single, legitimate births already studied. Multiple births were excluded because their numbers (180) were thought to be too few for analyses. Illegitimate births (672) were excluded because the high rate of adoption was thought to make future contact difficult. The sample then taken from the single, legitimate births comprised all those to wives of non-manual and agricultural workers and a random one in four of births to wives of manual workers, a total of 5,362 children. A weighting procedure compensates for the stratification by father's social class at the time of the study member's birth by multiplying the results of those in the sampled classes by the denominator value (4) of the sampling fraction. The study population has not been augmented in any way, and so aims now to be as far as possible representative of the single born, legitimate, native population of this age who are still resident in England, Wales, or Scotland.

The sample size has been adequate to maintain a good degree of representativeness, as described below, and not so large that frequent contacts in childhood would have been impossible. A larger sample would have provided more cases of particular illnesses and of other problems, but with a corresponding loss in data quality since numbers of data collectors would have had to be greatly increased, with an inevitable loss of the amount of time that could be spent in training and quality checking. Time spent in tracing lost study members would also have increased. Funding viability is closely associated with sample size.

## FREQUENCY AND METHODS OF DATA COLLECTION

Contact was most frequent during infancy and the school years when biological and educational change was rapid, and as the pace of change slowed in adult life contact frequency was reduced, as table 9.1 shows.

During the pre-school years local health authorities agreed that health visitors should collect information on behalf of the study, through visits to mothers at home and from clinic records. Although not all local health authorities had agreed to take part in the original maternity survey, all agreed to help in the follow-up studies. In the school years local education authorities and most headteachers agreed that tests could be administered to study children by their usual teacher, and headteachers answered questions about their school and the study child's class, and school doctors and nurses undertook medical examinations. Youth Employment Officers interviewed those who had left school at the earliest opportunity. In early adult life health visitors (community nurses) collected data at home visits, and thereafter information was collected by postal questionnaire (at ages 20, 22, 23, and 25 years), at home visits by specially briefed professional interviewers (at 26 years), and more recently by research nurses (56 nurses when study members were 36, and 58 nurses when study members were 43 years old) who were recruited and trained for each occasion.

Information describing the regions and areas of residence, and the extent of local atmospheric pollution from coal burning has been added from published statistical sources.

## MAINTENANCE OF CONTACT

During the pre-school years local health authorities and, in particular, health visitors were most helpful in finding children who had moved between study contacts. Similarly during the school years local education authorities frequently helped to trace children whose parents had moved. From the sixteenth birthday onwards a birthday card has been sent to each study member; this includes a description of current work, and a returnable card for checking current name and address. Study members known to live abroad are not included in data collections but receive the birthday card, and this has been a valuable source of information on returning migrants, who have then been included in subsequent data collections. Pamphlets describing current work and giving references to recent publications have been distributed on three occasions to all members of the study population. At the most recent contact 90 per cent of available study members were successfully interviewed and measured (table 9.2).

## DATA QUALITY

Data quality on hospital admissions has been enhanced, when study members' permission is given, by checking records of hospital admissions with hospitals. Other measures taken to ensure good quality of data collection include careful design and pilot study of questions, training sessions of up to five days of nurses and interviewers, checks during data collection of nurses' scoring of responses (by test tapes), checks on form completion, comparison of reports of illness and infant care with health authority records (Douglas and Blomfield 1956), use of physiological measuring instruments which reduce observer error (Wadsworth *et al.* 1985), and by checking internal logic of information.

Risks to data quality through frequency of contact, for example by increased use and awareness of health and educational services or through increasing sophistication in taking attainment tests, was checked by monitoring the health and school progress of a comparison sample. These children were examined at age 11 years by school doctors, their mothers were also interviewed at this time, and their educational progress and choice of occupation were monitored at the time of leaving school. This sample comprised one-third of the single, legitimate children who were not selected for follow-up after the maternity study, and so all were of manual class origins; there was no comparison sample for children whose fathers were in non-manual or agricultural employment in 1946. By the time they left school members of the comparison sample showed no significant differences in health or education from children in the follow-up group (Douglas 1976).

## POPULATION LOSS AND REPRESENTATIVENESS

Contact rates shown in table 9.1 have been maintained because of persistent tracing of study members who changed address, because of communication to study members of findings and information about the purpose and uses of the study through the birthday card and pamphlets, and because in a national study only emigrants leave the study area.

TABLE 9.1 *Contacts made with the whole population selected for follow-up after the birth survey of 1946*

| Year | Age in years | Data collector | Population not available (cumulative totals) | | | | Population available | | |
|------|------|------|------|------|------|------|------|------|------|
| | | | Dead | Emigrated | Living abroad | Permanent refusal | Population contacted | Population not contacted | Percentage contacted |
| 1948 | 2 | HV | 219 | 129 | 21 | 0 | 4,689 | 304 | 94 |
| 1950 | 4 | HV | 229 | 196 | 36 | 1 | 4,700 | 200 | 96 |
| 1952 | 6 | SD; SN or HV | 232 | 232 | 39 | 1 | 4,603 | 255 | 95 |
| 1953 | 7 | SN or HV; SD; T. | 232 | 249 | 42 | 1 | 4,480 | 358 | 93 |
| 1954 | 8 | SN or HV; T. | 236 | 259 | 40 | 1 | 4,435 | 391 | 92 |
| 1955 | 9 | SN or HV | 239 | 275 | 40 | 1 | 4,181 | 626 | 87 |
| 1956 | 10 | T. | 240 | 273 | 37 | 1 | 4,077 | 734 | 85 |

| | | | | | | | | |
|---|---|---|---|---|---|---|---|---|
| 1959 | 13 | T. | 247 | 292 | 28 | 1 | 4,127 | 86 |
| 1961 | 15 | SN or HV; T.; SD | 250 | 295 | 26 | 1 | 4,274 | 89 |
| 1965 | 19 | HV | 263 | 316 | 38 | 4 | 3,561 | 75 |
| 1966 | 20 | P. | 268 | 333 | 39 | 7 | 3,899 | 83 |
| 1968 | 22 | P. | 275 | 373 | 35 | 45 | 3,885 | 84 |
| 1969 | 23 | P. | 281 | 397 | 66 | 100 | 3,026 | 67 |
| 1971 | 25 | P. | 286 | 436 | 70 | 124 | 3,307 | 74 |
| 1972 | 26 | I. | 290 | 447 | 69 | 146 | 3,750 | 85 |
| 1977 | 31 | P. | 306 | 528 | 77 | 158 | 3,340 | 78 |
| 1982 | 36 | RN | 323 | 571 | 73 | 520 | 3,322 | 86 |
| 1989 | 43 | RN | 365 | 607 | | 540 | 3,262 | 85 |

*Note:*
HV = health visitor; SN = schoolnurse; SD = school doctor; T = teacher; P = postal contact; I = interviewer; RN = research nurse.

TABLE 9.2    *Contact with the cohort at age 43–4 years*

|  | No. |  | As % of total cohort |
|---|---|---|---|
| *Contact not attempted at 43–4 years for these reasons* |  | *As % of those not attempted* |  |
| Dead | 361 | 23.9 | 6.7 |
| Living abroad | 607 | 40.2 | 11.3 |
| Permanent refusal | 540 | 35.8 | 10.1 |
| Total | 1,508 | 100.0 | 28.1 |
| *Contact attempted at 43–4 years* |  | *As % of of those attempted* |  |
| Successful | 3,262 | 84.6 | 60.8 |
| *No success for these reasons* |  |  |  |
| Dead | 4 | 0.1 | |
| Living abroad | 11 | 0.3 | |
| Permanent refusal | 106 | 2.7 | 11.0 |
| Temporary refusal | 195 | 5.1 | |
| Untraced | 276 | 7.2 | |
| Total | 3,854 | 100.0 | 71.8 |
| GRAND TOTAL | 5,362 | | |

Changes in the size of the population available for study, and the extent of losses through death and emigration are described in table 9.1.

Deaths of study members have been discovered through parents and relatives, and causes of death checked with death certificates. Losses through death in childhood occurred at a rate comparable with that found in the national population (table 9.1). Rates of death at later ages have been difficult to compare with national rates because of the small numbers of deaths of study members, and because national rates include not only the native born but also immigrants, who first began to arrive in significant numbers in the early 1950s, after the sample for this follow-up study had been selected.

Losses through emigration follow a similar distribution to those of national rates. The national data show a high rate of emigration immediately after the end of the war and an overall falling trend from the late 1940s to the mid-1960s, with peaks in 1957 and in 1963 (Oversea Migration Board 1964), but poor national data (Coleman 1988) make further comparison impossible. Fathers of families who emigrated before study members were 20 years old had significantly better educational qualifications than those who continued to live in Britain. Women study members who emigrated after 20 years also had significantly higher educational qualifications than others, as expected (Committee on Manpower Resources for Science and Technology 1967). But men who emigrated did not differ significantly from others.

Losses through refusal comprise those which refer only to the current request for information, and those which are permanent refusals. Permanent refusals amounted to 510 (9.5 per cent of the total initial population) by age 36 years, and to 653 (12.2 per cent) by 43 years. Permanent refusals rose in adult life, particularly after a gap of ten years between home visits, when the largest number of such refusals (368) was added. More recently such refusals have risen only by 106 during a seven-year interval, and this may be the result of the shorter time interval between contacts and the more settled nature of life at these older ages. Refusals of a request for interview at 43 years because of current family or other problems, that is temporary refusals applying only to the most recent contact in 1989–90, amounted to 190 (5.2 per cent of interviews requested). Table 9.2 shows the balance sheet of contacts attempted in the most recent study.

As well as being reasonably representative in its losses through death and emigration the study population has been found to be representative of the national population in other ways. Study data were compared with census information nearest in age, or grouped age. Information on region of residence at 4 years and 36 years showed no significant differences from the national figures for people of those ages in 1951 and 1981. Similarly comparisons of the distribution of father's social class at 4 years and 15 years, and of own social class at 26 years and 36 years, of home overcrowding at 4 years and 15 years, and of numbers of children born to mothers aged under 26 years in 1972, all showed no statistically significant differences between the study data and published national census information. The study population, however, tended to over-represent those who had been married by 36 years, and to under-represent those who were single, perhaps because of the study's tendency to lose contact with those who were mentally ill and handicapped, and those who most often changed their addresses, since these groups contained a high proportion of single people.

Long-term studies are at risk of selective loss from particular sections of the population. Some of these kinds of loss may be impossible to assess; for example, parents may have withdrawn from the study because of anxiety about their child's capabilities or health, or because of a fear 'that home visits would show up dissension in the family: or young adults (may have withdrawn) because they felt they were unsuccessful' in their careers (Douglas 1976: 9). Other aspects of selective loss can be measured by comparing rates of loss among those from different socio-economic groups and family circumstances, and among those who experienced particular illnesses and educational attainments with those who did not.

Comparison of attributes up to age 4 years of study members for whom information was collected with those who could not be contacted, even though they were alive, resident in Britain, and had not so far refused, revealed no differences between the two groups. By age 15 years significant losses of contact had occurred among those who had lived in overcrowded circumstances up to age 4 years, and among those whose parents had the highest educational qualifications and lived as owner-occupiers. Losses of contact by 36 years were signficantly greater among those who had been relatively low scorers on the attainment tests (at 8 or 11 or 15 years), and among those who had been to schools for the educationally subnormal (Rodgers 1979), those with low levels of literacy (Rodgers 1986), and those who had had severe psychiatric disorders (Rodgers 1990c).

Any study which restricts its population to those born in one month will not fully represent all the births in that year, and will be subject to bias because illnesses and

Respiratory infections in early infancy, for example, are likely to be fewer among those born in the spring and in the autumn and so are accidental burns which are particularly likely when the child is learning to walk. In [this study] this would have been in the spring and summer when open fires were seldom used and the children less likely to be cooped up in the kitchen (Douglas 1976: 10).

When study children were 5 years old (in 1951) date of birth was a deciding factor in the age at which children began full-time education, and so comparison with educational attainment by children of the same age, but born at other times in the year, has to take account of differences in the amount of time spent in school.

The study has the advantage of a nationally distributed population and consequently losses of contact through moving house have been restricted mostly to those who emigrated. A national study population also allows analyses to separate geographical from socio-economic effects, for example in educational attainment, and has enabled the study to show that 'Where we live in Britain still influences survival, health, education and employment' (Douglas 1976: 14), a finding amply confirmed in extent and durability over time by more recent studies (Butler and Bonham 1963, Davie *et al.* 1972, Chamberlain *et al.* 1975, Townsend and Davidson 1982, Fogelman 1983, Osborn *et al.* 1984, Butler and Golding 1986, Whitehead 1987, Blaxter 1987, Shaper *et al.* 1988, Barker and Osmond 1986*a*, 1987, Davey Smith *et al.* 1990).

## COMMENTS ON THIS RESEARCH METHOD

It is a paradox of the long-term longitudinal research method that whilst being the most dynamic way of studying the life course, it is rooted in the time of any particular age of its study population. Thus in this study, when the population was aged 5–11 years (1951–7), the research team assessed health using the ideas and measures of the day. Children's health was then, for medical examination and recording purposes, usually described only by the absence of illness, by signs of disability or malfunction, and by the measurement of height and weight to assess growth rates and to compare them with population standards. Even twenty years later a government-appointed commit-tee on the future of child health services in Britain decided that health was 'not an absolute that can easily be measured. We can only point to increased survival, improved growth and the absence of particular forms of ill-health as indicators for progress' (Court Report 1976: 39).

Nowadays assessment of children's health would include not only a wider range of measures, but also the concept of future risk to health contained, for example, in information on the smoking habits of parents, and the child's and the family's dietary and exercise habits. Much as we would now like to know about these aspects of study members' childhood in the 1940s and 1950s they cannot for the most part be discovered adequately from recollection, although information on children's diet in general can be obtained from contemporary studies and books of advice for parents, from biographies, and from information on food sales. Information on smoking at particular times in the past is available in comparable ways, and from cigarette and tobacco production statistics (Wald *et al.* 1988).

The problem of not knowing which measures of health will come to be seen in later years as essential, but which are not yet seen as important or not yet available or discovered cannot be avoided, but may be reduced in a number of ways. Biological samples, such as blood, may be divided and some part stored until new analytical techniques become available. Information on diet may be stored both in the form of current knowledge of nutrient content and according to type, quality, and cooking method of food, so that further analyses may be undertaken in later years in the light of new knowledge. It should also be assumed that the study will continue for many years, and areas of information should then be outlined which it would be useful to know in later times on the study population at its present age. For example, current research on health in old age shows that were this study to continue into the retirement years it would be valuable to have collected data during middle life about the current state and subsequent rates of change of such cognitive processes as memory. Diet and exercise in middle life are also thought now to be important for health in later life. Even though the current methods of collecting information on memory and diet will probably not be as good as those to be developed in future years, such measures serve in a longitudinal study both as assessments of current status, whose antecedents may usefully be investigated, and as baseline measures against which future change may be assessed. This study's measures of blood pressure and respiratory function, as well as those of cognitive processes, and diet, smoking, and exercise all serve these two purposes.

To some extent, however, any measure will bring the problem in later years of whether to repeat exactly the same measure for comparative purposes, or whether to use a more recently developed and probably better technique; the option of using both methods is rarely viable because time spent on examination and interview is necessarily limited. The intergenerational comparison of verbal assessment at 8 years (in the study population in 1954 and in their first born offspring during 1977–82) presented this problem and was resolved, as described in Chapter 7, by updating and regrading the original test, in order to compare changes in average scores in the two populations, within groups in the two populations, and within families.

This illustrates one of the long-term longitudinal population study's dilemmas in wanting appropriately good serial measures to assess individual change over time, but having to collect such data in the usually less than optimal circumstances of school or home, which restricts choice of measurement methods. In this study equipment for measuring blood pressure and respiratory function has had to be portable, and is consequently not the most sensitive (Wadsworth *et al.* 1985). Similarly in measuring mental health decisions have had to be taken to use methods which suit the circumstances of the study's data collection. Most assessment methods take a long time to administer, and short versions have been used, for example, of the Maudsley Personality Inventory (Eysenck 1958) and of the Present State Examination (Rodgers and Mann 1986). This problem of restricted choice of measurement methods can be dealt with by using tests which reliably screen out a range of measures, for example those which indicate high blood pressure, and then returning to measure in greater detail those who score in the chosen range. In a national study this can be prohibitively expensive, and carries the risk of exposing some study members to far more contact hours than the study population's average. It was not used in this study for these reasons, and because the gains were not thought to be sufficient for the use to be made of the data. In using measures to assess change over time in the respiratory function of study members, for instance, the concern has been to describe movement between percentiles derived from measurements on the whole study population, and portable measures are adequate for these purposes.

The most desirable measures for clinical and laboratory purposes may not necessarily be those required in population studies. This is best illustrated in dietary assessment, where the possibilities include laboratory analysis of 24-hour urine samples, asking respondents to record and weigh all the food they eat over a number of days, asking them to keep a detailed diary of types and quantities of food and drink consumed over a week, or asking about frequency of eating particular foods. The longitudinal research designer must judge which is the most ˙desirable method for present and long-term purposes, which is the most practical in terms of time taken in data collection, in training interviewers and respondents in its use, and in coding the data, which method can be justified in terms of purchase of equipment such as weighing scales, and which will provide the most appropriate data for use in the study. In this study the seven day diary method has been used (Braddon *et al.* 1988), and information compared well with studies of weighed intake.

The passage of time is also a source of problems in the analysis of long-term longitudinal data. Illnesses, occupations, and qualifications are given coding numbers after each new data collection, using national and international classification methods. Unfortunately classifications are changed, added to, and regraded so that for comparative purposes information collected some years ago, such as father's occupation in 1950 and 1957, coded originally using the 1961 census classification, had to be coded again using the 1971 and later the 1981 classifications (Office of Population Censuses and Surveys 1980). Similarly the World Health Organization's *International Classification of Diseases, Injuries and Causes of Death* (e.g. World Health Organization

1977) has been changed and updated since its version of 1948 was first used in this study, and the versions of 1957, 1965, and 1977 have all been used. Diagnostic nomenclature used in medical records and in the study's data collections has also changed and so, for example, it is now difficult to understand exactly what was meant by the terms 'dyslalia' and 'inadequate personality' used by school doctors and others in the 1950s. Changes in boundaries of administrative districts during the course of the study have also made difficulties in comparisons with findings from other studies and with published statistics, and necessitated some reclassification of area codes.

Some of these problems associated with time passing may be avoided by using other ways of collecting data about many years of life, but other study designs also have their own difficulties. The catch-up design uses a population on whom data have been collected at earlier times and having recontacted them collects information once or more from then on. For example male members of a Swedish study, originally concerned in 1938 with intelligence in 10-year-old boys and girls and its relationship with social and family circumstances, were recontacted in 1976–8 in order to study the development of high blood pressure (Lindgarde *et al.* 1987). In America Robins (1966) traced adults who as children attended a guidance clinic, in order to investigate their mid-life mental health and behaviour, and McCord (1990) studied the personality and behaviour of men whose childhood home circumstances and behaviour had originally been studied between 1926 and 1933. Elder (1974) and Elder *et al.* (1984) investigated the relationship of behaviour of children born during the American depression in the 1930s with their adult experience of marriage, parenthood, and work. Quinton and Rutter (1988) studied the adolescent behaviour of girls brought up in institutions. Theorell and Floderus-Myrhed (1977) collected information to form a baseline on health and perceived stress, and followed up the subsequent health of a population of Swedish men through records. In Britain a study is beginning of the recorded causes of death of men and women who were children in families whose nutrition and health were studied between 1936 and 1941 (Boyd-Orr 1937). By contrast some catch-up investigations contact their study population in order to catch up on the past in relation to the present; Bury and Holme (1991) used this method in the study of the health and social circumstances of a national sample aged 90 years and over.

The high risk design starts to follow up a population from a time in life when a particular risk begins to increase, or selects a population believed to be at high risk; catch-up investigations may also be concerned with populations selected originally for their high risk status. The British Regional Heart Study (Shaper *et al.* 1988), for instance, began collecting information on heart disease risk from samples of men in middle age, in a prospective study of the origins of risk of heart disease in men. Following a first study of middle-aged male government employees and their risk of heart disease (Marmot *et al.* 1978) a prospective study of a similar population is being undertaken by the same team to investigate the relationships of work stress with heart disease risk. Weikart *et al.* (1970) studied the long-term effects of a specially designed education programme used during early childhood with children in very poor urban areas, and reported it to be of detectable and significant benefit at age 19 years (Berrueta-Clement *et al.* 1984).

A much less common study design begins with a random population sample or the population of a whole community and undertakes prospective research on change over time in some aspects of the subjects' lives. The study reported here of the health and development of men and women born in 1946 is an example, as are the studies of all children born in England, Wales, or Scotland in one week in March 1958 (Fogelman 1983) and in one week in April 1970 (Butler and Golding 1986). Similarly the investigations recently begun by Macintyre and her colleagues of three samples of residents of Glasgow, beginning at age 15 years, 35 years, and 55 years are also prospective studies of health (Macintyre *et al.* 1989). A study of children born in Newcastle upon Tyne in 1947 has investigated their health and development, so far to 1980 (Miller *et al.* 1960, Miller *et al.* 1974, Kolvin *et al.* 1990). In the United States two studies of communities have been concerned with health in their populations followed over many years (Montoye 1975) and even into a following generation (Feinleib *et al.* 1975).

All of these longitudinal study research designs rely extensively on recollection and on records for information about the years when they did not contact their study members, which may amount to half a lifetime, and this presents difficulties for a number of reasons. If a study continues over several years there are inevitably past experiences and circumstances on which information was not originally collected, but which are currently required and, as in catch-up studies, subjects are asked to recall aspects of their earlier life. The nature of information that can be collected in this way is limited, like the use of records. Recollection of weight several years back is, for example, likely to be inaccurate, earlier life self-concepts and reactions to experiences may be hard to remember, and recall of childhood circumstances is likely to have been influenced by older generations' reminiscences (Baddeley 1979). Yarrow *et al.* (1970) noted that

'Mothers have a significant role in determining the folklore of the family and, by extension, in shaping the nature of the findings in retrospective investigations' (p. 67). Limitations may also be imposed by the subjects' views of the importance of the topic, by the conscience of those interviewed, by the effects of the interviewer and the context of the interview (Thompson 1978), by respondents' age and stage in life (Cohler 1982), and by the chances of subjects' forgetting, reordering, or invention of past events (Robins 1988). Fussell (1975) gave an example of how recollection may change the perspective and evaluation of the past: 'Lillian Hellman testifies that during 1944 she kept copious and detailed diaries, hoping to register important experience. But reading them later, she found that they did not include "What had been most important to me, or what the passing years had made important"' (pp. 310–11). Diaries written during the war must have been subject to influence from newspaper and radio reports, which were themselves influenced by deliberate selection in efforts to boost home population morale, and perhaps also by the writers' need to 'whistle in the dark' (Thompson 1978). The extent of various kinds of distortion of recall has been assessed both in studies where subjects recalled events on which data had already been collected (Douglas and Blomfield 1956, Robins 1966, Yarrow *et al.* 1970, Cherry and Rodgers 1979), and in investigations of the risk of bias in recall because of reinterpretation in the light of more recent circumstances (Yarrow *et al.* 1970, Vaillant and McArthur 1972, Thompson 1978, Cohler 1982, Robins *et al.* 1985, Butler 1989, Baddeley 1989). Methods of minimizing and assessing the extent of such problems have been applied in study design (Thompson 1978, Robins 1988) and in techniques of interviewing (Hoinville and Jowell 1987).

Recollection may itself be a topic of study rather than a possible source of inaccuracy or bias, and in the study described here research into short- and long-term memory capacity in middle life forms an important part of the programme.

There are many other ways of studying long periods of lifetimes, ranging from those which use only data from records (Stein *et al.* 1975, Hareven 1978, Barker and Osmond 1986*a*, 1987), and those which use only recollected information (Thompson 1978, Plummer 1983). Reviews of longitudinal studies, that is studies which collect information about individuals on more than one or two occasions over a number of years, reveal the variety of concepts of study and methods of analysis, and show that it is misleading to think of longitudinal research as a homogeneous form of research method (Clarke and Clarke 1976, Brim and Kagan 1980, Schulsinger *et al.* 1981, Mednick and Baert 1981, Schaie 1983, Mednick *et al.* 1984, Nicol 1985, Plewis

1985, Blaxter 1986, Rutter 1988, Robins and Rutter 1990, Wadsworth and Rodgers 1989). There seems little doubt that the demand for such studies will continue as information is needed about the effects of social, technological, medical, and educational change, as the lengths of time of treatments and chronic illnesses increase, and as concepts of cause of illnesses extend back over many years of life, and into previous generations.

# Appendix 2

## Descriptions of Social Class Measures and Tests of Attainment

### SOCIAL CLASS MEASURES

1. Social class was first classified in this study using the family census groups designed for the Royal Commission on Population (Douglas and Blomfield 1958). The groups were

Non-manual
: Professional and salaried
: Blackcoated

Manual
: Skilled
: Semi-skilled
: Unskilled
: Agricultural
: Self-employed

2. *Composition of the indicator of social group.* This classification was constructed to make groups which did not change, and which took into account not only the father's occupation when the child was 11 years old (or an earlier occupation if necessary), but also for both parents the length of time spent at school and whether they had been brought up in a family in which their father had been a non-manual or manual worker (Douglas 1964). This classification is referred to as social group.

*Upper non-manual social group.* The father is a non-manual worker, and

(a) both parents went to secondary school and were brought up in non-manual social class families, or

(b) both parents went to secondary school and one parent was brought up in a non-manual social class family, or

(c) both parents were brought up in non-manual social class families and one parent went to secondary school.

*Lower non-manual social group.* The rest of the non-manual workers' families.

*Upper manual social group.* The father is a manual worker and either the father or mother or both of them had secondary school education, and/or one or both of them were brought up in a non-manual social class family.

*Lower manual social group.* The father is a manual worker, and both the father and the mother had elementary schooling only, and both the father and the mother were brought up in manual working class families.

3. The Registrar-General's social class groups have been used in most medical analyses, and in general from about 1960 onwards. The shorter Hope–Goldthorpe classification has also been used (Britten 1981).

## TESTS OF ATTAINMENT

Tests of attainment were taken in schools at ages 8, 11, and 15 years, and at home at age 26 years. First born offspring of study members also took tests at 8 years. Schools were asked to administer tests to study members, and the tests taken at home were given by trained interviewers. Detailed instructions were printed on each test booklet describing how to introduce the tests, how to offer encouragement and to avoid prompting, and where appropriate how to score the answers. The tests taken in schools were later marked again at the National Foundation for Educational Research (NFER).

At 8 years children took four tests; a 60-item non-verbal picture test (published by NFER as picture test 1 by J. E. Stuart), a 35-item reading comprehension test (published by NFER as sentence-reading test 1 by A. F. Watts), a 50-item word-reading test and 50-item vocabulary test, each of which was designed by NFER for the study. Information on the reliability and validity of these tests is given in Douglas (1964). In the picture test children were asked to identify the odd one out in a series of pictures, to continue a series of four pictures by choosing one from a group of five, and to continue a series of relationships between pictures. In the reading comprehension test children were asked to choose the appropriate word from five to complete a sentence. Sentences became progressively more difficult. The first item, for instance, was

1. Come with me to the shops to buy some (FIRE, WATER, STONE, SWEETS, MOTORS).

   And the last item was

35. The political dangers of monopoly seem to have been much (EXASPERATED, EXCISED, EXAGGERATED, EXPROPRIATED, EXPOSTULATED).

For the reading tests children read a series of words to the teacher, and for the comprehension test described what each of the same words meant. Teachers used an answer guide to assess acceptability of descriptions. The first two items on this test were 'cat' and 'egg', and the last two were 'ophthalmic' and 'haemorrhage'.

At 11 years a further four tests were taken; an 80-item verbal and non-verbal test designed for the study by NFER, a 50-item arithmetic test also designed by NFER, and the same word-reading and vocabulary tests as had been taken at the age of 8 years. Information on reliability and validity is given in Douglas (1964). In the first test children were asked to complete the series of three words or shapes with an appropriate fourth choice taken from five possibilities. The arithmetic test comprised fifty addition, multiplication, subtraction, and division sums, and problems ranging from

1. Add
   34
   +47
   ———

to

48. A cross-country runner runs at 4½ miles per hour. He begins running at 8 o'clock and runs for two hours. He rests for half an hour and then runs until 12 o'clock. How many miles has he run?

49. Find the product of 174 and 36.

50. This [diagram] is a plank of wood worth 4*s*. 6*d*. How much is the shaded piece worth?

The word-reading and vocabulary tests were the same as those used at 8 years.

At 15 years the three tests taken were a 130-item verbal and non-verbal test (group ability test AH4), a 35-item reading comprehension test (the Watts–Vernon reading test) and a 47-item mathematics test designed by NFER for this study. Information on reliability and validity is given in Douglas *et al.* 1968. In the first test the first 35 items comprised shape matching and selection tasks, and the second 35 were verbal and number problems, of which the first two items were

1. 1, 2, 3, 4, 5, 6, 7, 8, 9. Multiply the middle one of these figures by 2.

2. *Easy* means the opposite of . . . problem, simple, difficult,
                                                  1       2       3
   always, and cannot.
         4        5

The last two items were

64. The *day after tomorrow* is to *the day before yesterday* as *Wednesday* is
        1       2       3       4       5
to *Friday, Saturday, Sunday, Monday, Tuesday.*

65. Here are three figures; 9 4 8. Divide the biggest figure by the smallest and add the result to the figure printed immediately after the smallest figure.

The reading comprehension test required pupils to select an appropriate word from a group of five to complete the sentence. For example the first item was

1. You can buy stamps at a post (station, house, shop, man, office).

And the last was

35. Before we make a decision we must consider all (relevant, relative, competent, decisive, comparable) factors.

The mathematics test included arithmetic, geometric, trigonometric, and algebraic questions, beginning with

1. Underline the number below that means a quarter of a million;

2,500,000   250,000   $\dfrac{1}{4,000,000}$   25,225   40,000

The last item was

47. Sin A × cosec A =

At 26 years the same reading comprehension test that had been taken eleven years earlier was administered by trained interviewers to study members at home. In order to avoid the 'ceiling effect' of too many study members scoring correctly on every item, the test used at age 15 years was extended by ten items, and the last item in the 26-year test was

45. The historical records are kept in the (arches, interims, archives, inquest, sojourn).

The use of this test was described by Rodgers (1986).

First born offspring took the reading comprehension, word-reading, and vocabulary tests at 8 years which had been taken by their study member parent at the same age. Findings and alterations to the tests to make them generation fair are described in Chapter 7 and in Wadsworth 1986*b*.

# References and Author Index

*Numbers in italic refer to pages in this volume*

ABEL-SMITH, B., and TOWNSEND, P. (1965), *The Poor and the Poorest* (London, Bell); *85.*

ADDISON, P. (1985), *Now the War is Over: A Social History of Britain 1945–51* (London, BBC and Jonathan Cape); *1, 38–9.*

ATKINSON, P. B., MAYNARD, A. K., and TRINDER, C. G. (1983), *Parents and Children: Income in Two Generations* (London, Heinemann); *173.*

BADDELEY, A. (1979), 'The limitations of human memory: implications for the design of retrospective studies', in L. Moss and H. Goldstein (eds.), *The Recall Method in Social Surveys* (London, University of London Studies in Education, No. 9), 13–27; *219.*

—— (1989), 'The psychology of remembering and forgetting', in T. Butler (ed.), *Memory: History, Culture and Mind* (Oxford, Blackwell), 33–60; *220.*

BAERS, M. (1954), 'Women workers and home responsibilities', *International Labour Review*, 69: 338–55; *34.*

BANKS, A. L. (1952), 'The future of local authority health services', *British Medical Journal* (ii): 1007–10; *55–6.*

BARKER, D. J. P., BULL, A. R., OSMOND, C., and SIMMONDS, S. J. (1990), 'Fetal and placental size and risk of hypertension in adult life', *British Medical Journal*, 301: 259–62; *93, 128, 139, 195, 199, 204.*

—— and OSMOND, C. (1986a), 'Childhood respiratory infection and adult chronic bronchitis in England and Wales', *British Medical Journal*, 293: 1271–5; *6, 128–9, 136–7, 195, 199, 203, 215, 220.*

—— —— (1986b), 'Infant mortality, childhood nutrition and ischaemic heart disease in England and Wales', *Lancet* (i): 1077–81; *128–9, 199, 220.*

—— —— (1987), 'Death rates from stroke in England and Wales predicted from past maternal mortality', *British Medical Journal*, 295: 83–6; *128, 139, 215, 218.*

—— —— GOLDING, J., KUH, D., and WADSWORTH, M. E. J. (1989), 'Growth in utero, blood pressure in childhood and adult life, and mortality from cardiovascular disease', *British Medical Journal*, 298: 564–7; *6, 128.*

BARNETT, C. (1986), *The Audit of War: The Illusion and Reality of Britain as a Great Nation* (London, Macmillan); *3, 4, 70, 175.*

BARTLETT, C. J. (1977), *A History of Postwar Britain 1945–74* (London, Longman); *2.*

BERENSON, G. S. (1986), *Causation of Cardiovascular Risk Factors in Children* (New York, Raven Press); *6, 93, 128–9.*

BERRUETA-CLEMENT, J., SCHWEINHART, L. J., BARNETT, W. S., EPSTEIN, S., and WEIKART, D. P. (1984), *Changed Lives: The Effects of the Perry Preschool Project Program on Youths through Age 19* (Ypsilanti, Monograph of the High/Scope Educational Research Foundation, No. 8); *197, 219.*

BLACKSTONE, T. (1971), *A Fair Start: The Provision of Preschool Education* (London, Allen Lane); *175.*

BLAXTER, M. (1981), *The Health of the Children: A Review of Research on the Place of Health in Cycles of Disadvantage* (London, Heinemann Education Books); *21, 135, 170.*

—— (1986), 'Longitudinal studies in Britain relevant to inequalities in health', in R. G. Wilkinson, (ed.), *Class and Health: Research and Longitudinal Data* (London, Tavistock); *221.*

—— (1987), 'Evidence on inequality in health from a national survey', *Lancet* (ii): 30–3; *170, 215.*

BLOMFIELD, J. M., and DOUGLAS, J. W. B. (1956), 'Bed-wetting: prevalance among children aged 4–7 years', *Lancet* (i): 850–2; *67–8.*

BLYTHE, R. (1979), *The View in Winter* (London, Allen Lane); *12.*

Board of Education (1931), *Report of the Consultative Committee on the Primary School* (London, His Majesty's Stationery Office); *70–1.*

BOCK, G. R., and WHELAN, J. (1991) (eds.), *The Childhood Environment and Adult Disease*, Ciba Symposium No. 156 (Chichester, John Wiley); *6, 93, 195–6.*

BOWLBY, J. (1953), *Child Care and the Growth of Love* (London, Penguin Books); *34.*

BOYD-ORR, J. (1937), *Food, Health and Income* (London, Macmillan); *218.*

BRADDON, F. M., RODGERS, B., WADSWORTH, M. E. J., and DAVIES, J. M. C. (1986), 'Onset of obesity in a 36 year birth cohort study', *British Medical Journal*, 293: 299–303; *67, 94, 137.*

—— WADSWORTH, M. E. J., DAVIES, J. M. C., and CRIPPS, H. A. (1988), 'Social and regional differences in food and alcohol consumption and their measurement in a national birth cohort', *Journal of Epidemiology and Community Health*, 42: 341–9; *128, 137, 143, 217.*

BRANSBY, E. R., BLOMFIELD, J. M., and DOUGLAS, J. W. B. (1955), 'The prevalance of bed-wetting', *Medical Officer*, 94: 5; *67.*

BRIM, O. G., and KAGAN, J. (1980) (eds.), *Constancy and Change in Human Development* (Cambridge, Mass., Harvard University Press); *220.*

BRITTEN, N. (1981), 'Models' of intergenerational class mobility: findings from the National Survey of Health and Development, *British Journal of Sociology*, 32: 224–38; *224.*

—— DAVIES, J. M. C., and COLLEY, J. R. T. (1987), 'Early respiratory experience and subsequent cough and peak expiratory flow rate in 36 year old men and women', *British Medical Journal*, 294: 1317–20; *6, 136.*

—— MORGAN, K., FENWICK, P. B. C., and BRITTEN, H. (1936), 'Epilepsy and handicap from birth to age thirty six', *Developmental Medicine and Child Neurology*, 28: 719–28; *134–5.*

BROWN, G. W., and HARRIS, T. (1978), *Social Origins of Depression* (London, Tavistock); *141, 197.*

BURLINGHAM, D., and FREUD, A. (1965), *Infants without Families* (London, Allen & Unwin); *70.*

BURNETT, J. (1978), *A Social History of Housing 1815–1970* (London, Methuen); *171.*

—— (1989), *Plenty and Want: A Social History of Food in England from 1815 to the Present Day* (London, Routledge); *8, 36–7, 67.*

Burnham Further Education Committee (1980), *Grading of Courses and List of Courses 1980* (London, Local Authorities Conditions of Service Advisory Board); *111.*

BURY, M., and HOLME, A. (1991), *Life after Ninety* (London, Routledge); *218.*

BUTLER, N. R., and BONHAM, D. G. (1963), *Perinatal Mortality* (Edinburgh, Livingstone); *20, 90–1, 93, 122, 129, 215.*

—— and GOLDING, J. (1986) (eds.), *From Birth to Five* (Oxford, Pergamon); *6, 215, 219.*

BUTLER, T. (1989) (ed.), *Memory: History, Culture and Mind* (Oxford, Blackwell); *164, 220.*

BUTTERFIELD, W. J. H. (1968), *Priorities in Medicine: The Rock Carling Fellowship 1968* (London, Nuffield Provincial Hospitals Trust); *90–1.*

CALNAN, M. (1982), 'Delay in the diagnosis and treatment of cancer', in M. Alderson (ed.), *The Prevention of Cancer* (London, Edward Arnold); *135.*

—— DOUGLAS, J. W. B., and GOLDSTEIN, H. (1978), 'Tonsillectomy and circumcision: comparison of two cohorts', *International Journal of Epidemiology*, 7: 79–85; *96, 168.*

CARPENTER, H. (1985), *Secret Gardens: A Study of the Golden Age of Children's Literature* (London, Allen & Unwin); *178–9.*

CARR, E. H. (1964), *What is History?* (London, Penguin); *121, 198.*

CARR-SAUNDERS, A., JONES, D. C., and MOSER, C. A. (1958), *A Survey of Social Conditions in England and Wales* (Oxford, Clarendon Press); *58–61.*

CARTWRIGHT, A. (1967), *Patients and their Doctors* (London, Routledge & Kegan Paul); *91.*

—— and ANDERSON, R. (1981), *General Practice Revisited* (London, Tavistock); *91.*

Central Advisory Council for Education (1954), *Early Leaving* (London, Her Majesty's Stationery Office); *107*.

Central Statistical Office (1990), *Annual Abstract of Statistics 1990* (London, Her Majesty's Stationery Office); *125*.

CHAMBERLAIN, R., CHAMBERLAIN, G., HOWLETT, B., and CLAIREAUX, A. (1975), *British Births 1970* (London, Heinemann); *129, 215*.

CHERRY, N. (1974a), 'Components of occupational interest', *British Journal of Educational Psychology*, 44: 22–30; *113, 149*.

—— (1974b), 'Do careers officers give good advice?' *British Journal of Guidance and Counselling*, 2: 27–40; *114*.

—— (1976), 'Persistent job changing: is it a problem?' *Journal of Occupational Psychology*, 49: 203–21; *114, 141*.

—— (1978), 'The Determinants of Occupational Functioning and the Use of Job Skills' (Ph.D. thesis, University of London); *11, 148–9, 152*.

—— (1984a), 'Women and work stress: evidence from the 1946 birth cohort', *Ergonomics*, 27: 519–26; *152–3*.

—— (1984b), 'Nervous strain, anxiety and symptoms amongst 32-year-old men at work in Britain', *Journal of Occupational Psychology*, 57: 95–105; *152–3*.

—— and KIERNAN, K. (1976), 'Personality scores and smoking behaviour', *British Journal of Preventive and Social Medicine*, 30: 123–31; *94*.

—— and RODGERS, B. (1979), 'Using a longitudinal study to assess the quality of retrospective data', in L. Moss and H. Goldstein (eds.), *The Recall Method in Social Surveys* (London, University of London Studies in Education, No. 9), 31–47; *220*.

CLARKE, A. M., and CLARKE, A. D. B. (1976), *Early Experience: Myth and Evidence* (London, Open Books); *197, 220*.

COHLER, B. J. (1982), 'Personal narrative and the life course', in P. B. Baltes and O. G. Brim (eds.), *Life-Span Development and Behavior* (New York, Academic Press), iv. 205–41; *201, 220*.

COLEMAN, D. A. (1988), 'Population', in A. H. Halsey (ed.), *British Social Trends since 1900* (London, Macmillan); *60, 213*.

COLEMAN, P. G. (1986), *Ageing and Reminiscence Processes: Social and Clinical Implications* (Chichester, John Wiley); *202*.

COLES, E. C., COTTER, S., and VALMAN, H. B. (1978), 'Increasing prevalence of breast feeding', *British Medical Journal* (ii): 1122; *29*.

COLLEY, J. R. T., DOUGLAS, J. W. B., and REID, D. D. (1973), 'Respiratory disease in young adults: influence of early childhood lower respiratory tract illness, social class, air pollution, and smoking', *British Medical Journal* (ii): 195–8; *136*.

Committee on Manpower Resources for Science and Technology (1967), *The Brain Drain: Report of the Working Group on Migration*, Cmnd. 3417 (London, Her Majesty's Stationery Office); *213*.

CONNERTON, P. (1989), *How Societies Remember* (Cambridge, Cambridge University Press); *164, 193.*

COSTELLO, J. (1985), *Love, Sex and War: Changing Values 1939–45* (London, Pan Books); *59.*

COURT, D., and ALBERMAN, E. (1988), 'Worlds apart', in J. O. Forfar (ed.), *Child Health in a Changing Society* (Oxford, Oxford University Press); *169.*

Court Report (1976), *Fit for the Future: The Report of the Committee on Child Health Services*, Cmnd. 6684 (London, Her Majesty's Stationery Office); *169, 215.*

COX, B. D., BLAXTER, M., BUCKLE, A. L. J., and FENNER, N. P. (1987), *The Health and Lifestyle Survey* (London, Health Promotion Research Trust); *128.*

CRISP, A. H., DOUGLAS, J. W. B., ROSS, J. M., and STONEHILL, E. (1970), 'Some developmental aspects of disorders of weight', *Journal of Psychosomatic Research*, 14: 313–20; *94.*

Crowther Report (1959), *15–18: A Report of the Central Advisory Council for Education* (London, Her Majesty's Stationery Office); *88, 147.*

DAVEY SMITH, G., BARTLEY, M., and BLANE, D. (1990), 'The Black Report on socio-economic inequalities in health 10 years on', *British Medical Journal*, 301: 373–7; *205, 215.*

DAVIE, R., BUTLER, N. R., and GOLDSTEIN, H. (1972), *From Birth to Seven: The Second Report of the National Child Development Study (1958 Cohort)* (London, Longman); *29, 215.*

Department of Health and Social Security (1983), *Present Day Practice in Infant Feeding*, Reports on Health and Social Subjects No. 20 (London, Her Majesty's Stationery Office); *44.*

—— (1985), *Health and Personal Social Services Statistics for England* (London, Goverment Statistics Service); *23, 26.*

DE SWIET, M. (1986), 'The epidemiology of hypertension in childhood', *British Medical Bulletin*, 42: 172–5; *6, 93, 138.*

DOLL, R., and HILL, A. B. (1956), 'Lung cancer and other causes of death in relation to smoking', *British Medical Journal* (ii): 1071–81; *62.*

DOUGLAS, J. W. B. (1950), 'The extent of breast-feeding in Great Britain in 1946, with special reference to the health and survival of children', *Journal of Obstetrics and Gynaecology of the British Empire*, 57: 336–61; *44–5.*

—— (1951), 'Social class differences in health and survival during the first two years of life: the results of a national survey', *Population Studies*, 5: 35–58; *40–1.*

—— (1960), 'Premature children at primary schools', *British Medical Journal* (i): 1008–13; *66.*

DOUGLAS, J. W. B. (1962), 'The height of boys and girls and their home environment', in A. Hottinger and H. Berger (eds.), *Modern Problems in Paediatrics* (Basle, Karger), vii. 178–82; *94.*

—— (1964), *The Home and the School* (London, MacGibbon & Kee); *10, 11, 69–70, 73–81, 224–5.*

—— (1969), 'Effects of early environment on later development', *Journal of the Royal College of Physicians*, 3: 359–64; *47, 65.*

—— (1970), 'Broken families and child behaviour', *Journal of the Royal College of Physicians*, 4: 203–10; *116, 141.*

—— (1973*a*), 'Early disturbing events and later enuresis', in I. Kolvin, R. C. Mackeith, and S. R. Meadow (eds.), *Bladder Control and Enuresis* (London, Spastics International Medical Publishers), 109–17; *52, 68, 141, 196.*

—— (1973*b*), 'Prospective study of effectiveness of tonsillectomy in children', in *Proceedings of 6th International Scientific Meeting of the International Epidemiological Association* (Belgrade, Savremena Administracija), 941–50; *96.*

—— (1975*a*), 'Early hospital admissions and later disturbances of behaviour and learning', *Developmental Medicine and Child Neurology*, 17: 456–80; *97, 141, 168.*

—— (1976), 'The use and abuse of national cohorts', in M. Shipman (ed.), *The Organisation and Impact of Social Research* (London, Routledge); *209, 214–15.*

—— and BLOMFIELD, J. M. (1956), 'The reliability of longitudinal studies', *Milbank Memorial Fund Quarterly*, 34: 227–52; *209, 220.*

—— —— (1958), *Children under Five* (London, Allen & Unwin); *42, 46–56, 162, 171.*

—— and CHERRY, N. (1977), 'Does sex make any difference?' *Times Educational Supplement*, 9 December, 3261: 16–17; *7, 107.*

—— and MOGFORD, C. (1953*a*), 'The health of premature children during the first four years of life', *British Medical Journal* (i): 748–54; *43, 138.*

—— —— (1953*b*), 'The growth of premature children', *Archives of Disease in Childhood*, 28: 436–45; *138.*

—— and MULLIGAN, D. G. (1961), 'Emotional adjustment and educational achievement: the preliminary results of a longitudinal study of a national sample of children', *Proceedings of the Royal Society of Medicine*, 54: 885–91; *68, 99.*

—— ROSS, J. M., and SIMPSON, H. R. (1967), 'The ability and attainment of short sighted pupils', *Journal of the Royal Statistical Society*, Series A, 130: 479–503; *95.*

—— —— —— (1968), *All Our Future* (London, Peter Davies Ltd.); *69, 76, 94–5, 98–9, 101–7, 112–13, 177, 225.*

—— and SIMPSON, H. R. (1964), 'Height in relation to puberty, family size and social class: a longitudinal study', *Milbank Memorial Fund Quarterly*, 42: 20–35; *66, 94.*

—— and WALLER, R. E. (1966), 'Air pollution and respiratory infection in children', *British Journal of Preventive and Social Medicine*, 20: 1–8; *65, 95–6.*

DRUMMOND, J. C., and WILBRAHAM, A. (1959), *The Englishman's Food* (London, Jonathan Cape); *67.*

*The Economist* (1944), 'Condition of the people', 30 Dec.: 859–60; *2, 3, 206.*

*The Economist* (1968), 'Poor homes, bad schools, poor citizens' (review article), 12 Oct.: 63–4; *121.*

EDELSTON, H. (1943), 'Separation anxiety in young children: a study of hospital cases', *Genetic Psychology Monograph*, 28: 3–95; *97.*

EEKELAAR, J., and MACLEAN, M. (1986), *Maintenance after Divorce* (Oxford, Oxford University Press); *116, 141–2.*

ELDER, G. H. (1974), *Children of the Great Depression* (Chicago, University of Chicago Press); *199, 218.*

—— LIKER, J. K., and CROSS, C. E. (1984), 'Parent–child behaviour in the Great Depression: life course and intergenerational influences', in P. B. Baltes and O. G. Brim (eds.), *Life-Span Development and Behavior* (New York, Academic Press), vi. 109–58; *199, 204, 218.*

EMANUEL, I. (1986), 'Maternal health during childhood and later reproductive performance', *Annals of the New York Academy of Sciences*, 477: 27–39; *6, 11, 21, 93.*

EYSENCK, H. J. (1958), 'A short questionnaire for the measurement of two dimensions of personality', *Journal of Applied Psychology*, 42: 14–17; *217.*

FEINLEIB, M., KANNEL, W. B., GARRISON, G. J., McNAMARA, P. M., and CASTELLI, W. P. (1975), 'The Framingham offspring study', *Preventive Medicine*, 4: 518–25; *219.*

FENNER, N. P. (1987), 'Leisure, exercise and work', in B. D. Cox, M. Blaxter, A. L. J. Buckle, and N. P. Fenner (eds.), *The Health and Lifestyle Survey* (London, Health Promotion Research Trust); *6.*

FLOUD, J., and HALSEY, A. H. (1957), 'Intelligence tests, social class and selection for secondary schools', *British Journal of Sociology*, 8: 33–9; *78.*

FOGELMAN, K. (1983) (ed.), *Growing up in Great Britain* (London, Macmillan); *215, 219.*

—— (1985), 'After school: the education and training experience of the 1958 cohort', National Child Development Study, Working Paper No. 3; *161.*

FORD, L. R. (1976), 'The community's unmet child health needs', *Public Health*, 90: 59–64; *27.*

FORFAR, J. O. (1988), 'Changing paediatric perceptions and perspectives', in J. O. Forfar (ed.), *Child Health in a Changing Society* (Oxford, Oxford University Press); *169*.

FUSSELL, P. (1975), *The Great War and Modern Memory* (Oxford, Oxford University Press); *220*.

GAMBLE, D. R. (1980), 'The epidemiology of insulin dependent diabetes, with particular reference to the relationship of virus infection to its etiology', *Epidemiologic Reviews*, 2: 49–70; *203*.

GELLNER, E. (1964), *Thought and Change* (London, Weidenfeld & Nicolson); *164*.

*General Household Survey 1977* (London, Her Majesty's Stationery Office); *129*.

*General Household Survey 1983* (London, Her Majesty's Stationery Office); *129*.

*General Household Survey 1984* (London, Her Majesty's Stationery Office); *128–9*.

GIBBENS, J. (1947), *Care of Children from One to Five*, 3rd edn. London, J. and A. Churchill); *33–4, 47*.

GLASS, D. V. (1954) (ed.), *Social Mobility in Britain* (London, Routledge & Kegan Paul); *186, 189*.

GOLDING, J. F. (1987), 'Smoking', in B. D. Cox, M. Blaxter, A. L. J. Buckle, and N. P. Fenner, *The Health and Lifestyle Survey* (London, Health Promotion Research Trust); *6*.

GOLDTHORPE, J. H., LLEWELLYN, C., and PAYNE, C. (1980), *Social Mobility and Class Structure in Modern Britain* (Oxford, Clarendon Press); *70, 161, 186, 189, 204*.

GORER, G. (1955), *Exploring English Character* (London, The Cresset Press); *35–6*.

GRAHAM, H. (1984), *Women, Health and the Family* (Brighton, Wheatsheaf Books); *128*.

GREENBERG, E. F., and NAY, W. R. (1983), 'The intergenerational transmission of marital instability reconsidered', *Journal of Marriage and the Family*, 44: 335–47; *193*.

HABBAKKUK, H. J. (1953), 'English population in the eighteenth century', *Economic History Review*, 6: 117–33; *203*.

HALBWACHS, M. (1980), *The Collective Memory* (New York, Harper & Row); *193*.

HALSEY, A. H. (1987), *Change in British Society*, 3rd edn. (Oxford, Oxford University Press); *60, 87, 165, 183*.

——— (1988), *British Social Trends since 1900*, 2nd edn. (London, Macmillan); *88, 120–1, 125*.

——— HEATH, A. F., and RIDGE, J. M. (1980), *Origins and Destinations: Family, Class, and Education in Modern Britain* (Oxford, Clarendon Press); *70, 106–8, 118, 186, 189, 204*.

HARDYMENT, C. (1984), *Dream Babies: Child Care from Locke to Spock* (Oxford, Oxford University Press); *34–6.*

HAREVEN, T. K. (1978) (ed.), *Transitions: The Family and the Life Course in Historical Perspective* (New York, Academic Press); *199, 220.*

—— and ADAMS, K. (1982) (eds.), *Aging and the Life-Course Transitions* (New York, Guilford Press); *199.*

HARRISSON, T. (1978), *Living through the Blitz* (London, Penguin); *11.*

HETHERINGTON, E. M. (1988), 'Parent and children and siblings: six years after divorce', in R. A. Hinde and J. Stevenson-Hinde (eds.), *Relationships with Families: Mutual Influences* (Oxford, Oxford University Press); *141, 197.*

HOGGART, R. (1957), *Uses of Literacy* (London, Chatto & Windus); *183.*

HOINVILLE, G., and JOWELL, R. (1987), *Survey Research Practice* (Aldershot, Gower Press); *220.*

HOWARD, A. (1986), 'We are the masters now', in M. Sissons and P. French (eds.), *Age of Austerity* (Oxford, Oxford University Press); *5.*

HOWARTH, T. E. B. (1985), *Prospect and Reality: Great Britain 1945–1955* (London, Collins); *11, 36.*

ILLSLEY, R. (1956), 'The duration of antenatal care', *Medical Officer*, 96: 107–11; *21.*

—— (1980), *Professional or Public Health: Sociology in Health and Medicine* (London, Nuffield Provincial Hospitals Trust); *135.*

—— and KINCAID, J. C. (1963), 'Social correlates of perinatal mortality', in N. R. Butler and D. G. Bonham (eds.), *Perinatal Mortality* (Edinburgh, Livingstone); *93, 122, 157.*

—— and MITCHELL, R. G. (1984), *Low Birth Weight* (Chichester, Wiley); *11.*

International Labour Office (1955), 'International guarantees for working mothers: purpose and prospects', *Courrier*, 5: 71–82; *53.*

JACKSON, B., and MARSDEN, D. (1962), *Education and the Working Class* (London, Routledge & Kegan Paul); *10, 69.*

Joint Committee of the British Medical Association and the Magistrates' Association on Psychiatry and Law (Joint Committee (*b*)) (1948), *Supplement to the British Medical Journal* (i): 43; *67.*

Joint Committee of the Royal College of Obstetricians and Gynaecologists and the Population Investigation Committee (Joint Committee (*a*)) (1948), *Maternity in Great Britain* (London, Oxford University Press); *17–18, 20–5, 27–31, 129, 207.*

JOLLY, M. (1977), *Book of Child Care* (London, Sphere Books); *7.*

JOWELL, R., and AIREY, C. (1984) (eds.), *British Social Attitudes* (Aldershot, Gower Publishing); *205.*

—— WITHERSPOON, S., and BROOK, L. (1990) (eds.), *British Social Attitudes* (Aldershot, Gower Publishing); *205.*

KIERNAN, K. E. (1980), 'Teenage motherhood: associated factors and consequences: the experience of a British birth cohort', *Journal of Biosocial Science*, 12: 393–405; *158*.

—— (1986), 'Teenage marriage and marital breakdown: a longitudinal study', *Population Studies*, 40: 35–54; *115*.

—— COLLEY, J. R. T., DOUGLAS, J. W. B., and REID, D. D. (1976), 'Chronic cough in young adults in relation to smoking habits, childhood environment and chest illness', *Respiration*, 33: 236–44; *136*.

—— and DIAMOND, I. (1983), 'The age at which childbearing starts: a longitudinal study', *Population Studies*, 37: 363–80; *115, 158*.

KING, M. TRUBY (1934), *Mothercraft* (Sydney, Whitcombe & Tombs); *33, 44–5*.

—— (1937), *Feeding and Care of Baby* (Oxford, Oxford University Press); *33*.

KOLVIN, I., MILLER, F. J. W., SCOTT, D. McI., GATZANIS, S. R. M., and FLEETING, M. (1990), *Continuities of Deprivation? The Newcastle 1000 Family Study* (Aldershot, Avebury); *219*.

KUH, D., and MACLEAN, M. (1990), 'Women's childhood experience of parental separation and their subsequent health and socioeconomic status in adulthood', *Journal of Biosocial Science*, 22: 121–35; *141*.

—— POWER, C., and RODGERS, B. (forthcoming), 'Secular trends in height and their association with social class and sex'; *8, 11, 169, 199*.

—— WADSWORTH, M. E. J. (1989), 'Parental height, childhood environment and subsequent adult height in a national birth cohort', *International Journal of Epidemiology*, 18: 663–8; *11, 169*.

—— —— (forthcoming), 'Childhood influence on adult male earnings in a longitudinal study', *British Journal of Sociology*; *11*.

LAWRENCE, E. S. (1970), *The Origin and Growth of Modern Education* (London, Penguin Books); *70*.

LAZAR, I., and DARLINGTON, R. (1982), 'Lasting effects of early education: a report from the consortium for longitudinal studies', *Monographs of the Society for Research in Child Development*, 47; *197*.

LEIGH, G. K. (1982), 'Kinship interaction over the family life span', *Journal of Marriage and the Family*, 44: 197–208; *193*.

LIDDIARD, M. (1944), *The Mothercraft Manual* (London, J. and A. Churchill); *28, 33*.

LINDGARDE, F., FURU, M., and LJUNG, B. O. (1987), 'A longitudinal study on the significance of environmental and individual factors associated with the development of essential hypertension (The Malmo Study)', *Journal of Epidemiology and Community Health*, 41: 220–6; *218*.

LOWNDES, G. A. N. (1969), *The Silent Social Revolution*, 2nd edn. (Oxford, Oxford University Press); *3, 63*.

Lucas, A. (1991), 'Early nutritional programming: human evidence', in G. Bock and J. Whelan (eds.), *The Childhood Environment and Adult Disease*, Ciba Symposium No. 156 (Chichester, John Wiley); *196*.

McCord, J. (1990), 'Long-term perspectives on parental absence', in L. Robins and M. Rutter (eds.), *Straight and Devious Pathways from Childhood to Adulthood* (Cambridge, Cambridge University Press); *218*.

Macfarlane, A., and Mugford, M. (1984), *Birth Counts: Statistics of Pregnancy and Childbirth* (London, Her Majesty's Stationery Office); *23, 26, 32, 170*.

Macintyre, S. (1984), 'Consumer reaction to present-day antenatal services', in L. Zander and G. Chamberlain (ed.), *Pregnancy Care for the 1980s* (London, Royal Society of Medicine and Macmillan Press Ltd.); *21, 31*.

——— Annandale, E., Ecob, R., Ford, G., Hunt, K., Jamieson, B., Maciver, S., West, P., and Wyke, S. (1989), 'The west of Scotland twenty-07 study: health in the community', in C. Martin and D. MacQueen (eds.), *Reading for the New Public Health* (Edinburgh, Edinburgh University Press); *219*.

McKeown, T. (1979), *The Role of Medicine: Dream, Mirage or Nemesis?* (Oxford, Blackwell); *203*.

McKinlay, J. B. and McKinlay, S. M. (1979), 'The influence of a premarital conception and various obstetric complications on subsequent prenatal health behaviour', *Journal of Epidemiology and Community Health*, 33: 84–90; *21*.

Maclean, M., and Wadsworth, M. E. J. (1988), 'The interests of children after parental divorce: a longterm perspective', *International Journal of Law and the Family*, 155–66; *99, 141*.

McQueen, D. V., and Siegrist, J. (1982), 'Social factors in the etiology of chronic disease: an overview', *Social Science and Medicine*, 16: 353–67; *135*.

Magnusson, D. Stattin, H., and Allen, V. L. (1986), 'Differential maturation among girls and its relations to social adjustment: a longitudinal perspective', in P. B. Baltes, D. L. Featherman, and R. M. Lerner (eds.), *Life-Span Development and Behavior* (Hillsdale, NJ, Lawrence Erlbaum), vii. 135–72; *197*.

Mann, S. L., Wadsworth, M. E. J., and Colley, J. R. T. (forthcoming), 'Accumulation of factors influencing respiratory illness in members of a national birth cohort and their offspring', *Journal of Epidemiology and Community Health*; *6, 65, 96, 128, 136, 168, 170, 196, 203*.

Mansfield, K. (1918), 'A married man's story', repr. in C. Tomalin (1983) (ed.), *Katherine Mansfield: Short Stories* (London, Dent); *12*.

Marmot, M. G. (1986), 'Social inequalities in mortality: the social environment', in R. G. Wilkinson (ed.), *Class and Health: Research and Longitudinal Data* (London, Tavistock); *138, 196*.

.MARMOT, M. G., PAGE, C. M., ATKINS, E., and DOUGLAS, J. W. B. (1980), 'Effect of breast-feeding on plasma cholesterol and weight in young adults', *Journal of Epidemiology and Community Health*, 34: 164–7; *143*.

—— ROSE, G. A., SHIPLEY, M. J., and HAMILTON, P. J. S. (1978), 'Employment grade and coronary heart disease in British civil servants', *Journal of Epidemiology and Community Health*, 32: 244–9; *219*.

—— SHIPLEY, M. J., and ROSE, G. (1984), 'Inequalities in death: specific explanations of a general pattern?' *Lancet* (i): 1003–6; *129*.

MARSHALL, T. H. (1965), *Social Policy* (London, Hutchinson University Library); *62*.

MARTIN, J. (1978), *Infant Feeding 1975: Attitudes and Practices in England and Wales* (London, OPCS Social Survey Division, Report No. SS1064, Her Majesty's Stationery Office); *44*.

—— and MONK, J. (1982), *Infant Feeding 1980* (London, OPCS Social Survey Division, Report No. SS1144, Her Majesty's Stationery Office); *44*.

—— and WHITE, A. (1988), *Infant Feeding 1985* (London, OPCS Social Survey Division, Report No. SS1233, Her Majesty's Stationery Office); *44*.

MARTYN, C. N., BARKER, D. J. P., and OSMOND, C. (1988), 'Motorneuron disease and past poliomyelitis in England and Wales', *Lancet* (i): 1319–22; *196, 203*.

MARWICK, A. (1982), *British Society since 1940* (London, Pelican Books); *4, 37, 50, 57–8, 60, 84, 86, 107, 124–5*.

MATTOCK, C., MARMOT, M. G., and STERN, G. (1988), 'Could Parkinson's disease follow intra-uterine influenza? A speculative hypothesis', *Journal of Neurology, Neurosurgery and Psychiatry*, 51: 753–6; *203*.

MEADOW, R. (1988), 'Time past and time present for children and their doctors', in J. O. Forfar (ed.), *Child Health in a Changing Society* (Oxford, Oxford University Press); *166*.

Medical Research Council (1951), *Report of the Medical Research Council for the Years 1948–1950* (London, His Majesty's Stationery Office); *38*.

—— (1952), *Report of the Medical Research Council for the Years 1950–1951* (London, Her Majesty's Stationery Office); *38*.

—— (1953), *Report of the Years 1952–1953*, Cmnd. 9184 (London, Her Majesty's Stationery Office); *62*.

—— (1954), *Report of the Years 1953–1954*, Cmnd. 9506 (London, Her Majesty's Stationery Office); *62*.

—— (1957), *Report of the Years 1956–1957*, Cmnd. 453 (London, Her Majesty's Stationery Office); *90*.

—— (1958), *Report of the Years 1957–1958*, Cmnd. 792 (London, Her Majesty's Stationery Office); *61, 90*.

—— (1961), *Report of the Years 1960–1961*, Cmnd. 1783 (London, Her Majesty's Stationery Office); *90*.

—— (1986), *Annual Report 1985–86* (London, Medical Research Council); *130*.

—— (1987), *Infant Nutrition and Cardiovascular Disease*, Scientific Report No. 8 (Southampton, Medical Research Council Environmental Epidemiology Unit); *6*.

MEDNICK, S. A., and BAERT, A. E. (1981) (eds.), *Prospective Longitudinal Research* (Oxford, Oxford University Press); *220*.

—— HARWAY, M., and FINELLO, K. M. (1984) (eds.), *Handbook of Longitudinal Research*; vol. i: *Birth and Childhood Cohorts*; vol. ii: *Teenage and Adult Cohorts* (New York, Praeger); *220*.

—— MACHON, R. A., HUTTUNEN, M. O., and BONNETT, (1988), 'Adult schizophrenia following parental exposure to an influenza epidemic', *Archives of General Psychiatry*, 45: 189–92; *203*.

MILLER, F. J. W., COURT, S. D. M., KNOX, E. G., and BRANDON, S. (1974), *The School Years in Newcastle upon Tyne* (Oxford, Oxford University Press); *219*.

—— —— WALTON, W. S., and KNOX, E. G. (1960), *Growing up in Newcastle upon Tyne* (Oxford, Oxford University Press); *219*.

MILLER, K. M. (1968), *Manual for the Rothwell–Miller Interest Blank* (London, National Foundation for Educational Research); *113*.

Ministry of Health (1946), *Report of the Chief Medical Officer of Health*, Cmnd. 7119 (London, His Majesty's Stationery Office); *51*.

—— (1953), *Report of the Ministry of Health for the Year 1953*, Cmnd. 9307 (London, Her Majesty's Stationery Office); *82–3*.

MINNS, R. (1980), *Bombers and Mash: The Domestic Front 1939–1945* (London, Virago); *52–3, 59*.

MONTOYE, H. J. (1975), *Physical Activity and Health: An Epidemiologic Study of an Entire Community* (Englewood Cliffs, NJ, Prentice-Hall); *219*.

MORRIS, J. N. (1967), *Uses of Epidemiology* (Edinburgh, J. & S. Livingstone); *87, 91, 122*.

MURPHY, J. (1990), 'A most respectable prejudice: inequality in education research and policy', *British Journal of Sociology*, 41: 29–54; *118, 120*.

NELSON, M., and NAISMITH, D. (1979), 'The nutritional status of poor children in London', *Journal of Human Nutrition*, 33: 33–46; *170*.

NEWSON, J., and NEWSON, E. (1963), *Infant Care in an Urban Community* (London, Allen & Unwin); *29*.

—— —— (1968), *Four Years Old in an Urban Community* (London, Allen & Unwin); *176*.

—— —— (1973), 'Cultural aspects of childrearing in the English-speaking world', in M. P. M. Richards (ed.), *The Integration of a Child into a Social World* (Cambridge, Cambridge University Press); *33*.

NICOL, A. R. (1985) (ed.), *Longitudinal Studies in Child Psychology and Psychiatry* (Chichester, John Wiley); *220*.

Office of Population Censuses and Surveys (1980), *Classification of Occupations and Coding Index* (London, Her Majesty's Stationery Office); *217*.

—— (1989), *General Household Survey 1987* (Social Survey Division, London, Her Majesty's Stationery Office); *126*.

—— (1990), *Communicable Disease Statistics 1988*, Series MB2 No. 15 (London, Her Majesty's Stationery Office); *38*.

OSBORN, A. F. (1981), 'Under fives in school in England and Wales, 1971–9', *Education Research*, 23: 96–103; *176*.

—— BUTLER, N. R., and MORRIS, A. (1984), *The Social Life of Britain's Five Year Olds* (London, Routledge & Kegan Paul); *51–2, 215*.

OUNSTEAD, M. K., COCKBURN, J. M., MOAR, V. A., and REDMAN, C. W. G. (1985), 'Factors associated with the blood pressure of children born to women who were hypertensive during pregnancy', *Archives of Disease in Childhood*, 60: 631–5; *138*.

Overseas Migration Board (1964), *Statistics for 1963*, Cmnd. 2555 (London, Her Majesty's Stationery Office); *213*.

PECKHAM, C. S., STARK, O., SIMONITE, V., and WOLFF, O. H. (1983), 'Prevalance of obesity in British children born in 1946 and 1958', *British Medical Journal*, 286: 1237–42; *67, 137–8*.

PIACHAUD, D. (1988), 'Poverty in Britain 1899 to 1983', *Journal of Social Policy*, 17: 335–49; *125*.

PICKERING, G. W. (1955), *High Blood Pressure* (London, J. and A. Churchill); *90*.

PILL, R., and STOTT, N. C. H. (1982), 'Concepts of illness causation and responsibility', *Social Science and Medicine*, 16: 43–52; *135*.

PINTO-DUSCHINSKY, M. (1970), 'Bread and circuses? The conservatives in office, 1951–64', in V. Bogdanor and R. Skidelsky (eds.), *The Age of Affluence 1951–1964* (London, Macmillan); *57*.

Platt Report (1959), *The Welfare of Children in Hospital* (London, Her Majesty's Stationery Office); *97*.

PLESS, I. B., CRIPPS, H. A., DAVIES, J. M. C., and WADSWORTH, M. E. J. (1989), 'Chronic physical illness in childhood and psychological and social circumstances in adolescence and early adult life', *Developmental Medicine and Child Neurology*, 31: 746–55; *66, 135–6*.

—— and DOUGLAS, J. W. B. (1971), 'Chronic illness in childhood, epidemiological and clinical characteristics', *Pediatrics*, 47: 405–14; *42, 65*.

PLEWIS, I. (1985), *Analysing Change: Measurement and Explanation Using Longitudinal Data* (Chichester, John Wiley); *220–1*.

Plowden Report (1967), *Children and their Primary Schools* (London, Her Majesty's Stationery Office); *88–9, 121, 176*.

PLUMMER, K. (1983), *Documents of Life* (London, Allen & Unwin); *220*.

PRAWER, S. S. (1988), review of Ingmar Bergman, *The Magic Lantern: An Autobiography*, trans. J. Tate (London, Hamish Hamilton, 1988), in the *Times Literary Supplement*, 17–23 June: 670; *13*.

PRICE, R. and BAIN, G. S. (1988), 'The labour force', in A. H. Halsey (ed.), *British Social Trends since 1900* (London, Macmillan); *87, 125, 161.*

QUINTON D., and RUTTER, M. (1976), 'Early hospital admissions and later disturbances of behaviour', *Developmental Medicine and Child Neurology*, 18: 447–59; *97–8.*

—— —— (1988), *Parenting Breakdown: The Making and Breaking of Intergenerational Links* (Aldershot, Gower); *197, 198, 218.*

Registrar-General (1947), *Statistical Review of England and Wales for the Years 1938 and 1939* (London, His Majesty's Stationery Office); *52.*

Report of the Committee on Children and Young Persons (1960), Cmnd. 1191 (London, Her Majesty's Stationery Office); *89.*

RILEY, M. R. (1987), 'On the significance of age in sociology', *American Sociological Review*, 52: 1–14; *193.*

Robbins Committee on Higher Education (1963), *Higher Education*, Cmnd. 2154 (London, Her Majesty's Stationery Office); *108.*

ROBERTSON, A. J. (1987), *The Bleak Midwinter 1947* (Manchester, Manchester University Press); *30, 36–7, 40, 60.*

ROBINS, L. N. (1966), *Deviant Children Grown Up* (Baltimore, Williams & Wilkins); *216, 220.*

—— (1988), 'Data gathering and data analysis for prospective and retrospective longitudinal studies', in M. Rutter (ed.), *Studies of Psychosocial Risk: The Power of Longitudinal Data* (Cambridge, Cambridge University Press); *220.*

—— and RUTTER, M. (1990) (eds.), *Straight and Devious Pathways from Childhood to Adulthood* (Cambridge, Cambridge University Press); *140, 197, 221.*

—— SCHOENBERG, S. P., HOLMES, S. J., RATCLIFF, K. S., BENHAM, A., and WORKS, J. (1985), 'Early home environment and retrospective recall: a test for concordance between siblings with and without psychiatric disorders', *American Journal of Orthopsychiatry*, 55: 27–41; *220.*

RODGERS, B. (1979), 'The prospects for ESN(M) school leavers', *Special Education: Forward Trends*, 6: 8–9; *214.*

—— (1984), 'The trend of reading standards re-assessed', *Educational Research*, 26: 153–66; *148.*

—— (1986), 'Change in the reading attainment of adults: a longitudinal study', *British Journal of Developmental Psychology*, 4: 1–17; *7, 148, 214, 226.*

—— (1989), 'Life-History Factors and Inequalities in Affective Disorders: A Cohort Study' (Ph.D. thesis' University of Bristol); *140–1.*

—— (1990a), 'Influences of early-life and recent factors on affective disorder in women: an exploration of vulnerability models', in L. N. Robins and M. Rutter (eds.), *Straight and Devious Pathways from Childhood to Adulthood* (Cambridge, Cambridge University Press), 314–27; *140.*

242          *References and Author Index*

RODGERS, B. (1990*b*), 'Adult affective disorder and early environment', *British Journal of Psychiatry*, 157: 539–50; *140–1, 196*.

—— (1990*c*), 'Behaviour and personality in childhood as predictors of adult psychiatric disorder', *Journal of Child Psychology and Psychiatry*, 31: 393–414; *140–1, 196, 214*.

—— (1990*d*), 'Influences of early-life and recent factors on affective disorder in women', in L. N. Robins and M. Rutter (eds.), *Straight and Devious Pathways from Childhood to Adulthood* (Cambridge, Cambridge University Press); *141*.

—— and MANN, S. A. (1986), 'Reliability and validity of PSE assessments by lay interviewers: a national population survey', *Psychological Medicine*, 16: 689–700; *139–40, 217*.

RONA, R. J., SWANN, A. V., and ALTMAN, D. G. (1978), 'Social factors and height of primary schoolchildren in England and Scotland', *Journal of Epidemiology and Community Health*, 32: 147–54; *169*.

ROSS, J. M., and SIMPSON, H. R. (1971), 'The national survey of health and development: rate of school progress between 8 and 15 years and between 15 and 18 years', *British Journal of Educational Psychology*, 41: 125–35; *98–9*.

ROWNTREE, B. S., and LAVERS, G. R. (1951), *Poverty and the Welfare State* (London, Longmans Green); *173*.

ROWNTREE, G. (1955), 'Early childhood in broken families', *Population Studies*, 8: 247–63; *52*.

RUSSELL, B. (1926), *On Education, Especially in Early Childhood* (London, Allen & Unwin); *69, 175, 197*.

RUTTER, M. (1972), *Maternal Deprivation Reassessed* (London, Pelican Books); *34, 197*.

—— (1988) (ed.), *Studies of Psychosocial Risk: The Power of Longitudinal Data* (Cambridge, Cambridge University Press); *197, 221*.

—— MAUGHAN, B., MORTIMORE, P., and OUSTON, J. (1979), *Fifteen Thousand Hours: Secondary Schools and their Effects on Children* (London, Open Books); *102*.

SAMPSON, A. (1962), *Anatomy of Britain* (London, Hodder & Stoughton); *84–6, 88, 118, 147*.

—— (1971), *The New Anatomy of Britain* (London, Hodder & Stoughton); *127*.

SCAMBLER, G. (1982), 'Deviance, labelling and stigma', in D. L. Patrick and G. Scambler (eds.), *Sociology as Applied to Medicine* (London, Bailliere Tindall); *133*.

SCARR, S., and WEINBERG, R. A. (1983), 'The Minnesota adoption studies: genetic differences and malleability', *Child Development*, 54: 260–7; *7*.

SCHAIE, K. W. (1983) (ed.), *Longitudinal Studies of Adult Psychological Development* (New York, Guilford Press); *220*.

SCHOFIELD, M. (1968), *The Sexual Behaviour of Young People* (London, Penguin Books); *86.*

SCHULSINGER, F., MEDNICK, S. A., and KNOP, J. (1981) (eds.), *Longitudinal Research: Methods and Uses in Behavioural Science,* (Boston, Martinus Nijhoff); *220.*

SHAPER, A. G., ASHBY, D., and POCOCK, S. J. (1988), 'Blood pressure and hypertension in middle-aged British men', *Journal of Hypertension,* 6: 367–74; *215, 219.*

*Sheffield Telegraph* (1949), review by L. Roberts of *Maternity in Great Britain,* 10 Jan.; *31.*

SISSONS, M., and FRENCH, P. (1986) (eds.), *Age of Austerity* (Oxford, Oxford University Press); *36, 60–1.*

SKOLNICK, A. (1986), 'Early attachment and personal relationships across the life course', in P. B. Baltes, D. L. Featherman, and R. M. Lerner (eds.), *Life-Span Development and Behavior* (Hillsdale, NJ, Lawrence Erlbaum), vii. 173–206; *197.*

*Social Trends* (1971) (London, Her Majesty's Stationery Office); *63.*

*Social Trends* (1987) (London, Her Majesty's Stationery Office); *127, 167.*

*Social Trends* (1990) (London, Her Majesty's Stationery Office); *59, 126, 127.*

SPOCK, B. (1955), *Baby and Child Care* (London, Bodley Head); *34.*

STACEY, M. (1960), *Tradition and Change* (Oxford, Oxford University Press); *59, 82, 144, 183.*

—— BATSTONE, E., BELL, C., and MURCOTT, A. (1975), *Power, Persistence and Change: A Second Study of Banbury* (London, Routledge & Kegan Paul); *183.*

STARK, O., ATKINS, E., WOLFF, O. H., and DOUGLAS, J. W. B. (1981), 'A longitudinal study of obesity in the National Survey of Health and Development', *British Medical Journal,* 283: 13–17; *94.*

STARK, R., and GLOCK, C. Y. (1968), *American Piety: The Nature of Religious Commitment* (Berkeley, Calif., University of California Press); *173.*

STEIN, Z., SUSSER, M., SAENGER, G., MAROLLA, F. (1975), *Famine and Human Development* (New York, Oxford University Press); *195, 204, 220.*

STEVENSON, J. (1984), *British Society 1914–1945* (London, Penguin Books); *35.*

STEWART, A., WEBB, J., GILES, D., and HEWITT, D. (1956), 'Malignant disease in childhood and diagnostic irradiation in utero', *Lancet,* (ii): 447; *62.*

STEWART, S. (1988), *Lifting the Latch: A Life on the Land* (Oxford, Oxford University Press); *1.*

STEWART-BROWN, S., HASLUM, N. M., and BUTLER, N. R. (1983), 'Evidence for an increasing prevalence of diabetes mellitus in childhood', *British Medical Journal,* 286: 1855–7; *168.*

SUMMERFIELD, P. (1986), 'The "levelling of class" ', in H. L. Smith (ed.), *War and Social Change* (Manchester, Manchester University Press); *1.*

*Tablet* (1968), 'Educational opportunity' (review article), 23 Nov.; *121.*

TANNER, J. M. (1962), *Growth at Adolescence*, 2nd edn. (Oxford, Blackwell Scientific Publications); *11.*

TAYLOR, P. H., EXON, G., and HOLLEY, B. (1972), *A Study of Nursery Education* (London, Evans-Methuen Educational); *176.*

TAYLOR, S. J. L., and CHAVE, S. (1964), *Mental Health and Environment* (London, Longmans); *58.*

THEORELL, T., and FLODERUS-MYRHED, B. (1977), 'Work load and risk of myocardial infarction: a prospective psychosocial analysis', *International Journal of Epidemiology*, 6: 17–21; *218.*

THOMPSON, P. (1978), *The Voice of the Past: Oral History* (Oxford, Oxford University Press); *220.*

THOMSON, D. (1981), *England in the Twentieth Century* (London, Penguin Books); *17, 30, 48, 57–8, 70, 84, 87, 124–5.*

TITMUSS, R. M. (1943), *Birth, Poverty and Wealth* (London, Hamish Hamilton); *26, 46, 55, 129.*

—— (1958), *Essays on the Welfare State* (London, Unwin University Books); *82–3, 190.*

—— TITMUSS, K. (1942), *Parents Revolt: A Study of the Declining Birth-Rate in Acquisitive Societies* (London, Secker & Warburg); *18.*

TOLAND, S. (1980), 'Changes in living standards since the 1950s', in *Social Trends 10* (London, Her Majesty's Stationery Office); *85, 94.*

TOWNSEND, P., and DAVIDSON, N. (1982), *Inequalities in Health: The Black Report* (London, Penguin Books); *122, 129, 135, 170, 205, 215.*

TROLL, L., BENGTSON, V., and McFARLAND, D. (1979), 'Generations in the family', in W. R. Burr, R. Hill, F. I. Nye and I. L. Reiss (eds.), *Contemporary Theories about the Family* (New York, The Free Press), i. 127–61; *193.*

Universities Funding Council (1990), *University Statistics 1988–1989* (Cheltenham, Universities' Statistical Record); *112.*

University Grants Committee (1957), *Returns from Universities and University Colleges in Receipt of Treasury Grant, Academic Year 1955–1956*, Cmnd. 211 (London, Her Majesty's Stationery Office); *63.*

University Grants Committee (1986), *University Statistics 1984–1985*, i (Cheltenham, Universities' Statistical Record); *63, 109.*

VAILLANT, G., and McARTHUR, C. (1972), 'Natural history of male psychologic health: the adult life cycle from 18–50', *Seminars in Psychiatry*, 4: 415–27; *220.*

VAN DER EYKEN, W. (1974), *The Pre-school Years* (London, Penguin Books); *175–6.*

VATTER, H. G. (1986), *The U. S. Economy in World War II* (New York, Columbia University Press); *5.*

WADSWORTH, M. E. J. (1981), 'Social class and generation differences in pre-school education', *British Journal of Sociology*, 32: 560–82; *149, 177–8.*

—— (1984), 'Early stress and associations with adult health, behaviour and parenting', in N. R. Butler and B. D. Corner (eds.), *Stress and Disability in Childhood* (Bristol, John Wright), 100–4; *157*

—— (1985), 'Inter-generational differences in child health', in *Measuring Socio-Demographic Change* (London, Office of Population Censuses and Surveys Occasional Paper No. 34), 51–8; *128, 137, 168, 214.*

—— (1986a), 'Serious illness in childhood and its associations with later life achievements', in R. G. Wilkinson (ed.), *Class and Health: Research and Longitudinal Data* (London, Tavistock); *42, 66, 96, 135, 157.*

—— (1986b), 'Effects of parenting style and pre-school experience on children's verbal attainment: a British longitudinal study', *Early Childhood Research Quarterly*, 1: 237–48; *54, 178, 181, 226.*

—— (1988), 'Inequalities in child health', *Archives of Disease in Childhood*, 63: 353–5; *129.*

—— CRIPPS, H. A., MIDWINTER, R. A., and COLLEY, J. R. T. (1985), 'Blood pressure at age 36 years and social and familial factors, cigarette smoking and body mass in a national birth cohort', *British Medical Journal*, 291: 1534–8; *138, 209, 216.*

—— and FREEMAN, S. R. (1983), 'Generation differences in beliefs: a cohort study of stability and change in religious beliefs', *British Journal of Sociology*, 34: 416–37; *173–4.*

—— and MACLEAN, M. (1986), 'Parents' divorce and children's life chances', *Children and Youth Services Review*, 8: 145–59; *116, 141.*

—— MACLEAN, M., KUH, D., and RODGERS, B. (1990), 'Children of divorced and separated parents', *Family Practice*, 7: 104–9; *116, 141–2.*

—— and RODGERS, B. (1989), 'Longterm follow-up studies: a critical overview', *Revue d'épidémiologie et de santé publique*, 37: 533–40; *221.*

WALD, N., KIRYLUK, S., DARBY, S., DOLL, R., PIKE, M., PETO, R. (1988) (eds.), *U.K. Smoking Statistics* (Oxford: Oxford University Press); *215.*

WALLERSTEIN, J. S., and KELLY, J. B. (1980), *Surviving the Break-Up* (London, Grant Macintyre); *53, 118, 140.*

WARNOCK, M. (1987), *Memory* (London, Faber & Faber); *12.*

WATSON, C. (1954), 'Population policy in France: family allowances and other benefits II', *Population Studies*, 8: 46–73; *53.*

WEDGE, P., and PROSSER, H. (1973), *Born to Fail* (London, Arrow Books); *27.*

WEIKART, D. P., DELORIA, D., LAWSER, S., and WIEGRINK, R. (1970), *Longitudinal Results of the Ypsilanti Perry Preschool Project* (Ypsilanti, Monographs of the High/Scope Educational Research Foundation, No. 3); *219.*

246 *References and Author Index*

WHITEHEAD, M. (1987), *The Health Divide: Inequalities in Health in the 1980s* (London, Health Education Council); *129, 135, 170, 205, 215.*

WHITEHEAD, R., and PAUL, A. A. (1987), 'Changes in infant feeding in Britain during this century', in *Infant Nutrition & Cardiovascular Disease*, Scientific Report No. 8 (Southampton, Medical Research Council Environmental Epidemiology Unit); *29, 44.*

WOLFENSTEIN, M. (1955), introduction to the section on child rearing literature in M. Mead and M. Wolfenstein, *Childhood in Contemporary Cultures* (Chicago, University of Chicago Press); *13.*

World Health Organisation (1951), *Expert Committee on Mental Health: Report on the Second Session* (Geneva); *34, 51.*

—— (1977), *International Classification of Diseases, Injuries and Causes of Death* (Geneva); *217–8.*

YARROW, M. R., CAMPBELL, J. D., and BURTON, R. V. (1970), *Recollections of Childhood* (Chicago, Monographs of the Society for Research in Child Development No. 138, vol. xxxv); *13, 193, 219–20.*

YOUNG, M. (1965), *Innovation and Research in Education* (London, Routledge & Kegan Paul); *71, 89.*

—— and WILLMOTT, P. (1962), *Family and Kinship in East London*, (London, Pelican); *1, 58, 81–2.*

—— —— (1973), *The Symmetrical Family* (London, Routledge & Kegan Paul); *183.*

# Subject Index

Acts of Parliament:
  Abortion Law Reform (1967)  124
  Arts Council Establishment
    (1946)  5
  Betting and Gaming (1960)  86
  Clean Air (1956)  10, 63, 95
  Divorce Law Reform (1989)  124
  Education (1902)  70
  Education (1918)  70
  Education (1936)  70
  Education (1944)  3, 4, 60, 63, 70,
    78, 118, 160, 205–6
  Equal Pay (1975)  126
  Family Allowance (1945)  4
  Housing (1949)  5
  Legal Aid (1949)  5
  Matrimonial Causes (1937)  51
  Matrimonial Property (1970)  126
  National Assistance (1948)  4
  National Health Service (1946)  4
  National Health Service Family
    Planning (1967)  124
  National Insurance (1946)  4
  National Parks (1949)  4
  New Towns (1946)  5
  Obscene Publications (1967)  86
  Sex Discrimination (1975)  126
  Town and Country Planning
    (1947)  4
adolescence  7, 9, 12–14, 92–123, 140,
  184, 193–4
age:
  middle  162, 170, 191–3, 201–2
  old  13, 87, 129–30, 170, 201
ageing  vi, 8, 14–15, 90, 206
alcohol consumption  9, 15, 127–8,
  143, 162, 200
Alzheimer's disease  130
ambition and aspiration  13, 70, 177
  in occupation  112–14, 149, 158
anaemia  46
antenatal care  19–21, 25, 29, 31, 43,
  48, 91
arthritis  130
asthma  65, 168
atheroma  143
atmospheric pollution  10, 64–5, 95–
  6, 165, 196, 208

attainment tests  77, 120, 149, 189,
  224–6
  generation differences in  179–81,
    190, 226
  regional differences  105
  taken at 8 years  72–4, 107–8, 144–
    6, 150–1, 224–5
  taken at 11 years  76–80, 102,
    224–5
  taken at 15 years  95, 98–101, 104–
    6, 109, 112–15, 149, 156, 177,
    225–6
  taken at 26 years  148–9, 226
attitudes:
  to authority  13, 82–3, 190, 121
  to health  9, 13–14, 91–2, 127–9,
    193–4
  to school work  64, 75, 77, 104

back trouble  152
bed wetting  51, 53, 67–8, 77, 116,
  140, 178, 196
Beveridge Report (1942)  4, 62, 85,
  165
birth:
  pain at delivery  24–5, 31, 63
  rate, see fertility
  weight  25–6, 40, 43, 54, 66, 138–9,
    170, 204
blood pressure  vi, 6, 15, 90, 93, 128,
  138–9, 162–3, 199, 204, 206,
  216–17
breast feeding  20, 28–9, 44–5, 54, 94,
  143
bronchitis  64, 95, 136–7, 199
  see also respiratory illness

cancer  61–2
career advice  92, 114, 160
cerebral palsy  42
child guidance  68, 218
child health clinics  8
  see also infant welfare
child rearing, see upbringing
children of cohort  5–6, 15–16, 135,
  157–8, 163, 168, 176–84
children's allowances  4

chronic illness 9, 41–2, 65–6, 92, 96, 129, 133–6, 166
  and life chances 135–6
  mortality 133
circumcision 96
Committee on Children and Young Persons (1960) 89
community life 1, 3, 5, 120, 153–6, 161
congenital problems 42
Conservative government 57–8, 85
contraception 86, 90, 124
cost:
  of medical care of the elderly 130
  of medical care of infants 130
  of pregnancy 19, 21–2, 29–31
Court Report (1976) 169, 215
crime 89, 127
crowding at home 21, 23–4, 42, 48–50, 68–9, 74, 107, 119, 136, 147
Crowther Committee (1959) 87–8, 147
Curtis Committee (1946) 2

deafness 42
death, *see* mortality; parents
depression:
  depressive illness 58, 139–42, 162–3
  economic 5, 199, 204
  *see also* emotion, problems
diabetes 91, 168–9, 203, 206
diarrhoeal disease 40, 45
diet, *see* nutrition
diphtheria 38
disability or impairment 38, 42–3, 61, 65–6, 130, 196, 203
disfigurement 68
divorce 51–2, 87, 124, 127, 140–2, 156–7, 159, 170, 183, 190, 198
  *see also* parents, separation/divorce
Down's syndrome 134

eating habits, *see* nutrition
eczema 65, 168–9
education 2, 7, 8, 14, 69–72, 118–23, 150–2, 160–1, 197, 202
  qualifications 116–17, 135, 141, 144–53, 160–1
  service development and planning 8, 62–3, 87, 118–21, 204–6
  *see also* generation differences; school

'effects' of education v, 4, 7–8, 11–12, 15, 69–70, 82, 107–8, 118–21, 160–3, 175–8, 181–2, 190–4, 197, 200, 202, 204–6
  on family contacts 82, 157, 182–3, 192
  on fertility 157–8
  on health 54, 95, 142–3, 160–2, 190
  on housing 159, 172, 190
  on income 10, 121, 150–2, 160
  on leisure time 153–6, 191–2
  on life review 159–60
  on marriage 156–7
  on opportunities and employment 10, 85, 87–9, 112–15, 144–9, 160–1, 186–92, 204
  on religious beliefs 173–5, 192–3
  on voting 174
emigration 19, 59–60, 213
emotion:
  coping 7, 128, 139–42, 197, 199
  problems 67–8, 77, 97, 99–101, 115–16, 128, 139–42, 162–3, 196–7
  strain at work 152–3
emphysema 137
employment, *see* occupation
epilepsy 9, 42, 133–5
exercise 6, 15, 92, 128–9, 154–6, 162–3, 201
expectation of years of life 166–7, 169, 191

fertility 15, 17–19, 30–2, 115, 157–8, 165

gender differences 1, 126
  in age at first parenthood 157–8
  in alcohol consumption 127
  in beliefs and attitudes 174
  in education and attainment 11–12, 72–7, 80, 99, 102–12, 118–21, 147, 179–81
  in emotional problems 67–8, 77, 139–41
  in expectation of years of life 167
  in family life and marriage 115, 156–7, 182–4
  in growth 47, 94, 137–8
  in health 40, 42, 92–4, 131–5, 137–9, 168
  in income 150
  in leisure activities 153–6

in life review 159–60
in nutrition 137, 143, 162
in occupation 114–15, 125, 141, 144–7, 149, 161, 163, 165, 184–9
in smoking 127, 142, 162
in teachers' assessments 75, 112–13
general practice 24, 35, 39, 91
generation differences 5–6, 13, 124, 163–94
in ambitions 13, 164
in behaviour and beliefs 10, 13–14, 173–5
in child upbringing 13, 33–6, 178–82
in education 9–10, 12–13, 70–2, 119–20, 123, 175–82, 190–3, 199–201
in health 9–11, 55–6, 122–3, 139, 165–70, 190–3, 199–201
in housing 170–3
in occupation 12, 184–9, 191
grandparents iv, 35, 177, 183–4
Guillebaud Committee (1956) 62

Hadow Committee (1926) 70
health services 6, 9, 11, 14, 31–2, 38–9, 41, 55–6, 62–3, 87, 90–2, 121–3, 129–32, 162, 169–70, 204–6
health visitors viii, 18–20, 28, 31, 35, 39, 45, 68, 82–3, 92, 142, 171, 208, 210–11
heart disease 62, 65, 90, 195, 201
height 7, 11, 14–15, 43, 45–7, 54, 66–7, 82, 92–5, 122, 129, 157, 162, 169, 191, 196, 199, 204, 206
intergeneration differences 8–9, 11, 169, 199–200
in low birth weight children 43
mothers' 43, 93
hospital:
admission 23–4, 41–3, 51, 55, 65–6, 96–8, 122–3, 135, 139, 166–8, 209
birth in 23–4
generation differences in admission 166–8
visiting 23, 41, 97, 166
housing 2, 48–50, 58, 65, 68–9, 74, 125–6, 131, 140–1, 159, 163, 165, 170–3, 190
*see also* crowding

illegitimacy 25, 27, 39–40, 86, 90, 207
immunization 3, 200
income 2–3, 10–11, 29–30, 46, 57–8, 85, 107, 124–6, 131, 140–2, 144, 147, 150–2, 160, 163–4, 184, 189, 191
infant welfare services 8, 19, 27–8, 44, 55, 162, 200, 208
infections 1, 38, 40–2, 45–6, 51, 54, 61–2, 91, 126, 130, 136, 166, 168–9, 191, 196, 200, 205
influenza 203
injury 42–3, 64, 130, 168

labour force skills 4, 10, 12, 14, 47–8, 87–8, 113–15, 125, 147–9, 160–1, 184–92, 198, 206
Labour government 4–5, 30, 37, 57, 85, 89
leisure time 14–15, 58, 153–6, 160, 163, 192
leukaemia 62
life review 12–13, 16, 159–60, 164, 193, 201–2

marriage 10, 87, 115, 134–6, 141, 156–8, 163, 170, 197–9
*see also* partner, choice of
maternity services 17–32, 43, 55, 90–1, 93, 122, 129, 162, 204
benefits 21–2, 31
measles 38, 42, 45, 54, 61, 203
medical manpower 2, 62–3, 166
memory:
change with age vi, 15, 216
of childhood 12, 201, 219–20
forgetfulness 130
and identity 12–13, 201
*see also* recollection
mental health 42, 196–8, 216–17
*see also* emotion
midwifery 20, 23–5, 27, 31, 45, 63
morals, morality 9, 13, 59, 142, 183
mortality 38, 42, 62, 64, 92, 122, 128–9, 131–3, 136–7, 161, 165–7, 169–70, 191, 202, 205, 210–13
awareness of 13, 202
infant 26–7, 40–1, 55–6, 132–3, 136–7, 169–70
maternal 20
neonatal 20–1, 26, 40, 132–3, 170
perinatal 20–1, 90–1

motor neurone disease 203
multiple births 12, 25, 39, 205
mumps 42

Newsom Report (1963) 88–9
nurseries, pre-school 3, 22–3, 34, 51,
      53–4, 175–82, 190
nutrition 2, 8–9, 11, 15, 20–1, 25, 35,
      46–7, 67, 92, 128–9, 130, 136–7,
      143, 162, 166, 169, 170, 189, 195–
      6, 199–201, 204, 215–17
   post-war rationing 1, 9–10, 20, 36–
      7, 57, 67, 137, 200

obesity 67, 91, 94, 137–8, 162, 168
occupation 11, 15, 97, 112–15, 144–
      9, 160, 163, 184–90, 197–8, 200–
      2, 217
   changing nature 4, 8, 60, 87, 125,
      165, 184–9
   and illness 134–5
   mother's 21–3, 50–1, 53–4, 205
   and parental separation 141, 183–4
   in pregnancy 21–3, 25, 30
   women's 1, 3, 35, 57, 59, 125, 144–
      9, 184–90, 200–2
   *see also* unemployment

parents v, vi, viii, 5
   aspirations for children's
      employment 112–13
   attitudes to education 11, 69–70,
      119–20, 147, 190
   death 20, 68, 115–18, 136, 138,
      140, 159, 182, 199, 202
   education 8, 10, 12, 46, 48, 99, 108,
      110–12, 119–20, 177, 181, 189,
      190, 200
   emotional state 140
   height 9, 11, 43, 93, 169, 191
   illness 65, 99, 136, 138, 159, 199
   interest in child's school work 10,
      70–7, 79–82, 98, 104–5, 119–20,
      123, 147, 160, 189–90, 198, 200
   occupation 47–8, 69, 74, 115, 144,
      184–9
   relations with children 15, 34–5,
      176–8, 181–4
   separation/divorce 9, 51–3, 68, 99,
      115–18, 140–1, 159, 163, 196,
      199
   smoking 65, 136, 196
   social mobility 47–8, 69, 73–4, 189

Parkinson's disease 203
partner, choice of 15, 156–7, 159, 198
personality 94, 99–101, 134–5, 140,
      152, 176, 217–18
phenylketonuria 169
Platt Report (1959) 97, 166
Plowden Committee (1967) 88–9,
      121, 176
pneumoconiosis 61
pneumonia 37, 40, 65, 95, 136–7
poliomyelitis 38, 61, 97, 203
postnatal care 19, 27–8
poverty 1–2, 25, 70–1, 85, 119, 125,
      162, 165, 172–3, 190
pregnancy:
   age at first 157–8
   care during 11, 19–23, 93, 195–6,
      199, 204
   cost 18, 21–2, 29–31
   employment during 21–3
present state examination 139–40,
      217
private health insurance 126
puberty 92, 94, 101, 109

recollection 1, 5, 12–13, 16, 193, 198,
      201–2
   as a source of information 16, 19,
      219–20
   *see also* memory
religious beliefs 10, 59, 126, 173–5,
      192–3, 195, 201–2
representativeness of sample 205,
      209, 212–15
respiratory function vi, 6, 10, 136,
      206, 216
   illness 45, 51, 64–5, 95–6, 122,
      128, 136–7, 162, 168, 195–6, 199,
      203, 214
   *see also entries for specific disorders*
response rate 19, 39, 64, 92, 131,
      205–15
retirement 14, 183, 216
rickets 46, 201
Robbins Committee Report
      (1963) 88, 108, 121
Royal Commission on Population
      (1949) 17

scarlet fever 42
schizophrenia 203
school:
   comprehensive 89

health service viii, 64, 68, 92, 208
independent 72, 79, 85, 102–3, 106, 126, 144–7
junior or primary 71–6, 79–80, 88, 104, 106, 147
leaving 5, 7, 87, 103, 106–8, 114–15, 119, 120, 147–8, 158
parents' choice of school 75, 78, 81–2
record of achievement 75–6, 77
secondary modern 78–9, 89, 102–3, 144–7
selective (grammar, direct grant, and technical) 11, 78–82, 101–7, 113, 118–19, 144–7, 150, 192
sex segregated schools 103–4, 109
streaming by attainment 77–8, 89
technical 79, 101
self-esteem 140–1
sexual behaviour 8, 86, 158, 200
attitudes to 10, 124, 163
sexually transmitted disease 127
sleep problems 77, 140, 153
smoking 6, 9–11, 15, 92–4, 122, 136–8, 142, 162, 196, 200–1, 215
habit change 10–11, 127–9
social class classification 217, 223–4
social class and social differentiation 1, 86, 190
in beliefs and attitudes 173–5
in birth circumstances 19–32
in birth weight 43, 66
in breast feeding 44–5
in education and attainment 3–4, 69–82, 87, 98–115, 118–21, 123, 144–52, 175–81, 190, 197, 200, 206
in emotional problems 67–8, 141–2
in family circumstances 115–18, 156–8, 182–4
in growth 45–7, 66–7, 94–5, 170
in health and illness 41–3, 54–6, 64–6, 82–3, 92–6, 121–3, 127–9, 131–9, 142–3, 161–2, 170, 190–5, 198–201, 206
in hospital admission 23–4, 41, 97–8
in housing 48–50, 68–9, 159, 172–3
in income 150–2, 173
in leisure time 153–6
in mortality 26–7, 40–1, 64, 131
social mobility 73–4, 86, 135, 184–9
*see also* parents

social workers 2–3, 82, 122
speech problems 68, 218
Spens Report (1938) 78
spina bifida 42
squint 65, 168–9
stomach trouble 77, 153
stroke 139, 199

teachers vii, 64, 73–6, 78–9, 81, 88–9, 99, 101–4, 109, 112, 134, 142, 147, 160, 176–7, 181, 208, 225
teachers' assessments of study members 64, 79–82, 89, 99, 101, 104, 119, 134, 142, 147, 177
technical colleges 4, 88, 192
tonsillectomy 96, 168
training for occupation 4, 15, 87, 114–15, 144–9, 160–1, 175, 184–9
tuberculosis 38, 41, 61, 91, 97, 201

unemployment 1, 48, 69, 74, 125, 141, 173, 184–5, 187–8, 199, 202
*see also* occupation
university 3–4, 60, 63, 85–8, 109, 112, 118–21, 160, 174, 192
proportions of male and female students 108–12, 116–21, 160, 192
undergraduate students 3, 60, 63, 107–12, 116–17, 119–21
upbringing:
generation differences in 13, 31–6, 59, 70–1, 89, 159–60, 164, 173–84

vaccination 38, 61, 200
vision 42, 65, 94–5
voting 174

waste of talent 70, 80–1, 88–9, 119–21, 147–9, 161, 206
*see also* social class and social differentiation
weight 9, 37, 43, 47, 67, 93–4, 96, 137–8, 162, 168
*see also* birth weight
whooping cough 38, 42, 54, 61, 137
Willinck Committee (1957) 62
Wolfenden Committee (1957) 86

Youth Employment Service viii, 92, 114, 160, 208